The Billion Dollar Game

BEHIND THE SCENES OF THE

GREATEST DAY IN AMERICAN SPORT

SUPER BOWL SUNDAY

ALLEN ST. JOHN

DOUBLEDAY

NEW YORK   LONDON   TORONTO   SYDNEY   AUCKLAND

CD

DOUBLEDAY

Published in the United States by Doubleday, an imprint of The Doubleday Publishing Group, a division of Random House, Inc., New York.
www.doubleday.com

DOUBLEDAY and the DD colophon are registered trademarks of Random House, Inc.

Book design by Tina Henderson

Library of Congress Cataloging-in-Publication Data
St. John, Allen
  The billion dollar game : behind the scenes of the greatest day in American sport—Super Bowl Sunday / Allen St. John.
    p. cm.
  1. Super Bowl. 2. Super Bowl—Social aspects. 3. Super Bowl—Economic aspects. I. Title.
  GV956.2.S8S7 2009
  796.332'648—dc22

                                        2008044582

ISBN 978-0-385-52354-7

PRINTED IN THE UNITED STATES OF AMERICA

10 9 8 7 6 5 4 3 2 1

First Edition

CONTENTS

For Rose Mercuro,
a giant in all the ways that count

A portion of the author's proceeds will be donated to Spinal Muscular Atrophy research. For more information on SMA, please visit www.fsma.org.

Baseball is what we were.
Football is what we have become.

—MARY McGrory

Let the Games Begin

For a brief moment on Super Sunday inside the University of Phoenix Stadium, time stood still.

The game clock high above the field in the rafters near the retractable roof stopped with just one second on it. New England Patriots coach Bill Belichick either didn't notice or didn't care; he came out to congratulate Giants coach Tom Coughlin and then disappeared. Football's ultimate celebration had started. Sort of.

But like teachers caught in the middle of a cafeteria food fight, the referees had to stop it. Rules are rules—the game wasn't over. With that single second remaining on the clock, Eli Manning would have to take a knee once more. Then and only then would the greatest upset in Super Bowl history be complete. Better than anyone else, Giants fans understood the reason to play out that last tick of the clock. Thirty years ago, in one of the most preposterous moments in sports history, they lost a game when their quarterback fumbled the ball with just a tick on the clock. No, they'd play it out.

And yet this awkward moment was somehow perfect. It provided a rare moment of reflection. It was almost as if the game itself were trying to shake us and say, "Pay attention. You'll want to remember where you are right now so you can tell your grandchildren about it." For the less sentimental, it still provided an all-too-rare moment of unity. It was a perfect turn-of-the-millennium moment: 100 million Americans squinting at the television, scratching their heads, and saying "Huh?" in unison.

But the moment didn't last long. The referees restored order. The players got back on the field. The ball was snapped, and Celebration 2.0 began.

If this was the end of Super Bowl XLII, let's rewind almost a year to the minute to the beginning, or at least *a* beginning—to Miami and the end of Super Bowl XLI. The raindrops were glistening like a swarm of fire-flies in the lights above Dolphin Stadium, but they'd also driven half of the fans in the most coveted seats in sports to take cover, leaving the hard core huddled under garbage bags. It was the same story where I was sitting, in the press section, the now-unattended TV monitors bleat-ing to no one in particular and sodden press releases sitting in puddles on now-empty makeshift Formica desks.

It was a moment of dreams waxing and waning. Colts fans had been waiting for this for thirty-eight years, since Johnny Unitas was the quar-terback and the team called Baltimore home. Peyton Manning and his dad and his brother had been waiting for this for two generations, a fam-ily of quarterbacks hoping to finally end a season with a win that meant something. Bears fans, still channeling Walter Payton and William

"Refrigerator" Perry, were hoping against hope for a miracle, but for them, the clock was their enemy. Mine too, as I hustled down from the press box to field level for the postgame interviews.

As I shoved my iBook and my commemorative seat cushion into my black Targus backpack, I spied the sparkly silver band on the handle. It was one of those security tags. The band had been affixed by a smiling security guard earlier that afternoon after my laptop passed muster with a metal detector, an X-ray machine, and a bomb-sniffing dog, who lingered awhile, perhaps catching a whiff of the many hero sandwiches that have ridden shotgun next to my laptop. In one way, this tag was a symbol of the sometimes dangerous world in which we live. In another, it carried a message. Just above the NFL logo was the Super Bowl's official motto: "One Game, One Dream."

As mottos go, it's actually a pretty good one (better than "The Road to Forty," the motto of Super Bowl XL). But while it's catchy—so catchy that the 2008 Beijing Olympics adopted "One World, One Dream" as its catchphrase—it's also wrong.

The Super Bowl is anything but one game. It's the championship of America's Game. It's the world's biggest single-day sporting event. It's an unofficial national holiday. It's a billion-dollar economic engine that's bigger than the GDP of many nations. It's an opportunity for a couple of hours of unity in an increasingly fragmented world. It's America's most widely watched live television broadcast. It is an unrivaled marketing opportunity. It's the world's biggest party.

And more.

Most of all it's the vessel for an even greater multitude of dreams, from the winning cornerback to the college kid making a few extra bucks as the night watchman for a display of Super Bowl merchandise.

This is the story of all of those games and all of those dreams.

It's a story that starts with an innocent phone call to the *enfant terrible* of modern architecture and ends with that second hanging precariously

3

on the scoreboard. It chronicles months and even years of intense preparation, moments of behind-the-scenes panic, and the strange web of
connections that runs through an enterprise this enormous.

It's also a story that's never been told before.

And it's a story that's best told by picking a few of the key elements
of this extravaganza, and exploring them in painstaking detail. Over
the course of more than a year of reporting, thousands of miles of travel,
and hundreds of hours of interviews and observation, I was granted
unprecedented behind-the-scenes access, watching the game's movers
and shakers at work, and then listening as they explained how and why
a Super Bowl comes together. And in the process I learned this simple
and profound truth: Most of the real heroes of a Super Bowl will never
even touch a football.

During that time I came to understand what the Super Bowl is and
what it is not. In polite disagreement with that security tag, I would
argue instead that there are actually three Super Bowls: The Game, The
Show, and The Celebration.

The Game is the first piece of the puzzle and the most obvious.
Wikipedia might call it a game of American football, played eleven-
on-eleven at a neutral venue between the champions of the American
Football Conference and the National Football Conference for the championship of the National Football League. The cynical among us would
suggest that it's an anticlimactic and often lopsided contest played in
front of a crowd of scene makers sprinkled with ordinary fans who called
in favors and/or dipped into the kids' college fund for the right to be
there.

In sharing the story of The Game in its 2008 incarnation, we'll start
with a visit with one of the world's greatest architects and the improbable story of the state-of-the-art stadium designed with the Super Bowl
in mind. We'll meet the local officials who have bet everything on the
chance of getting into the Super Bowl business. We'll meet the anony-

mous guy with a tiny, cluttered office on Park Avenue who on Super Bowl Sunday might be the most powerful man in sports.

Then there's The Show. That's the version of The Game that ends up on television, played not in front of 70,000 spectators but before 100 million or more. It's one of the strangest broadcasts in television, a day of reversals when network executives cheer for their competition and viewers wait with bated breath for the next commercial.

We'll go behind the scenes with the FOX Sports team, from the gregarious Australian who runs the ship to quarterback-turned-color-guy Troy Aikman to the guys in the truck who are faced with a preposterous real-time high-wire act yet make it seem almost easy. We'll also talk to the company that has turned Super Bowl advertising into an art form.

And finally, there's The Celebration. Over the span of four decades this game has morphed from a simple sporting event into an unofficial national holiday. Super Bowl Sunday has become an excuse for ordinary Americans to gather around the bean dip while A-list celebs party with unimaginable indulgence. We'll show you both sides of The Celebration. We'll get an exclusive insider's look at the hottest party of Super Bowl week, where a spot on the guest list can sell for more than a game ticket. At the other extreme, we'll also get down and dirty with a crew commemorating the Super Bowl by building a replica of the stadium out of canned goods.

And what powers it all? Cold hard cash. As we follow each of the story lines, we'll follow the money as well, Woodward and Bernstein style. So sit back in your Barcalounger with the beverage of your choice. It's time for *The Billion Dollar Game* to begin.

1

THE GAME

If You Build It...

"It all started with an innocent phone call," says Peter Eisenman.

Wearing a navy blue cashmere sweater with a small hole, Eisenman is sitting in the sunny, unpretentious Manhattan loft space that he calls his office, perched in an old black Breuer chair, at one end of a conference table big enough for a game of platform tennis. (Just the thing for spreading out pages of blueprints, I assume.) Eisenman is one of the major figures in contemporary architecture. He is also the first of many auteurs of Super Bowl XLII.

The man on the other end of that phone call in September 1996 was Mike Rushman. Rushman is a Phoenix-based lawyer who had worked briefly with Eisenman on a proposed, and ultimately abandoned, project at the Boston Navy Yard. Now he came to the architect with a proposition.

"Are you interested in football?" Rushman asked.

"Yes," Eisenman replied.

"Well, the Arizona Cardinals are thinking of building a new stadium. And we're going to have a competition, with Frank Gehry and Will Bruder, who's a local architect," Rushman explained.

"Frank Gehry doesn't know anything about football," Eisenman countered.

"This season is the fiftieth anniversary of the Cardinals winning their first NFL championship, so it's a good time to kick this thing off."

"Yeah, I know. I saw that team play," said Eisenman casually.

"Really?" said Rushman.

"Not only did I see that team play, I can name the starting backfield. Paul Christman, who played at Missouri. Elmer Angsman, the fullback who played at Notre Dame. Pat Harder, who played at Wisconsin. Charley Trippi, who played at Georgia. And the fifth one was . . ." Eisenman paused, more for effect than anything else. "Marshall Goldberg, who played at Pittsburgh."

Unlike Frank Gehry, Peter Eisenman knew a thing or two about football.

He went on to tell Rushman how the Cardinals had gotten their name. "They were an Irish club on the South Side of Chicago, and they had no money for jerseys." Believe it or not, a half century ago, the National Football League was just a ragtag organization that took a backseat to the big college programs of the day. How ragtag? When Jay Berwanger of The University of Chicago, winner of the very first Heisman Trophy in 1935, was selected first overall by the Chicago Bears in the first round of the first NFL draft, he decided against playing pro football and became a successful foam rubber salesman instead.

"The University of Chicago was called the Maroons," Eisenman continued. "And they would give their hand-me-down jerseys to the local pro team. But after being washed all year, by the end of the season they were no longer maroon, they were cardinal red."

And with that casual phone call began an odyssey that would see a sleepy desert farming town become a place where, a dozen years later, the worlds of professional sports, high finance, and mass culture would come together on a sleet-gray January Sunday for Super Bowl XLII, not only the biggest Super Bowl but also the best. For a brief shining moment at least, Glendale, Arizona, would become the center of the universe.

The truth is that Super Bowls don't really have a beginning, or at least one single beginning. A lawyer in search of a creation myth might settle on the day when bid contracts were signed. A football fan might consider the countdown to the next Super Bowl under way when the last one ends. A guy in the street might settle on the moment when the banners go up on the light posts.

But most years, it really is impossible to pin down where a Super Bowl starts. Super Bowls intersect and overlap, building on each other in a bumpy continuum that stretches all the way back to that first game between Vince Lombardi's Packers and Hank Stram's Chiefs.

But Super Bowl XLII is unique in this regard. It really does have a beginning, and it harks back to that fortuitous phone call between Eisenman and Rushman. This marked the moment when Arizona entered the Super Bowl business and the very first stadium built to host a Super Bowl began taking shape. It's no coincidence that this conversation came only a few months after Arizona first hosted the Super Bowl, at Sun Devil Stadium in Tempe in January 1996.

The buildup to that first Super Bowl was rocky, to say the least. The NFL originally awarded the Cardinals Super Bowl XXVII, which was to be played in January 1993. But a growing controversy regarding the state's refusal to recognize Martin Luther King Jr.'s birthday as a holiday intensified. Facing a broad-based boycott of the state, which included both national convention planners and entertainers such as Stevie Wonder, the NFL took action. They made the unprecedented move of pulling the Super Bowl from Arizona and moving it to the Rose Bowl. This was a most uncharacteristic action. The NFL avoids taking public stands on political issues at all costs, but once the NFL Players Association weighed in, this one couldn't be ignored. It was only after the state reversed its position on the King holiday that Arizona got its Super Bowl, three years late.

Swamped by all this brouhaha was an important truth: The greater Phoenix area was an almost ideal Super Bowl host city. The warm, dry midwinter climate was a huge attraction, as were the many golf courses and resorts in the area. There was a reason why professional athletes including Randy Johnson, Curt Schilling, and Steve Nash would ultimately choose to play in Phoenix, and other superstars such as Kobe Bryant would seriously consider it. And the growing city had plenty of hotel rooms, restaurants, and convention facilities as well to handle the 89,000 visitors who flocked to the city during Super Bowl week. Before the game the organizers projected an economic impact of $187 million, but their final tally—$305 million—was even rosier.

But Arizona lacked one thing. The Cardinals were the only NFL team not to have its own stadium. They played in Sun Devil Stadium in Tempe, home of Arizona State's college team. Despite several expansion projects, the forty-year-old facility was subpar even by big-time college standards, featuring backless bleachers instead of seats in some sections. It wasn't the kind of place that would impress someone paying $5,000 a ticket for the world's premier single-day sporting event.

Still, on balance, the first Arizona Super Bowl was a success, and the message from the NFL was clear: "You've got a shot at getting into the Super Bowl business, but only if you get a new stadium."

This was easier said than done. More than anyplace else in the league, building an NFL stadium in Arizona was a gamble. The price tag of a state-of-the-art football stadium can be $400 million or more. But unlike baseball, basketball, and hockey, where that expenditure can be recouped over as many as eighty-one home games every season, an NFL stadium hosts only eight home games per year. And in the 1995 and 1996 seasons, the Cardinals' attendance lagged at only 65 percent of capacity, despite ticket prices that were among the lowest in the league. Getting a Super Bowl every five years or so could make all the difference in that equation.

The phone call between Rushman and Eisenman set in motion a roller coaster, a procession of false starts and dead ends, political intrigue, and simple whims all moving in the direction of getting that stadium completed and fitting the last piece of Arizona's Super Bowl puzzle. Fast-forward a dozen years and the result is something singular: a landmark stadium unlike any other and the first one ever built to host the Super Bowl.

At first it seemed almost easy. After hearing Eisenman rattle off the names of Elmer Angsman and Charley Trippi, Rushman could see the next move clearly. The next day he called back and invited Eisenman to Cincinnati, where the Cardinals were playing that weekend, to meet the Bidwill family, who owned the team. Eisenman accepted, although it meant missing the season opener for his beloved football Giants.

Peter Eisenman seems to delight in keeping people a little off balance. Just take his Web site. The home page features nothing more than the firm's name in stark sans serif capitals, all white except for the second N, which is red, all set against an inky black background. It's certainly sleek, but it's also a tad sterile at the same time.

The firm's offices are anything but, however. The building is a nondescript brick structure in the mid-twenties, just off Fifth Avenue, a part of Manhattan where the scale is more intimate and even the tallest buildings don't top ten stories. Next door sits a shockingly large parking lot that somehow escaped a developer's attention, and across the street is a passel of antique dealers. The small lobby has seen better days. The elevator is the size of a phone booth, seemingly built when people were smaller, and features plastic wood paneling that's the antithesis of style. It always seems ready to stop unexpectedly between floors, and you're thankful when it doesn't. The building is the kind of place where you'd expect to see struggling talent agents and private eyes.

Opening onto Eisenman's office, the cramped elevator spills onto a bright and spacious top-floor space with lofty ceilings, big windows, and an open floor plan—no cubicles here—that enhances the sense of space. But the wood floors haven't seen a sander or a coat of finish since the Eisenhower administration, and the computers sit on metal desks that could have come from the nearby shops that sell surplus office furniture. But for the computers, the Eisenman offices hark back to the days when architects were men in white shirts and skinny ties carrying briefcases, rather than black-clad hipsters slinging messenger bags. Here, it's clear, form follows function.

And Eisenman himself continues the contradictions. With round black-framed glasses, short-cropped graying hair, and a serious mien, he cuts a stern, almost Randian figure. If you were casting him in a movie, he might be played by Ian Holm. Favoring tailored fashions from Paul Stuart worn in a slightly rumpled, academic way, he looks every bit the part of a Yale professor, and his booming baritone is perfectly suited to the lecture hall, a living alarm clock for snoozing students. But if you keep peeling away the layers of the onion, deconstructing the deconstructionist, you'll find something surprising at the center. At heart, he's a sports fan first and foremost.

"My father was a Dodger fan," he says. "In the thirties and forties, if you were a lefty, you read the P.M. [the afternoon edition of the daily newspaper], you were close to the Communist Party, and you were a Dodger fan," he says. "No one in my house could be a Yankee fan."

And his knowledge of football goes well beyond that old Cardinals championship team. When I tell him that I live in Montclair, New Jersey, just down the road from South Orange, where he grew up, he starts citing chapter and verse about half-century-old teams from his high school days, recalling how Montclair's star Aubrey Lewis broke Eisenman's brother's leg.

"I have this photographic memory for total wacko nonsense," he admits.

And his appetite remains undiminished. Eisenman confesses, almost sheepishly, that the night before, with pro sports having a rare dark night during baseball's All-Star break, his wife, Cynthia, had to drag him away from watching a high school baseball game on cable.

But the center of his sports obsession is pro football. And to Eisenman, pro football means the New York Giants. He's been a season-ticket holder for fifty years, and his first season ended with a game that was at once iconic and heartbreaking. In that 1958 NFL Championship Game the Giants lost to Johnny Unitas and the Baltimore Colts in the first sudden-death game ever played in the NFL. Many have called it The Greatest Game Ever Played.

Eisenman combines cutting-edge architecture credentials with an almost childlike love of the game. Some architects wouldn't deign to build a stadium. Not Peter Eisenman. The University of Phoenix Stadium is the building that he was born to build.

And for most NFL teams, none of that would have mattered at all. It's useful to think of NFL owners as one of the most exclusive—and expensive—clubs on earth, a literal billionaire boys' club. In 2007, *Forbes* magazine valued the average NFL club at $957 million, and gaining control of a franchise took not only huge wealth but also significant connections, because any franchise purchase must be approved by the league's other owners.

In most other NFL teams, if Eisenman somehow managed to get the meeting at all, he would have sat down with the vice president of operations and immediately faced tough questions about cost control as well as his reputation for designing high-concept buildings that proved impractical once constructed. They would have talked seriously, and Eisenman would have become one of the marquee names in their nationwide search. The VP would have dropped Eisenman's name on background to a few reporters and then moved on to a blander but safer choice.

But the Arizona Cardinals are not most football teams, and that was even more the case a dozen years ago. They were a mom-and-pop operation. The Bidwill family had owned the team since 1932. The Cardinals are the oldest continuously operating professional football franchise and, along with the Chicago Bears, are one of two remaining charter teams from the founding of the NFL. Indeed, Eisenman will remind you that Bill's brother Stormy Bidwill loaned George Halas the money to buy the Bears.

But the Cardinals were different from the other venerable franchises in the league. George Halas cut a larger-than-life figure, and the 1985 Bears were one of the great teams of all time. Pittsburgh Steelers owner Art Rooney built one of the sport's great dynasties during the 1970s, with his Steelers winning four championships. Wellington Mara's New York Giants won two Super Bowls, and Mara himself was widely respected throughout the league. He was famous for putting the good of the game over his own personal gain, like the time he strongly advocated for the sharing of television revenues. That move was one of the keys behind the success of the league, allowing teams in small cities such as Green Bay to compete on an even playing field with franchises in New York and Chicago, but it also cost Mara money, and likely cost his big-market Giants at least a few championships. Mention any of these old-school owners, and football fans get a warm, fuzzy feeling.

Not so with the Cardinals. At the time of the conversation between Eisenman and the Bidwills, they were one of only four NFL teams that had never been to a Super Bowl. (The Cleveland Browns, Detroit Lions, and New Orleans Saints were the others, while the expansion Jacksonville Jaguars and Houston Texans would soon join that list.) Just as important, they'd never seriously challenged for the honor. Indeed, in 1996, they hadn't celebrated a single playoff win since 1947 (that string would be broken with a wild-card victory in 1998). Unlike teams such as the Chicago Cubs and the Boston Red Sox, who appealed to their fans as lovable losers, the Cardinals were simply losers. On ESPN.com Tom Friend pondered the franchise's highlights:

> I was sitting here trying to think of the greatest and most famous Cardinals game of all time, and it hit me: *Jerry Maguire*! In the movie, Rod Tidwell [played by Oscar winner Cuba Gooding Jr.] made that catch to beat the Cowboys, and the team had to show Rod the money. Come to think of it, it was just another bad Cardinals contract negotiation. It never ends, just never ends.

For the better part of half a century, the Cardinals bumped along, neither loved nor hated, mediocre at best, and often much worse than that. There was a reason why the team was focused on celebrating the anniversary of that 1947 championship: It was the team's last.

This is what Peter Eisenman encountered when he walked into the owner's box at Riverfront Stadium that late-summer afternoon.

"Bill Bidwill is a nonstop nostalgia guy," Eisenman recalls. "All he likes to talk about is the old days. And I was fresh meat for him."

So as they watched the Cardinals jump out to an improbable lead against the Bengals, Eisenman and Bidwill matched each other anecdote for anecdote, reminiscence for reminiscence. Eisenman listened as Bidwill told him about his days as the team's ball boy back on the South Side of Chicago. Bidwill told Eisenman why an official's flag is yellow. Then he told him again. They were kindred spirits.

The Bidwill family wasn't just ready to hire him, they were all but ready to adopt him. "Ma Bidwill was there, and she kept asking me if I could find a nice Catholic girl for her son Mike to marry," Eisenman recalls.

And so they talked about football and blind dates and the good old days, but not much about stadiums or architecture, and not at all about cost overruns. In the modern NFL, teams are run like Fortune 500 companies, and a team's on-the-field accomplishments are directly related to the management's ability to put every problem, big or small, through the wringer. Seat-of-the-pants decision making? It gets you nothing but grass stains. This casual management style, basing big decisions about players and coaches on emotion rather than cold hard facts, had helped put the Cardinals in the predicament they were in. But this time, Bill Bidwill's instincts served him well. He'd stumbled upon one of the world's great architects and because they hit it off, he offered him the chance to build a landmark project.

The Cardinals lost the game to the Bengals—and to this day the Bidwills still teasingly blame Peter Eisenman for that. But they gained much, much more.

2

THE GAME

Location, Location, Location

Before Peter Eisenman could design the state-of-the-art stadium that would host Super Bowl XLII, there was the not-so-small matter of finding a place to put that stadium. This was a process that would take the better part of a decade, involve politics at the highest levels and billions of dollars, and ultimately have a huge impact on the future development of one of America's fastest-growing cities.

The first thought in 1997 was to locate the Cardinals' new home near their old one, on the border between Tempe and Mesa. The 1,000-acre multi-use project called Rio Salado Crossing would have included a convention center. According to the developer, the project would "exceed your wildest dreams"—unless your wildest dreams included a blimp hangar, an exploding scoreboard, and a stadium built so that each end zone was in a different city. The project would have housed not only the Cardinals but also the Suns basketball team, the NHL's Phoenix Coyotes, the arena football team the Arizona Rattlers, the WNBA's Mercury, hockey's minor league Mustangs, the Thunder of the National Public Safety Football League, and even the Desert Mamas of the Women's World Roller Derby League. The non-sports aspects of the project would include shopping, restaurants, two indoor eighteen-hole golf courses, a funeral home, a prayer chapel, and a 20,000-plot cemetery located below a retractable floor.

The next step, of course, was funding the $1.8 billion project. And in the words of the artist sometimes known as Prince, "Money changes everything."

The public funding of sports stadiums in the United States has been a hot-button issue, to say the least. It hinges on a fundamental question: Is a sports franchise a private business or a public trust? The answer to that depends on whom you ask and under what circumstances.

This question first arose in the mid-1950s when baseball's Brooklyn Dodgers were looking for a new place to play and established a precedent that still applies to all professional sports today. Ebbets Field, for all its charms—charms subsequently burnished by the rouge of memory—was dilapidated. As far back as June 1952, Dodgers owner Walter O'Malley sent a letter to Frank Schroth, the publisher of the *Brooklyn Eagle*, foreshadowing his plan. "I believe Brooklyn needs a modern athletic stadium seating approximately 52,000. A modern stadium with a movable roof would provide convention facilities unequalled elsewhere. Such a stadium could house motor boat, automobile, flower, sportsman, and other shows and attractions."

In 1955, O'Malley made a formal proposal to Robert Moses, point man for Mayor Robert Wagner. The proposed stadium was to be located in downtown Brooklyn at the intersection of Atlantic and Flatbush

Avenues and cost $6 million—big money for the day. The proposal was rejected.

O'Malley called the city's bluff: He'd move the Dodgers to Los Angeles for the 1958 season. This was the first moment that manifest destiny became practical in professional sports. At that point, St. Louis was the westernmost outpost of Major League Baseball, and for that matter major league sports as a whole. The advent of air travel and television made the country smaller, and O'Malley found a travel partner in Giants owner Horace Stoneham, who agreed to move his team, led by a young Willie Mays, to San Francisco.

The move shocked the city, the fans, and everyone in the business of sports. In some quarters, O'Malley became public enemy number one. *New York Times* writer Sam Roberts suggested, "There was a time in Brooklyn when the name Walter O'Malley would be muttered only in the same breath as Hitler or Stalin." By doing the unthinkable, he set the stage for a half century of stadium and arena building in all sports. Owners wanting a new, publicly funded home now carried a big stick. If they didn't get one, they would simply threaten to move the franchise. And city fathers, not wanting to be tarred with the legacy of having lost a team, by and large caved in.

One of the very few cities that didn't capitulate was St. Louis, old home of the NFL Cardinals. They wouldn't build the team a new stadium. In 1988, the league's owners voted "reluctantly, but overwhelmingly" to approve the team's move to Phoenix. This was in stark contrast to the acrimony surrounding other NFL franchise moves. In 1980, Raiders owner Al Davis moved the team from Oakland to Los Angeles, prompting an injunction from the league, which was countered by a massive antitrust suit from Davis. (Unlike Major League Baseball, the NFL doesn't enjoy a congressional antitrust exemption.) Soon after, Robert Irsay moved the Colts from Baltimore to Indianapolis on fifteen hours' notice, with Mayflower moving vans showing up in the middle of a snowy night. By contrast, the Cardinals' move generated the barest measure of controversy. The NFL had quietly encouraged the Bidwill family to move to Baltimore, hoping to fill the gap left by the Colts' departure, rather than Arizona, so that the league could locate an expansion franchise in Phoenix and collect a $60 million franchise fee that would be divvied up by the existing owners. Team owner Bill Bidwill teared up at the league meetings, calling himself "mixed up," but there were few tears shed on the banks of the Mississippi. The Cardinals were neither greatly missed in St. Louis nor eagerly welcomed in their new hometown.

The Cardinals would play their games at Arizona State's Sun Devil Stadium in Tempe, where early-season games were often contested in the scorching heat and the amenities were hardly NFL-quality. Virtually every week that the then Phoenix Cardinals played at home during the early years of the franchise, most of greater Phoenix would use that opportunity to catch up on yard work or squeeze in a round of golf. As a bone to teams looking to maximize ticket sales, the NFL imposed blackout rules on television broadcasts. Before 1973, all games were blacked out in the city in which they were played. This meant that fans of the New York Giants, which sold out every game for decades, would have to flock to Connecticut to watch their team on the tube. After some legal jostling, in 1972 Congress compelled the league to slacken the blackout rules. Only if a team failed to sell out a home game within seventy-two hours of kickoff would that game not be televised. In some NFL markets, such as Green Bay, where every game is sold out before the season even starts, the blackout is a nonissue. And in most markets, it's still largely a formality, with the NFL selling out more than 90 percent of its games.

But that was not the case in Phoenix in the 1990s. The Cardinals ranked consistently near the bottom of the league's attendance rankings, and their average attendance in most cases only filled Sun Devil Stadium a little more than halfway.

It became a cycle of indifference: The games didn't sell out, so they weren't televised, which made it more difficult to sell tickets, which led to more blackouts, and so it went.

This was the climate in which the Rio Salado stadium project was presented in 1997. Voters were asked to approve a one-quarter-cent increase in the state sales tax for twenty years to pay for $320 million in infrastructure improvements associated with the project. On one side was a group called Yes on Rio Salado Crossing, which raised almost $900,000, including $476,000 from the Cardinals themselves. The opposition in this largely blue-collar town was more grassroots, piggybacking on public outrage over a sales tax increase, not subject to a public vote, that had financed the Arizona Diamondbacks' home, then called Bank One Ballpark. Countering the suggestion that the development would put the area on the map, Rand McNally, the aptly named president of a group called NO NO NO, argued, "We're already *on* the map."

Tired of taxes and having little affection for the Cardinals, the citizens of Tempe and Mesa rejected this proposal resoundingly, and the giant project, of which an Eisenman-designed sports complex was the centerpiece, was very much in danger before it started.

Fearing that the Cardinals would leave—Los Angeles and San Antonio were seen as likely destinations for the franchise—Arizona governor Jane Hull formed the Plan B Task Force. The idea was to rethink the stadium project and present it to the voters in a way that was more palatable, knowing that a second defeat at the voting booth would all but doom the prospects for a stadium. The project was reduced in scale to a football-only stadium. Gone were the arena (the Suns and Coyotes would soon move to the American Airlines Arena downtown), the hotels, the indoor golf courses, and even the cemetery. The stadium's price tag would be $331 million, with the Cardinals providing $85 million in funding. Income tax revenue from players' salaries and revenues from a surcharge on Fiesta Bowl tickets would also be thrown into the kitty. The major source of public revenue was no longer an increase in the general sales tax but an increase in taxes on hotel rooms and rental cars, costs to be borne largely by out-of-towners. As for the project itself, it was no longer linked to the Tempe site, and several alternative locations were put back into the running, ranging from the existing Tempe-Mesa site to a location on the Yavapai Nation Indian reservation not far from a casino. Also rolled into the project were other popular items, including funding for Cactus League baseball, tourism development, and youth sports. Despite this extensive reworking, the project fared miserably in early polls, with as many as 65 percent of voters opposing the new proposal.

Supporters of the plan launched an expensive and glitzy public relations campaign. An independent economic analysis was commissioned, which "calculated the average annual economic impact from Prop 302's sports, entertainment and tourism activities at $1.95 billion per year over a period of 30 years." This detailed study annualized the impact of the Super Bowl at $101 million. This was grounded in the naively optimistic assumption that Arizona would get a Super Bowl every three years.

Full-page ads featured the slogan "A New Stadium Is a Touchdown for Arizona's Economy." One of the five key points, along with the Cardinals remaining in Arizona and the Fiesta Bowl retaining its place among the elite college football games, was that Arizona would enter the Super Bowl rotation. Attached to that prospect was a number: $305 million.

This connection to the NFL's biggest game became a rallying cry for supporters of Proposition 302. "The stadium itself, since it's multipurpose, will not only be the home for the Cardinals and the Fiesta Bowl," team owner Mike Bidwill told ESPN's *Outside the Lines* in 2000. "But it will also host a Super Bowl about every five years." For Proposition 302 to work, the state of Arizona not only *wanted* but *needed* to crack the NFL's unofficial Super Bowl rotation.

What is a Super Bowl worth to a host city? It's a simple question with a very complex answer. The number can vary by a factor of ten, depending upon whom you ask and how they count. Ask the host committee from a city that's been awarded the game and the number will have many zeroes. Miami's host committee, for example, projected a figure of $350 to $400 million, and other host committees have come up with similar numbers. (Interestingly, the numbers have generally stayed the same over the years or even decreased somewhat, so in inflation-adjusted dollars the projected impact seems to be decreasing slightly.) To put this number in some perspective, that weeklong economic impact number is roughly equivalent to the GSP (gross state product) from arts, entertainment, and recreation for the state of Alaska for the entire year of 2004.

Studies by academics have been far less optimistic. The more generous economic impact estimates are about one-half of the NFL's (Jeffrey Humphreys of the University of Georgia put it at $166 million), while at least one economist (Phil Porter of the University of South Florida) has suggested that the net effect is closer to zero. Holy Cross economist Victor Matheson and Robert Baade of Lake Forest College summarized these studies and discussed the issues involved in undertaking this kind of analysis in a 2004 paper entitled "Padding Required: Assessing the Economic Impact of the Super Bowl."

In exploring the issue, Matheson and Baade cite any number of effects that account for the differences between the NFL's robust figures and the more conservative ones proposed by the academics. For example, the "substitution" effect theorizes that an event such as the Super Bowl doesn't so much increase the amount of money spent in a city as it concentrates it during a particular time frame. People coming to Miami may choose to visit the city during Super Bowl week instead of the third week in February.

"Crowding out" suggests that while the game attracts many consumers, it also drives some away. Some would-be visitors and spenders, especially locals, stay away from the host city because of the "limited hotel rooms and high hotel prices, rowdy behavior of football fans, and peak use of public goods such as highways and sidewalks."

"Leakage" suggests that much of the money that is spent on hotels and rental cars, and to a lesser degree at stores and restaurants, goes not to locally owned businesses but to the national corporations that own the local outlets.

The money that is spent can be divided into direct spending by consumers and visitors and the indirect spending that stems from it. An example of direct spending is the money that a corporate sponsor pays to a local caterer. Indirect spending is when the caterer decides to spend that money on a new stove purchased from a local retailer and installed by a local contractor.

Matheson and Baade and other academics argue that the NFL and host committee studies overestimate the effects of indirect spending and ignore or underestimate the aforementioned effects that temper a city's gain from the game.

"Can a study either commissioned or performed by the NFL be unbiased if the NFL has used the promise of a future Super Bowl as an enticement for cities to build new facilities?" the professors ask rhetorically. "Modern sports stadiums generally receive some form of public funding, and the NFL at least indirectly has rationalized public financial support on the grounds that the economic impact from a single Super Bowl approximates the cost of building a new stadium. Coincidence?"

On the other hand, scholars are hardly disinterested analysts either. An academic study that refutes a widely accepted claim is much more likely to gain wide attention than one that supports the conventional wisdom. Biases aside, the economic impact figures posited by academics vary wildly and, as we've seen above, can disagree by $100 million or more. Indeed, Baade and Matheson did two separate studies that addressed the Super Bowl economic impact question, and the $92 million projection in their 2002 study was more than three times their 1999 estimate of $30 million.

Ultimately, the answer can be found in that word: *estimate.* The Nobel Prize–winning physicist Enrico Fermi used to give his students this quiz on the first day of class: How many piano tuners are there in New York City? While the question may seem totally irrelevant, it requires the student to make the same kind of estimates—how many people? How many pianos? How often do they have to be tuned?—that are at the heart of a discipline such as physics, which lies in the realm of the uncountable.

Fermi's out-of-left-field question strikes at the very heart of the art of economics as well. Each of these studies begins with estimates of how much money was actually spent. This kind of calculation involved comparing a city's economy in a Super Bowl year to its economy in years before and years after. While that task seems formidable enough on the surface, there's one significant monkey wrench: While the economic impact of a Super Bowl may seem plenty large compared to the annual economy of a medium-to-large city, it's really just a drop in the bucket, as Baade and Matheson explain. "For the cities in question, a one percent error translates into a $200 to $500 million difference for the smallest cities such as Miami and New Orleans and over a $2 billion difference for Los Angeles, the largest host city. Given the size of these large, diverse economies, the effect of even a large event with hundreds of millions of dollars of potential impact is likely to be obscured by natural, unexplained variations in the economy."

The next level of analysis involves trying to divine those things that *would* have happened. This requires a leap of faith, or more accurately, several of them. How do you parse cause and effect within the context of a system as complex as an economy? Did a city's economy grow *because of* or *despite* the Super Bowl? At its core, it relies on that most unpredictable of all elements: human behavior. How would people have spent their money in an alternative universe in which the Super Bowl was played in some other city? It's a dauntingly complex question. Perhaps the only sure thing is that smart people can make an honest effort to search for an answer and still not even come close to agreeing.

Still, the bottom line is simple enough. Unlike the Olympic Games, which won't return to a city for decades, if ever, the Super Bowl is played every year. If the game's impact truly was as minimal as most academics argue, cities would have caught on by now and wouldn't still be competing for the right to host the game.

How much was the prospect of hosting a Super Bowl worth to the people of greater Phoenix? About $322 million, as long as that money was raised largely from visitors. On Election Day, Proposition 302, which provided for that amount of stadium funding, passed by a narrow margin, with 52 percent of voters approving the plan.

But the vote was hardly the end of the story. The task force settled rather quickly on a site in Tempe, not too far from the proposed location of Rio Salado. The site was smaller, big enough for a stadium and a couple of small office buildings, but not much else.

And then September 11 happened. The stadium site was on the flight path to one of the runways at Sky Harbor Airport. So was the Diamondbacks' stadium, Chase Field (then called Bank One Ballpark), and the potential security risks were put into stark relief as the Diamondbacks and the Yankees played the World Series there only a few weeks after the attacks. While a Cardinals regular-season game might not have been at the top of a terrorist hit list, the Super Bowl was the very definition of a target-rich environment.

The first suggestion was to move the stadium 1,200 feet to the east on the same site to keep it out of the flight path. But the combination of post-9/11 paranoia and some lingering local resentment about both the airport and the stadium project doomed this potential fix as well.

Which meant that the stadium project was back to square one. Sort of. "We had ordered the steel for the roof," says Eisenman's partner Rick Rosson. "The site was being graded. Construction was under way." With the clock very much ticking, the Cardinals needed another site and they needed it now.

The answer was to be found with another team that had relocated to Phoenix. When they came to Phoenix from Winnipeg, the Coyotes played hockey in America West Arena in downtown Phoenix, which was originally designed for basketball. When outfitted for hockey, its 16,000-seat capacity made it the smallest facility in the NHL. Size matters, so when developer Steve Ellman bought the team, he made it a priority to build an arena, and he chose Glendale, a sleepy bedroom community in a less-than-chic area west of Phoenix. The $180-million arena, built on the site of a former alfalfa farm, would be the centerpiece of a larger mixed-use development called Westgate. The project included 6.5 million square feet of retail, restaurant, and entertainment space, complete with a 400-foot-long man-made lagoon that features a synchronized fountain like the ones at the Bellagio hotel in Las Vegas, all at a cost of $1 billion.

Ellman landed in Glendale after he experienced difficulties securing support for his arena in tony and well-developed Scottsdale, and ultimately viewed the open space near the Loop 101 highway as a tabula rasa. There was acreage aplenty, and the locals in Glendale, used to taking a backseat to the upscale communities to the east, were especially welcoming. And their support for the project wasn't just a fruit basket. They set aside $36,623,470 for sewage, utilities, roads, and traffic signals, including more than $23 million for the construction of parking lots and a pedestrian plaza.

The Arizona Cardinals, and ultimately Super Bowl XLII, finally had a place to call home.

3

THE GAME

I've Just Seen a Place

Over the course of more than two centuries, no other building type has evolved less than the stadium. Homes have changed. Workplaces have changed. But the stadium dates back to the Roman Empire. While the Colosseum was designed to host gladiatorial games, it is also a virtual prototype of a modern football stadium argues architecture critic Jeffrey Kipnis. The perfection of that early design is both awesome and frustrating for architects like Peter Eisenman who pride themselves on innovation.

"If we could tilt the playing field, that would be something," says Eisenman playfully. "Or create a seating area with a rake that is so steep that you feel like you're going to fall out of your seat. Except that as football fans, we wouldn't want to sit in those seats." In a stadium, the field has primacy, and even an architect as bold as Eisenman understands that. The sports nut in him knows that the game has to be the center of attention. At fourth down and two, form must follow function. What is so remarkable about the University of Phoenix Stadium is the degree to which it does exactly that.

Eisenman's landmark stadium features a flexible, modular design, but, unlike many modern buildings, all of its flexibility serves a purpose. "People want flexibility, but when they get it they don't have any idea how to use it," Eisenman explains. In the architect's view, too often flexibility is about allowing the client the opportunity to delay the frightening prospect of making a real decision, the wisdom of which—or lack thereof—will end up memorialized in glass, stone, and steel for generations to come. So faced with this uncertainty, the client punts, opting for an auditorium with movable walls and seating that can be configured and reconfigured as easily as a Lego set. Then within a couple of years the client realizes that what they wanted was really just a traditional auditorium with a fixed proscenium. So they bolt the chairs down, build a stage, and live with a building that doesn't work quite as well as it should and cost a lot more than it needed to.

That's not the case with Eisenman's stadium. The very things that make it state-of-the-art also make it a magnificent place to watch a game. From the beginning, the Cardinals decided that their new stadium would have air-conditioning and a roof. The fans' number one complaint at Sun Devil Stadium—aside from the team's play—was the oppressive heat in the late summer and early fall.

"Peter and I argued with Mike Bidwill that the Arizona desert could be a huge home-field advantage for the Cardinals," laughs Eisenman's partner, Rick Rosson. "The Chicago Bears would never build a dome because they view a winter football game as being to their advantage. Not that we were going to win the argument."

Contemporary fans tend to think of a domed stadium as an umbrella, something that provides shelter from the rain and the snow. But the very first domed stadium—the Astrodome—featured a roof that was more of a parasol, designed to deflect the heat of the Texas summer. And several other early domes, most notably the New Orleans Superdome, were built at least partly with that idea in mind. But the Cardinals' Stadium takes this notion to an extreme. The Phoenix area gets virtually no rain, and the winter temperature rarely dips below 40 degrees, but early in the football season temperatures can top 100 degrees. You needn't be a marketing expert to understand that air-conditioned comfort could be a key to attracting new fans.

However, during those temperate days of autumn and early winter in Arizona, a parasol roof isn't necessary or even desirable. So why not simply make it disappear? The idea of a retractable roof was hardly a new one. The Roman Colosseum featured a retractable canvas canopy that provided some measure of protection from the sun and the elements. The Buckminster Fuller-designed stadium, commissioned by Walter O'Malley for the Brooklyn Dodgers in the mid-1950s but never built, also featured a retractable roof. But the first modern sports arena with a retractable roof option was actually the home of a National Hockey League team. The Pittsburgh Civic Arena, which opened in 1961, was originally built for the Pittsburgh Civic Light Opera, which found the acoustics sorely lacking with the roof open. The NHL Penguins began playing in the building in 1967, but didn't take advantage of the possibility of hockey al fresco. The first modern retractable-roof sports venue was Olympic Stadium in Montreal, built for the 1976 Summer Games, but the tentlike roof wasn't completed until 1988 and even then was plagued with engineering problems. Ultimately, the Toronto SkyDome, now the Rogers Centre, became the prototypical retractable-roof stadium, featuring large rectangular panels that slide open like a very large automobile sunroof. Since then the retractable roof has become, if not exactly standard equipment, at least a viable option for NFL stadiums.

Eisenman's initial conceptions of the Cardinals' Stadium included a huge roof opening, one that was larger than the field itself. While structural—and financial—considerations meant that the opening had to shrink, the retractable roof remained an integral part of the finished building. Eisenman's early conception of the stadium, when the stadium was still located in Tempe, also included an open end zone that featured a view of Camelback Mountain. "The Bidwills—who were really our client—loved it because you could see the desert," says Rosson. "The landscape was an extension of the stadium interior. This made it unique from Houston and Detroit and every other stadium that has a roof."

It was a striking idea, but one that ultimately ended up on the cutting room floor. It added only incrementally to the fan experience while significantly increasing both complexity and cost. When the stadium was moved from that initial Tempe site to the Glendale location with a less scenic view, the open-air end zone was eliminated.

The other design touchstone was all about accommodating the players. In the mid-1990s there was a significant backlash against artificial turf, with many players concerned about the increased injuries from playing on the rock-hard surface. And given the fact that NFL teams were burdened by a hard salary cap and thus can't outbid their rivals for free agents, playing conditions became an important factor in luring players to a franchise. This prompted some teams such as the New York Giants, which played in *al fresco* stadiums, to tear up their Astroturf in favor of natural grass.

But a grass field in a dome? That's a different matter. The very first indoor stadium, the Astrodome, tried to grow natural grass inside. Originally, the building had a translucent roof, which caused so much sun glare that it was impossible for outfielders to see fly balls. When they painted the roof to provide relief to outfielders, the grass died, and they replaced it with plastic grass, henceforth known as Astroturf. With a few exceptions, it has been a package deal: a domed facility requires artificial turf.

Which got Eisenman thinking outside the box. "Rick and I worked on a stadium for a German Olympics in Leipzig," he explains. "It was a segmented stadium that could be taken apart." While the Olympic bid was unsuccessful, the concept of a modular stadium, which included a movable field, continued to percolate. When the Cardinals insisted on the roof but still longed for a natural grass field, the defining element of the stadium took shape. The result was a stadium that pleased everyone—the players got their natural turf, the fans got their air-conditioning, and reducing the size of the retractable roof saved $50 million.

The movable field concept was simple and elegant. The field would be grown in what appeared to be a giant baking pan, complete with its own in-ground irrigation system. The field tray, which would weigh 18.9 million pounds including the turf, would slide in and out on a track system composed of 13 rails, powered by 42 high-torque one-horsepower electric motors. Combined, the wheel assemblies produced less horsepower than a single Toyota Prius, but managed to move the field in and out in about 75 minutes.

The movable field provided a huge side benefit for the facility during those weeks when the Cardinals weren't playing there. The building could play host to anything from a trade show to a rock concert to a high school graduation and the event could take place on a hard floor while the field was rolled out to bask in the Arizona sun.

"Architects don't have many ideas," says Eisenman, almost apologetically.

Actually, Eisenman has nothing but ideas. Sometimes, however, they haven't always been terribly practical ones. Once Eisenman designed a house for a friend with a big slot in the floor of the master bedroom. The friend was, shall we say, quite large. One night, he got out of bed in the middle of the night on the wrong side and fell into the slot. "He couldn't get out," says Eisenman, savoring the punch line. "They had to call the fire department to extricate him."

That's the sort of rebellious image that Eisenman actually cultivates. It's a useful persona in a world in which genius and an artistic temperament are often thought to go hand in hand. Eisenman is one of the eminent figures in contemporary architecture—one of a handful of true giants in the field. But as practiced in the second half of the twentieth century, contemporary architecture is as much about thinking about buildings as it is actually building them. In the first half of the twentieth century, modern architecture had its roots in the work of designers such as Frank Lloyd Wright and Charles Rennie Mackintosh, who placed their primary emphasis on form rather than decoration, and moved toward the spare glass-and-steel boxes of Bauhaus designers such as Le Corbusier and Ludwig Mies van der Rohe. In the 1950s, Eisenman and other architects began nudging the pendulum back the other way, rejecting the equally strict rules set down by the modernists. (Eisenman's colleague Robert Venturi turned Van der Rohe's famous "Less is more" maxim on its head, arguing, "Less is a bore.") While many of the buildings built by Eisenman's contemporaries such as Michael Graves are characterized by a return to the use of purely ornamental forms and elements, it's really much more than that. It's a rejection of the rules, both the doctrine of classical architecture and the equally strict modernist dogma that replaced it. Eisenman's work embraces the idea that buildings aren't just glass and stone and steel but *meaning*.

For example, House VI, the aforementioned house with the slot in the floor, incorporates other playful elements, such as a column that doesn't extend all the way to the floor and an upside-down staircase. That infamous slot that runs through the middle of the master bedroom "forced us to sleep in separate beds, which was not our custom," said Suzanne Frank, the client, who, despite a variety of technical problems discussed at some length in a book called *Peter Eisenman's House VI: The Client's Response*, pronounced herself largely pleased with the house. Some whimsical, some jarring, these elements are all about provoking the viewer, challenging his or her assumptions about conventions in architecture and ultimately the world at large.

For a long time, Eisenman was a full-fledged paradox: an architect who didn't build anything. But around his fiftieth birthday, Eisenman, who teaches at Yale and has collaborated with French philosopher Jacques Derrida, made a radical change, entering contests and vying for large-scale commissions. No longer satisfied to talk the talk, he felt the need to walk the walk as well.

"Architects have to build," he states simply.

His Wexner Center for the Arts at Ohio State University was one of his first grand-scale buildings. At one level, it's nuanced—the building's floor plan plays with the idea that the university's grid system sits just a few degrees askew from the grid of the city of Columbus. On the other hand, the experience of the building is anything but subtle—the use of colliding planes is so disorienting that some visitors become nauseated. Typically, Eisenman delights in talking about how his building makes people vomit.

He followed the Wexner Center with what may prove to be his most enduring work: The Memorial to the Murdered Jews of Europe in Berlin. It's typically knotty. Although Eisenman is Jewish, he claims little affinity with what he calls "the Holocaust industry." But the collection of concrete plinths located near the Brandenburg Gate rises above his professed indifference. Some have likened it to a sea of identical gravestones in a military cemetery, but Eisenman insists that his inspiration was being lost in an Iowa cornfield. In any case, the work strikes a balance between the literal and the symbolic that is truly profound.

The design concept Eisenman presented for the World Trade Center site seems downright whimsical at first glance—from a distance it looks like two of the world's largest tic-tac-toe boards set at a right angle to each other. But the building's use of negative space, and the way it sits on the perimeter of the old World Trade Center site, conveys meaning. Eisenman's proposed tower, like the ground upon which it would have stood, is all about what *isn't* there.

The University of Phoenix stadium represents a balancing act for Peter Eisenman. It's a bold design with definite limitations. The retractable roof and the movable field set it apart, but there are plenty of aesthetic details for an architecture critic to gnaw on. Its proportions were inspired by the ancient ballcourts used by the Hotapi Indians. From above, the asymmetrical configuration looks like a coiled snake (although at least one architecture critic has likened it to a cinnamon bun). Why a snake? The serpent is revered by the native Americans because its head and tail are thought to represent birth and death. And the 21 vertical striations around the stadium's perimeter, which vary in width from 30 to 65 feet, are reminiscent of small round barrel cactus that grows in the Arizona desert.

But the interior of the stadium allowed fewer opportunities for self-expression. Seeing this, Eisenman forged an unlikely alliance with HOK, the nation's preeminent stadium architect. The firm, which has achieved acclaim for bringing retro style to stadiums like Baltimore's Camden Yards, is accustomed to being the design architect on projects, but after a little persuasion by Hunt Brothers, the project's construction firm, HOK agreed to design the concrete bowl that would sit inside Eisenman's state-of-the-art shell.

The collaboration wasn't without its challenges. On a less-ambitious stadium HOK would simply design one quadrant of a building and clone it four times with minimal modifications. That wouldn't work with Eisenman's asymmetrical footprint, which meant more design time, more documentation, and more oversight.

And while Eisenman and Rosson settled on a budget material for the outer skin—aluminum sandwich panels that are usually used for warehouses—they employed it in a most unconventional way. They discovered that the sheets could be bent just a little to conform to the building's curves. However, curving the panels meant that when they were installed, the pieces would no longer be simple rectangles, and indeed no two of the building's 8,000 panels were exactly the same shape. Hunt Brothers had to devise a computer program that would spit out the exact measurements of each panel, which was then cut to size on a table saw. Peter Eisenman had created the world's largest jigsaw puzzle.

But the end result of this give-and-take is a design that's ambitious in all the right ways. In much the same way that a football player accepts the rules of the game, Eisenman came to embrace the age-old strictures that are part and parcel of every stadium. Perhaps that's because he's spent so much of his life sitting in one. "It's vanilla ice cream," he says. "Just like in a hospital, there are lots of things that have to function in a certain way. But it's important to me because I'm a football fan."

4

THE GAME

Believe the Hype

"If Jesus were alive today, he would be at the Super Bowl." That's what Norman Vincent Peale, Protestant minister and the father of Positive Thinking, once said about the Big Game.

It's hard to refute or confirm this kind of elaborate claim, but amid all the Super Bowl hype, truth and fiction stand side by side and it's hard to separate the two. Indeed, a full-blown mythology has evolved around the Super Bowl that rivals anything the Greeks or the Romans ever conjured up.

Most Super Bowl myths are simply white lies or half-truths, the result of a game of telephone in which a crucial fact is omitted, a number is exaggerated, and some altered form of the myth—usually simpler, more compelling, and bigger than the truth—is repeated.

For example, you'll hear that the potential television audience for a

Super Bowl is more than a billion viewers worldwide. Which is true, but with a huge caveat: Just because a billion people *can* watch the Super Bowl doesn't mean that anywhere near that many actually *will*. The broadcast is available to a huge number of viewers in Africa, Asia, Europe, and South America, but there is no reliable worldwide ratings system similar to the Nielsens to determine how many of them are actually watching. The reality is that while most of the residents of Bangor, Maine, may be watching the game, a much smaller percentage of the population of Bangalore is tuning in, and most of those who do are expatriate Americans.

Do giant sewer lines explode on Super Bowl Sunday when everyone gets up to go to the bathroom at the same time? No, but there's also a grain of truth in this one as well. During the 1930s, when radio serials drew massive audiences and sewage systems were still quite primitive, there were occasions when so many listeners would take a bathroom break at the same time that the overtaxed pipes would indeed burst. However, with today's modern plumbing, that's simply a nonissue. And, of course, during most recent Super Bowls plenty of viewers stay around the television just *for* the commercials. Still, some news outlets choose to believe the myth. When a sixteen-inch water main broke in Salt Lake City on Super Bowl Sunday of 1984, causing significant local flooding, local media outlets, as well as some national ones, invoked this myth, even though public works officials blamed it on old rusty pipes rather than a Super Bowl–related overload in the system.

Does Disneyland become a ghost town on Super Bowl Sunday? While it sounds like a Yogi Berra–ism turned inside out—"It's so empty that everyone goes there"—it's also untrue. The California theme park is a little less busy than on a normal Sunday, but Disney spokespeople, girding to answer this question yet again, note that Super Sunday seems to be getting busier as more families, hearing and believing the myth, head to the park expecting to find it deserted.

And what about offices on the day after the Super Bowl? Is it really the biggest call-in-sick day of the year? One survey suggested that 1.4 million people call in sick on the day following the game, but the information is rather sketchy. Still, the lack of reliable statistics hasn't kept anyone from making and repeating this claim. Indeed, one grassroots group, www.superbowlmonday.com, proposes taking it a step further. The Web site suggests that Super Bowl Sunday be made an official national holiday and that the Monday afterward be designated as a formal day of observance.

"Super Bowl Sunday is not just an ordinary day in America," the site argues. "It has gained a *significance* that transcends the game itself. It is a *shared*, national event, organized around a single stage at a single time." Suggestions for the name run the gamut from Super Monday to National Sports Day to Lombardi Day. By early January 2008, 15,655 people had signed an online petition (with 498 voting no) to be sent to Congress in support of the new holiday. One of the sponsors of the site, Marc Kinley of nMotion Technologies, has put his money where his mouth is, giving his employees half a day off on Super Bowl Monday.

Do Americans eat two-thirds of the year's crop of avocados as guacamole while they're watching the game? More like 4 percent, and it turns out that Cinco de Mayo is actually the biggest avocado-eating day of the year in the United States. Still, the 49.5 million pounds of avocados consumed on Super Bowl Sunday is enough to fill a stadium nineteen feet deep with guacamole.

What's the common thread running through these myths? It's all about the sheer size of the event.

"As folklore, the truth of a legend is unimportant," argued the late anthropologist Alan Dundes. "Every culture's legends express that culture's values. Super Bowl legends usually involve numbers and a sense of enormity. The idea of big numbers, of being bigger than other people, is very American."

For the most part, the exaggerations about guacamole and theme parks are relatively harmless. But what about those times when myths truly take on a life of their own, affecting something as large and fundamental as the stock market? Enter the Super Bowl indicator for the Dow Jones Industrial Average.

Here's the theory. When a team from the old NFL wins the championship, the Dow Jones Industrial Average will rise in the year ahead. When an AFL team wins, the bears will come out of hibernation and the Dow will fall.

It turns out that this indicator holds true a shocking amount of the time. In a venue where billions of dollars will change hands on an edge measured in fractions of a percentage point, the Super Bowl indicator predicts the direction of the market more than 80 percent of the time. Legendary sportswriter Leonard Koppett noted the idea rather casually in the *New York Times* in 1978, and Robert Stovall, then of Dean Witter, reported the theory in a marketing piece for the banking firm. "There is no apparent reason for this directional signal to be correct," says Stovall. "It just happens that way."

New York Times writer Floyd Norris agreed, arguing that the indicator was mere coincidence masquerading as causation, the equivalent of a coin coming up tails eight times in ten. "The Super Bowl indicator provides proof not of what will happen to stocks, but of the fact that it is sometimes possible to correlate two completely unrelated events." But that was before the indicator, which was well known among stock professionals, had become common knowledge among the investing public.

A later study by John Sheppard and Thomas Krueger of the University of Wisconsin-La Crosse argues that what may have started out as mere coincidence has morphed into something more. They have found that investors are clearly buying and selling with the Super Bowl indicator in mind. The researchers call it a "Pygmalion Effect": a "phenomenon that does not have any substance by itself but takes on . . . meaning because humans assign importance to it."

The professors report that market activity increases in the weeks before the game as well as immediately after. Volume spikes after an NFC team wins—with a 2.24 percent increase on the Monday after an NFC win, and an overall 11 percent increase in volume over the following week. However, volume still increases even after an AFC win—1.37 percent on the day, almost 7 percent over the following week, with some investors dumping stocks bought before the game and others seeing a short-sell opportunity. "This is fairly strong evidence that investors are acting on this phenomenon," the researchers suggest.

Why is the indicator so appealing to the average investor? Perhaps it's because of its inherent simplicity. The conventional wisdom is that Wall Street runs on unobtainium. In order to make money, an investor needs a roomful of analysts crunching numbers through proprietary metrics—or, a cynic might suggest, insider information. On the other hand, the Super Bowl Index is the ultimate *outsider* information. It's dirt simple and available to everyone. And more often than not, it's right.

Then there's a far more disturbing Big Game myth: a widely reported increase in domestic violence on Super Bowl Sunday.

In 1993, the media watchdog group Fairness and Accuracy in Reporting (FAIR) persuaded NBC to run a thirty-second public service announcement about domestic violence during the Super Bowl. The spot featured a well-dressed man sitting in a jail cell and the warning "Domestic Violence Is a Crime." Before the game, FAIR issued a press release that asserted, "The Super Bowl is one of the most widely viewed television events every year. Unfortunately, women's shelters report that Super Bowl Sunday is also one of the worst days of the year for violence against women in the home." FAIR followed that release with a press conference during Super Bowl week in Pasadena. One of the speakers at the event, Sheila Kuehl of the California Women's Law Center, cited a study by Old Dominion University that showed an increase in the number of police reports and hospital admissions in the Washington, D.C., area due to domestic violence on game days in 1988 and 1989 when the Washington Redskins won. In a widely disseminated wire story about the press conference, the Associated Press reported that domestic violence complaints rose by 40 percent on Super Bowl Sunday. A wide variety of news organizations began reporting this figure as fact and continue to do so to this day.

A year later, a *Washington Post* reporter, Ken Ringle, began investigating this claim, and his reporting poked holes in this 40 percent figure. He noted that the data sample in the Old Dominion study was minuscule—the number of expected cases was fifteen and the number of actual cases was twenty-one, which meant that the 40 percent increase represented a difference of only six cases. His research further indicated that most experts, including those with hands-on experience in women's shelters, found little anecdotal information suggesting that Super Bowl Sunday caused an increase in domestic violence. Ringle's front-page story set off a firestorm of its own, drawing criticism from women's groups, but when it was analyzed by the *Post*'s ombudsman and later by the *American Journalism Review*, his conclusions largely held up.

The truth, it seems, is complex and not easily reduced to a sound bite. Prompted in part by the controversy, Indiana University researchers did a larger study of domestic violence reports in fourteen NFL franchise cities on Sundays during football season. Their conclusion? "The number of domestic violence cases was inversely related to the point spread." In other words, on those days when the home team was expected to lose, the number of police dispatches related to domestic violence tended to increase.

"Not all football games are alike," the researchers concluded. "The nature of the game, the time of year, the consequences of the outcome, the expectations going in; these factors and others make the relationship between NFL football games and domestic violence quite complex." They further add that other days of the year outrank Super Bowl Sunday in terms of the increase in domestic violence—most notably Christmas.

5

THE CELEBRATION

It's My Party...

It's rare to first meet someone at a moment when they're under siege. Most introductions are kind of pedestrian—a quick handshake at a business meeting, hovering over the hors d'oeuvres at a cocktail party. It sometimes can take years before you truly understand what someone is made of. How often do you get your first glimpse of a person during one of their defining moments?

"Hi, how are you? *Incoming!*"

But that's how I met Donna Tavoso, one of the masterminds behind Playboy's Super Bowl party. It was at half-court on the floor of Miami's American Airlines Arena at around 1:00 P.M. on Super Bowl Saturday 2007, and even though the Miami Heat were nowhere to be found, it was very much crunch time.

To my right was a scissor lift. To my left was an army of carpenters frantically assembling plywood platforms. Dangling above them was a crescent moon, but at this moment it wasn't a storybook moon but one out of a Creedence Clearwater Revival song: "I see the bad moon a-risin' . . ." Walking out onto the floor of a building this big is guaranteed to make you feel a little insignificant, but now the frantic activity made me worry that if I sat down for a second, someone might just start building a platform on top of me. The whirr of cordless drills and saws echoed through the cavernous building, punctuated by the occasional shout above the din. It was pretty scary.

When I finally found her amid the confusion, Tavoso, whose title is vice president of special projects and creative services, was sweating, wearing a T-shirt and sweats, a bandanna pulling back her curly brown hair. Her attire suggested that this was an all-hands-on-deck situation. But her eyes and her voice said something different.

"Yeah, we're a little behind," she said almost matter-of-factly.

She ticked off a quick list of the things that still needed to be done: lighting, sound, construction, decor. In other words, everything.

"Over there!" she'd bark at someone looking for direction and then turn her attention back to me.

"It'll get done," she said, and her eyes said that she truly believed that.

I've hung around arenas enough to recognize the look. It was an I-want-the-ball look. Don't believe what you read in those as-told-to autobiographies. What an athlete really wants is a twenty-point lead with thirty seconds to go. But if it has to be a one-point game with eight seconds on the clock, some players would just as well watch their teammates get the call, and others want the ball. Donna Tavoso wanted the ball. Even if the ball was a sequined disco ball that wasn't quite hung yet.

Sure, she would much rather be sitting on that twenty-point lead, which in party parlance would mean that they'd be setting out the liquor bottles at this hour instead of building the bar. But if it had to be so, she wanted to be here, making the decisions, taking the heat, literally and figuratively.

How did this all happen? It was inevitable, a fundamental conflict of the time-space continuum. There was a Wednesday night game at the venue. Then a Thursday night event. And Miami has twenty-four-hour liquor laws, so the Thursday party wasn't over until almost dawn, and thus most of the day Friday was spent tearing down the other event. And as you might imagine, the load-out is not always pursued with the same energy and zeal, not to mention deadline focus, as the load-in. It was a party planner's Perfect Storm.

But at that moment, none of it seemed to matter to Donna Tavoso. She wanted the ball.

The Super Bowl party has become a part of modern American culture, perhaps our largest and most significant secular holiday. While gathering around the television may not be quite as ingrained as gathering around the turkey on Thanksgiving, it's making rapid progress in that direction. And there's very much a different feel to it—while many other holidays feel like an obligation, Super Bowl Sunday still seems like a pure celebration.

Last year 36 percent of Americans told pollsters they'd be attending a Super Bowl party. The average Super Bowl party had eighteen revelers in attendance. Many of them were gathered around a newly purchased television, since more than two million sets are sold in the week before the Super Bowl, more than five times the usual number. Half of Americans polled suggested that they would rather go to a Super Bowl party than a New Year's Eve party.

In America at large, the Super Bowl party is a multitasking event:

Eat junk food and schmooze with friends while keeping one eye on the television. It's the second-largest stuff-your-face day, behind only Thanksgiving, prompting a 20 percent boost in antacid sales the Monday after.

In the Super Bowl city, however, this sort of multitasking isn't on the agenda. So during Super Bowl week, there will be upward of a hundred parties during the nights leading up to the big game, ranging from a small bash at the local club to gala black-tie fund-raisers featuring top-line celebrities. The best parties are generally invitation-only events, usually sponsored by companies to entertain clients and their friends, and, of course, the firm's upper management.

Perhaps the most coveted invite of all is to the Playboy party, which starts on Super Bowl Eve and continues until the wee hours of game day. "Players would tell me before the season that they were torn," Tavoso tells me. "They wanted to be in the game, but if they were, they'd miss the party."

For what seems like a no-brainer of an idea, the Playboy Super Bowl party is a surprisingly recent innovation. It was 2000, the peak of the dot-com frenzy, and the people at Playboy knew they needed to get in on the act. Playboy.com had just launched, and they decided that they'd provide some special Web content during halftime of the Super Bowl. This was long enough ago that this seemed like a good idea. On the other hand, it was also long enough ago that there was no wireless broadband Internet access, so interacting with Playboy's Web content meant that you couldn't interact with your friends or even your television set. Hardly a slam dunk, in retrospect, but the days of dot-com were nothing if not heady.

In support of this venture, Playboy hosted a modest party. They worked out a deal to cosponsor a party at a small Atlanta club. Nothing fancy—a few logos, a few Playmates, and a little bit of Playboy swag to give away.

But a strange thing happened. While the Web site didn't generate nearly the excitement that the magazine had hoped, the party created a disproportionate buzz. There was a line around the block, and they ultimately had to turn away far more revelers than they let in.

It was an accident, but like the Benedictine monk Dom Pérignon, who fumbled with a few fermented bottles and turned wine into champagne, or Columbus, who came to realize he had discovered something even more significant than a shortcut to India, the Playboy Party Team had the foresight to understand the importance of what they'd stumbled upon. What they stumbled upon was the beginning of not *a* Super Bowl party but *The* Super Bowl party.

Indeed, if there's one thing that Playboy knows how to do, it's throw a party. The parties thrown by magazine founder Hugh Hefner at the Playboy Mansion virtually redefine the term. Super Bowl fans understood almost instinctively, even before the magazine's marketing staff did. Even if a Regular Joe didn't stand a chance of scoring an invite to the Mansion, he figured that this was the next best thing, a way to get a little piece of Hef's vision of paradise, and perhaps a 3-D encounter with the impossibly perfect girls of a *Playboy* pictorial.

The concept really gained traction in 2002, when the party was moved to Anne Rice's mansion after the Super Bowl was rescheduled in the aftermath of September 11. The guest list topped 1,000, and while that's hardly the biggest party of Super Bowl week—some of the biggest parties approach 10,000—at Playboy the trick is to host a large-scale party that's still intimate enough that every guest feels like a VIP.

It also helped that competitors were starting their own exclusive Super Bowl parties. The most notable was *Maxim*, the American version of the British laddie magazine that was stealing attention and circulation away from *Playboy*. The Super Bowl party became a competitive event. Which party was hotter? Which one attracted more A-list celebrities and athletes? Which one had more buzz? Which one would make a regular Joe contemplate selling a kidney? Call it the drool factor. And to compete in this league, a party had to go big.

What is it that makes a Super Bowl party go? I would have thought that money was the answer. But earlier that week, four nights before the Playboy bash in Miami, I discovered that piles of cash aren't nearly enough.

The Tuesday night before Super Bowl XLI, South Beach played host to an astonishingly great midweek party. The organizers shut down five blocks of the beach itself, but once you got inside the sand fence, it became clear that this was no ordinary beach party. One section of the beach was furnished with couches and upholstered chairs arranged in front of a stage with a steel drum band and Latin dancers gyrating on platforms. Just to one side, chefs churned up paella with shovels, rolling the yellow rice around in comically large six-foot frying pans. In another cabana, they were handing out Super Bowl commemorative Crocs— blue with orange or orange with blue, all gratis. The party felt busy, but there was never a line, whether it was for the roast pig at another savory station, the decadent bittersweet chocolate truffles on the dessert tray, or the top-shelf liquor at one of the bars. Wretched excess was exactly enough.

Another quadrant housed a makeshift beach volleyball court, aglow with black lights, and a few leggy female college volleyball players wearing white bikinis. This probably cost only a few thousand dollars as part of a party budget that ran to seven figures. But what could be more enticing than watching attractive young ladies hitting expert sets and spikes while they and the ball glow in the dark?

The only decision was how often to turn away from the luminescent volleyball and toward the Jack Daniel's bar. There a particularly attractive young woman was pouring bourbon gratis. She was notable for what she was wearing, or more accurately how much. With a long-sleeved black top that covered her elbows and her shoulders, if not her navel, she seemed almost prim by comparison to most of the other women working the party. We dubbed her the "Amish girl."

The grand finale was a Mardi Gras parade, with only a few square inches of strategically positioned cloth keeping this from an NC-17 rating. The giant video screens and the fireworks display were the icing on the cake, or maybe the gilding on the lily. This magical evening struck that elusive balance between buzz and chill. And like any other great party, it was totally grounded in time and place: Miami, the Tuesday before the Super Bowl.

The next night, Super Bowl week's movable feast moved to the Gulfstream Park racetrack. They shipped us out on buses, and I should have seen what was in store when I saw the NFL bloopers reel running on the VCR. We were greeted by a red carpet with a Joan Rivers impersonator interviewing incoming partygoers over closed-circuit TV.

"So don't you look *mahvelous* tonight, darling. Where are you from?"

"Um, Kansas City," came the pained reply from a Dockers-clad scribe.

The steam table buffet featured the same kind of one-step-up-from-the-dining-hall fare that would have elicited yawns in an office park cafeteria. The skydivers who landed on the track had roughly 8 percent of the visual impact of the volleyball girls in the glowing bikinis at maybe ten times the cost.

I scanned the bars in search of the Amish girl. No such luck.

"It's a pregame spread without the game," I overheard one reporter saying to another.

It turns out that these parties were sponsored by different arms of the Super Bowl host committee—the first put on by Dade County, the second by Homestead County, where Dolphin Stadium is located. Dollarwise, the second party probably cost every bit as much as the first, maybe more, once you factor in the substantial lost revenue from keeping the track dark for a night. But per unit of fun, it was an amazingly expensive evening, judging by the number of would-be revelers waiting impatiently for the first bus back to the city.

The difference between Tuesday night and Wednesday night? Someone like Donna Tavoso.

When I showed up at the door for the Miami Playboy party on Saturday night, having seen things as a work in progress only a few hours earlier, I was expecting the worst.

I registered at the press table and walked down the red carpet. After taking only five or six steps, I was frozen by a flurry of flashbulbs. I looked up. The center of attention was the attractive young woman walking a few steps ahead of me. I squinted for a second. Alyssa Milano.

"Alyssa has a sore throat, so she won't be taking any questions," said her publicist.

So Alyssa just stood there smiling as the herd of photographers shot hundreds, no, thousands of identical frames.

Smile. *Click.* Smile. *Click.* Smile. *Click.*

Two minutes. Three minutes. Four minutes.

Still she smiled and the photographers shot, hoping perhaps that she'd sneeze and the result would be a celebrity blooper photo. I could see the headline now: "What's Alyssa Wearing? Mucus."

But eventually the photographers ran out of digital storage space and Alyssa ran out of patience. I followed her through a tunnel past a fog machine for the big reveal.

This truly was an alternative universe. A leggy Playmate was perched in the crescent moon, now securely hung from the rafters, while others staged pillow fights down below. Body paint as evening wear? Why not?

In the party's VIP area, Alyssa settled on a couch, canoodling with *Entourage*'s Jeremy Piven while trying to be tactful with David Spade, who was being as annoying as he was on *Just Shoot Me*. *Sopranos* star Joe Gannascoli, the actor who plays the ill-fated Vito in the season's tragic subplot, snuck a smoke while keeping an eye out for fire marshals. "Terrible what happened to you, man," said a fan. "I haven't played pool since." Vito didn't look amused.

It was a great party, even by standards of the Amish girl blowout on South Beach.

But whether it was the slightly rushed preparation, the space itself, or just some missing X factor, this party fell slightly short. It was as if just a tiny bit of the tension from the afternoon lingered on into the night. The bar area by the entrance seemed a bit crowded, the VIP area was strangely empty, and some revelers retreated to the arena seats for a respite. A feng shui expert would have figured it out in a flash.

Great? Yes. Magic? Not quite.

For Donna Tavoso and friends, next year, and the buildup to the Arizona Super Bowl party, began on Sunday morning.

6

THE CELEBRATION

Making a List

Just call it the List of Things We Have to Ask. That's what Donna Tavoso and the rest of the Playboy Super Bowl team took away from the Miami Super Bowl party. As the party has grown over the years—so does the planning and preparation time. And the first round of brainstorming for the 2008 Arizona party begins in the hours immediately following the 2007 Miami Party.

The list is a work in progress, the sum of the collected knowledge of parties past. It isn't written down or kept on someone's laptop. It is the bounty of hard experience, lessons generally learned the hard way, through disasters averted. The list is the thing that will make this year's party better than the last . . . they hope.

And the 2008 list includes several big questions. The first: When can they start setting up? "With the level our decor is at, we need two days to load into a venue," says Tavoso, with the vision of Miami's late load-in still fresh in her mind. "I say that without knowing 100 percent if we're going to achieve that this year."

But you get the sense that if they can possibly help it, they won't book a venue in Phoenix where their preparation time is at the mercy of someone else's cleanup. Tavoso is quick to admit that the hurried prep led to a less-than-optimal flow. The entrance area, by the so-called Stiletto Seduction bar, was a little crowded, made more so by the late addition of a car from last-minute sponsor Dodge. On the other hand, the VIP room to the side was largely empty, with most of the guests drifting to the cabanas and the dance floor on the far end of the room. If they had been able to set up on Friday, she would have looked at the layout from a bird's-eye view and moved the bar back just a little. With a Saturday setup, there wasn't any point in reviewing the big picture because there was no time for large-scale changes.

And, of course, Tavoso and the Party Team are serving many masters. The partygoers and the magazine itself are the obvious constituencies. But the event's sponsors are every bit as important. "It's about branding for Playboy, but it's also about them," says Tavoso. "And if we can't deliver for Cuervo and Sony, then we've failed."

Miami's other takeaway lesson? Security. The arena had a contract with its own security firm, while Playboy is used to providing the security at their own events. Despite the fact that Shaquille O'Neal played there and VIPs are a constant presence at NBA games, the American Airlines Arena guards weren't particularly subtle in dealing with delicate situations: *Do you have a ticket? Okay, you're in . . . No ticket? Go away.* Their emphasis was making sure that the wrong person didn't get in. While that's a consideration for Playboy, an even bigger problem is when the *right* person gets turned away or hassled unnecessarily.

"Our security people know how to deal with a client who swears he has a ticket and can't get in, all when there are 2,000 people screaming at you," says Tavoso. "It's a very different kind of security. Did any person who came into the party know we had a problem? No," says Tavoso. "Did we know? Yes."

And then there's the issue of overseeing Playboy's own VIPs. "Watching the Playmates is its own special, unique—I hate to say it—art form," she says. "There is really a kind of a skill to being close enough to them so that the girls feel safe, so that people aren't grabbing at them, and far enough away so that consumers can interact with them."

Beyond those two large items, the debriefing focused on satisfying successes and small glitches of the sort that are inevitable in an undertaking of this magnitude.

"The liquor service and the bar service were great—you never waited for a drink. That's one of my and Dana's pet peeves," says Tavoso, referring to Events Marketing Director Dana Rosenthal, her partner in crime on the Party Team. "We tell every caterer, 'However much staff you think you need, add fifteen more,' because that's what we're going to want, because I never want someone waiting for a drink."

On the media side, Senior Vice President of Public Relations Lauren Melone found the setup for the photographers at the red carpet less than ideal. "We always ask for adjustable risers, so we need them to go all the way down to a foot or a foot and a half," she explains. "Well, they did get us an adjustable riser, but the lowest it went was three feet. Which is too high for people to get their shots. So we had to end up pushing the riser back."

The DJ was, on the whole, a big success—and already booked for the 2008 party. One thing would have to be changed, though. The DJ booth and a platform for the go-go dancers had been built at the same level, which created visual interest. But there'd been a problem: When the girls would dance, the vibrations would sometimes cause the records to skip.

That's the level of detail that has to be distilled into the plans for next year. In the grand scheme, vibration in the DJ booth is a modest problem, but Tavoso doesn't take it lightly. Except for the fact that the issue involved a DJ and go-go dancers, Tavoso could have been a head football coach breaking down film from last week's closer-than-it-should-have-been 27–21 win, or a COO reviewing operations at a plastics factory. It's about closing the gap between acceptable and perfect.

And like Bill Belichick, Tavoso understands that her team has to set the bar higher than the pickiest partygoer. "If I'd told someone who was at the party, they might have been like, 'Oh yeah, it was a little crowded when you walked in the door, but then it was fine. I don't know what you're talking about, you crazy girl.'"

Looking forward to Phoenix, Tavoso and the Party Team have another problem: This year's issues don't have plug-and-play solutions for next year's party. The fact that the Super Bowl is a traveling circus is perhaps the Team's biggest challenge. Take one of Playboy's other big events. Every year Playboy's Golf Scramble ends at the Mansion, so if there's a small issue, it's a clear and easy fix for next year. Not so with the Super Bowl party, where Murphy's Law seems to be a member of the Party Team.

For instance, two weeks before the Detroit Super Bowl in 2006, the Party Team discovered that in Michigan it's illegal for caterers to own liquor licenses and getting a license for a party is just about as difficult as getting one to open a bar. "It's one of six states that has that law," says Tavoso, still incredulous more than a year later. "I've never thrown a party where the liquor license did not belong to the caterer." While Playboy doesn't sell tickets to the party on anything like a mass scale, there are a few that are paid for as part of sponsorship deals. As far as the state liquor officials are concerned, that constitutes a paid admission ticket, which is illegal.

"We worked out a deal with a charity where we gave them a percentage of what would have been the liquor distributed at the party for whatever tickets were sold, but you still have to get that liquor license approved," Tavoso explains. So two days before the party, Dana Rosenthal drove to Lansing to get a special liquor license. If the wrong bureaucrat looked askance at the paperwork, the party could have been thrown into last-minute chaos.

And indeed, when it came time to begin thinking about Phoenix, they looked at dozens of sites all over the area. They came pretty close to booking one, and then asked one of the questions on their list. It turned out that the property, like many venues around Phoenix, was on an Indian reservation. As such, it was subject not to Arizona state law but to *tribal* law, which prohibits serving alcohol except in the casino, in the hotel, and on the golf course—not at the proposed party venue. Chalk one up for The List.

There are other details that need to be nailed down in advance. Some are pedestrian, like the eighty-five hotel rooms at a nearby Marriott Residence Inn that need to be booked a year out and the black limousines—"white limos are for the prom," says Melone—that get booked up when a big event comes to a medium-size city like Phoenix. And some details are more exotic. Like girls.

"We bring thirty Playmates to the Super Bowl. We have twenty booked right now because if we didn't put them on hold we'd lose those girls, and we wouldn't want that," says Tavoso.

Then there's the delicate question of female guests. An optimal male-female ratio is vitally important to the vibe of the party, and balancing the guest list is a key challenge. "As you can imagine, at any Playboy party, every guy you know wants to come, and so to balance out the party you have to have pretty girls," Tavoso explains. "There's a whole art and science of recruiting women for the party."

One of the jobs on the flow chart of this operation is "girl outreach," or "girl wrangler," as it's known informally in the party-planning business. Playboy prints special girl-only tickets that are distributed to local modeling agencies and models who've appeared at Playboy.com and other magazine properties, as well as friends of the Playmates.

"You want the girls who will go up and talk to all the guys at the party and who will go on the dance floor and get the things going, get it all moving and jump up that excitement level a little bit for you," Tavoso says.

The Party Team will even go out into the city distributing girl tickets on Wednesday, Thursday, and Friday nights before the party. The next step is on-campus recruiting at Arizona State. "Their deal is that if the campus recruiters can fill a bus with fifty attractive women— twenty-one and over—they can come to the party with a friend," says Tavoso. "So on the night of the party, this huge bus pulls up, and fifty attractive co-eds get out."

With tickets to the Playboy party even more in demand than Super Bowl game tickets, and often commanding more on the black market, sometimes this seemingly foolproof system goes awry. "Even though they're bright pink and say 'Admits Women Only' at the top of it, every year I'd say at least five men come to the door with that ticket, telling me that he paid for it," laughs Tavoso.

The Playboy Party Team is made up almost exclusively of women, so they have an interesting perspective on this issue. The Playboy brand is all about attractive young women. But they make a clear distinction be- tween actively recruiting hotties and excluding those who aren't twenty-two years old and 105 pounds. Before the Detroit party in 2006, *Maxim* actually screened photos of prospective female guests—"If you offend in spandex, you need not apply"—and only abandoned the practice after a minor media backlash. Playboy's policy is clear: Anyone who has a ticket gets in.

"We would never be like, 'If you can't fit into a size two, don't come,'" says Tavoso. "I say this as a forty-four-year-old woman. You have to be there when someone tells a woman she's not pretty enough to come into a party to appreciate how horrifying it is."

7

THE CELEBRATION

In the Beginning

Let it be noted that Playboy doesn't hold a World Series party, an NBA Finals party, a Daytona 500 party, or a party for college football's BCS National Championship Game. And the meta message of that is clear: The Super Bowl is clearly more than just any old championship game.

And the other American professional sports have clearly stood up and taken notice. For example, on April 15, 2007, baseball superagent Scott Boras sent a letter to baseball commissioner Bud Selig. His suggestion: Make the World Series more like the Super Bowl. He proposed turning the Fall Classic into a best-of-nine affair and having the first two games held at a neutral site, to be chosen from advance bids. The weekend would kick off with the announcement of the MVPs and other major awards on Friday night and the opening game on Saturday.

While that proposal is likely going nowhere for now, Boras was clearly onto something. The Super Bowl is a perfect holiday. Its exact date is known far in advance. It always falls on a weekend. It occupies an ideal niche in the calendar, squeezing into the holiday gap between New Year's and Valentine's Day. Its midwinter date makes it an ideal excuse to escape to some warm-weather venue while the snow is on the ground, or at least throw a party to help forget about it. And, of course, it's got a near-perfect name.

While the Super Bowl may seem like it could have been planned by a marketing task force, in reality, the things that make the Super Bowl the ultimate holiday are the result of a series of happy accidents, seat-of-the-pants decisions made decades ago that have since proven to be prescient.

Rewind for a moment to 1958, when this all began. The National Football League was a moderately successful professional sports league, but not much more than that. Baseball was still the undisputed national pastime, and pro football was vying with the college game for fan support.

The first turning point that marked the rise of modern football and the ascendancy of its championship game was the December 28, 1958, NFL championship game between the New York Giants and the Baltimore Colts.

According to Peter Eisenman, then a young architect who had just purchased his first Giants season tickets, the game was quite a spectacle in its own right. The Colts band arrived at Grand Central and marched up Park Avenue to Yankee Stadium, blaring their fight song the whole way. The fans? They wore suits and ties, protected from the elements by camelhair overcoats, fedoras, and the occasional hip flask. It was a far cry from the team jerseys and face paint of today.

In the third quarter of the cold and snowy contest, the Giants took the lead when Frank Gifford caught a long pass from Charlie Conerly.

But with two minutes remaining, Colts quarterback Johnny Unitas got the ball on his own 14-yard line. Three long passes to tight end Raymond Berry moved Baltimore into field goal position with seven seconds to play. Kicker Steve Myhra booted a 20-yarder to tie the game.

What came next would make history. "When the game ended in a tie, we were standing on the sidelines waiting to see what came next," Unitas recalled. "All of a sudden, the officials came over and said, 'Send the captain out. We're going to flip a coin to see who will receive.' That was the first we heard of the overtime period." At this point in football history there were no overtime sessions during the regular season, and games would frequently end in ties. And while the NFL instituted a provision for a sudden-death overtime period in a title game in 1941, no championship game had ever been tied after regulation. This was new, and new is always exciting.

The Giants won the coin toss but were forced to punt. The Colts then proceeded to drive the ball 80 yards on thirteen plays, and when Alan Ameche plunged over the goal line at Yankee Stadium to win the game, he broke Eisenman's heart in the process. The Greatest Game Ever Played (as it would eventually become known) was now history.

While some still debate the quality of the game itself, with its conservative play calling and sometimes sloppy play, there is no doubt about one thing: Through the magic of television, this game captured America's imagination. It was the first nationally televised championship game, and it attracted a remarkable 50 million viewers (although none in New York because the league's blackout rules at the time prohibited a local broadcast of even a sold-out game). This was the first hint that the NFL's championship game could turn into something more than sixty minutes of fullback sweeps and post patterns.

But just as the NFL was beginning to move into the public consciousness, a threat to the league's very existence was taking shape. Like many such threats, it started with a powerful man and a perceived slight.

Throughout NFL history, the Chicago Bears, owned and run by George "Papa Bear" Halas, has been one of the league's best and most profitable franchises. Not so their then-crosstown rivals the Cardinals. In the early 1960s, the Bidwill family was entertaining offers for the team, and one of the potential bidders was a young Texas oil millionaire named Lamar Hunt, who planned on moving the team to Dallas. When he couldn't secure more than a minority interest in the Cardinals or a promise that the team could be moved, Hunt changed tactics. He approached the NFL Expansion Committee, headed by Halas. NFL commissioner Bert Bell was concerned about diluting his newly popular product with new teams, and Hunt returned to Texas empty-handed, at least for the moment.

"The idea just hit me while I was flying home from my last attempt to buy the Cardinals," Hunt recalled. "I knew that other cities were interested in getting pro football teams, and I decided the answer had to be a new league."

The twenty-six-year-old Hunt approached another young oilman, Bud Adams, who also had tried without success to buy the Cardinals and move them to Houston, and with six other owners they formed what Hunt called "The Foolish Club." Their fledgling American Football League held its first meetings in August 1959 and began play in 1960.

A natural rivalry sprang up between the NFL and Hunt's well-funded rival league. (When informed that his son's football team was losing a million dollars a year, Hunt's oil baron father H.L. copped a line from *Citizen Kane* and replied, "At this rate he'll only last 150 years.") The AFL also had another acronymed ally: ABC. The league signed a $1.7 million deal with the network, giving the AFL crucial exposure on television.

The NFL went after Hunt, locating an expansion team in Dallas— named the Cowboys—which ultimately forced him to move his Dallas Texans franchise to Kansas City, where they would become the Chiefs. The Minnesota Vikings ownership group had initially agreed to play in the AFL, but the NFL made them an offer to join the senior league, and they did.

The first and most furious battle between the two leagues was over the rights to college players. The NFL began to literally babysit each of its draftees, sending a league representative to shadow the player and keep him away from AFL scouts until he could sign. The elaborate program didn't always work.

"The Dallas Cowboys were babysitting [Otis Taylor] in a motel room to keep him away from the AFL scouts," Hunt told *Pro Football Weekly*. "But one of our scouts, Lloyd Welles, went into the motel and found a janitor to give a message to Otis. Otis climbed out the window of the motel, got into Lloyd's car, and was on the next flight to Kansas City. We signed him the next day."

This battle over players proved costly to both sides, with players' salaries skyrocketing because they could play one league against the other in contract negotiations. Sometimes it went to extremes, as in the case of Heisman Trophy winner Billy Cannon, who signed deals with teams in both leagues.

Still, while the AFL was winning these skirmishes, its day-to-day survival wasn't ensured until January 29, 1964, when the league signed a $36 million television deal with NBC. That influx of cash led to another coup for the AFL the following year, when the New York Jets signed quarterback Joe Namath to a then-unprecedented $427,000 contract, snatching him away from the St. Louis Cardinals, who owned his NFL rights.

The bold moves by the top AFL teams were putting the NFL's poorer teams—such as the Washington Redskins and the Pittsburgh Steelers—in a financial bind. With the television deal making it clear that their rival wasn't about to fold anytime soon, the NFL sought peace. On April 4, 1966, a clandestine meeting was scheduled between Hunt and Cowboys owner Tex Schramm at Dallas' Love Field. They met at the airport's Texas Ranger statue and retired to Schramm's car in a dark parking garage. Schramm talked about the problems that their competition was causing for both leagues, and the Cowboys' owner again broached the idea of a merger. A year earlier, the NFL had put out feelers about a potential merger, but their offer included several poison-pill provisions, including a $50 million indemnity fee and the relocation of the New York Jets and Oakland Raiders to cities without NFL teams. Hunt told Schramm he thought that the AFL owners would be amenable, at least in principle, to an agreement without these kind of deal killers, and with that he hopped his connecting flight to Houston.

Even on the verge of a lasting peace, there were still a few post-truce salvos yet to be fired in the AFL-NFL war. Throughout their rivalry, the two sides abided by an informal agreement not to poach players already under contract. In 1966, the New York Giants breached the peace, signing placekicker Pete Gogolak, a pioneer of the now-ubiquitous soccer-style technique, away from the Buffalo Bills. Thus provoked, new AFL commissioner Al Davis, who was in the dark about Hunt's secret merger discussions, went to the mattress. He proceeded to sign eight top NFL quarterbacks, including John Brodie and Roman Gabriel, as well as Bears tight end Mike Ditka. Gabriel's deal was worth a whopping $400,000, while Brodie stood to make a quarter of a million, a monumental raise from the $38,000 he was making with the 49ers. This bidding war didn't seal the deal on the merger, but it did make clear the financial consequences of continued hostilities between the two leagues.

On June 8, 1966, the National Football League and the American Football League signed a formal merger agreement. Under the terms of the deal, which would bring the two leagues together beginning in 1970, Pete Rozelle would become the commissioner of the expanded league. The AFL would pay an $18 million indemnity to the NFL, but all franchises in both leagues would remain in their current locations, and there would be a combined draft that would end the bidding wars over players. With the pact came one other order of business: a champion-ship game between the NFL and AFL champions at the end of the 1966 season.

So what to call this new title game? If Commissioner Rozelle, the ac-knowledged father of the Super Bowl, had his way, it would have been called the AFL-NFL Championship Game, which isn't so much a name as a description. Briefly, there was some sentiment in favor of The Big One, which, at best, sounds like something on a fast-food chain's menu. Then Lamar Hunt got into the picture. Hunt was nothing if not full of ideas. At one point, the billionaire tried to buy Alcatraz Prison and turn it into a shopping and tourist destination. Around the time of the merger negotia-tions, Hunt saw his son Lamar junior and his daughter, Sharron, playing with a new ball from Wham-O that was almost impossibly bouncy. It wasn't such a leap from Super *Ball* to Super *Bowl*. Hunt brought it up at an own-ers' meeting, and—over Rozelle's strong objections—the name stuck.

"I was smart enough to understand that it was a corny term that would never catch on with the public," he later recalled with character-istic self-deprecation. In a nod to Rozelle, who was concerned that the term wasn't appropriately dignified, Hunt half-jokingly suggested add-ing a Roman numeral at the end. While the name Super Bowl was still a nickname during the first two Super Bowls—the game tickets bear Rozelle's unwieldy choice of name—the moniker became official with Super Bowl III.

Four decades later, there is great irony in all this. What started out as an almost offhand riff on the name of a children's toy has become one of the most valuable and rigorously protected trademarks in history. For the 2008 game there were only twenty-two national sponsors who are authorized to use the phrase "Super Bowl" or the game's logo in ads or promotions. Protecting the name, once derided by the league's commis-sioner, has become a full-time job for the NFL's staff of lawyers.

Every year they send out hundreds of cease-and-desist letters to infringers large and small. Those who have drawn the ire of the NFL run the gamut. The easy targets are vendors looking to make a quick profit on bootleg T-shirts. More problematic are national corporations looking to test the line between free speech and protected trademarks. Coors was hauled into court by the NFL in 1993 over the use of "Super Sunday" in an ad campaign and again in 1999 over the use of the phrase "the official beer of NFL players," a designation purchased from the marketing arm of the NFL Players Association. After the NFL prevailed in court, Coors took the high road and the company paid the NFL a reported $300 million in 2002 to become the league's official beer. The deal was renewed for five years in 2005 for a reported $500 million.

A favorite loophole in this unofficial ambush marketing war is "The Big Game." Advertisers ranging from Radio Shack to FOX (in a year when another network was broadcasting the game) have used this euphemism to refer to the Super Bowl. In 2007, the NFL attempted to close the loophole by trademarking the phrase. Only one problem: Stanford and Cal call their annual college football meeting The Big Game, a tradition that's been going on since 1892. When the schools objected, the NFL quietly abandoned its efforts.

At the other end of the spectrum, the NFL ran up against an enforcement nightmare in trying to deal with organizations holding large-scale Super Bowl parties. The league prohibits "mass out-of-home" gatherings in front of a television larger than fifty-five inches. That provision ensnared both a Las Vegas casino and the New England Aquarium. The controversy came to a head in 2007, when the Falls Creek Baptist Church in Indianapolis canceled its annual Super Bowl gathering after receiving a cease-and-desist letter from the league only days before the party. Ironically, the national attention surrounding the incident seems to have helped the church. Pastor John Newland reported that in the wake of the controversy his average Sunday congregation grew from 275 to 350, and a series of church-sponsored in-home football parties have proven popular with believers and nonbelievers alike. "We're not going to let the NFL stop us from doing what God called us to do," Newland said. "Satan can throw up obstacles, but with God's spirit we can't be stopped."

And then there's the saga of Spike the Super Ball. The Arizona host committee invented Spike, a bigger-than-life football wearing oversized sunglasses, "to generate awareness . . . and to unite the community in support of Super Bowl XLII." With various staffers inside the costume, Spike traveled the state, high-fiving children of all ages at 158 events ranging from the Ostrich Festival Parade in Chandler to Wyatt Earp Days in Tombstone to lower-profile appearances at local grammar schools and community centers. Spike has been a hit by all standards.

And while the NFL was fine with Spike per se, they did have an issue with his epithet: the Super Ball. Earlier in the year, the host committee received a cease-and-desist letter from the Wham-O company, the maker of the Super Ball, which inspired Lamar Hunt. The host committee countered by suggesting that Wham-O's trademark applied to a narrow market segment: balls that bounce. Spike, for all his other virtues, is not particularly bouncy. However, the NFL's objection was taken much more seriously, and soon Spike was being called the Team Captain. "We're just a non-profit trying to help the NFL put on a Super Bowl," host committee president Bob Sullivan told the *Arizona Republic*. "If we have to pull back on his full name, we will."

Until that first Super Bowl between the champions of the two leagues, both NFL and AFL championship games were played at the stadium of the team with the better record. Indeed, it was this home field advantage that actually separated NFL games from their college counterparts, where bowl games were almost always played at a neutral site. That legendary Giants-Colts championship game was played at Yankee

Stadium, and until the merger talk arose, the league was perfectly happy to treat its championship game as an extension of the playoff system.

But this had its limitations. The ultimate example of this was the 1967 NFL Championship Game, which has since come to be known as the Ice Bowl. Played in a New Year's Eve blizzard at Lambeau Field, the contest featured the most brutal conditions ever for a professional football game: a game-time temperature of –13 degrees and a windchill of –48 degrees. The referee's whistle froze to his lips on the opening play, and from then on, stoppages in play were signaled by shouting. Packers quarterback Bart Starr suffered frostbite and Dallas Cowboys quarterback Don Meredith was hospitalized with pneumonia after the game. The University of Wisconsin-La Crosse band was scheduled to perform, but their halftime show was canceled after seven members suffered hypothermia. And the conditions likely gave the Packers the NFL title. Green Bay coach Vince Lombardi is said to have decided that attempting a game-tying field goal on fourth down, which could have sent the game into a frigid sudden-death overtime, would have been too cruel for the Green Bay fans, so he went for a touchdown instead. Quarterback Bart Starr called for a handoff to running back Chuck Mercein, but Starr deemed the field conditions too treacherous. He kept the ball and basically stumbled in for the score.

On one hand, Starr's quarterback sneak was the stuff of legend, with many football purists calling the play one of the greatest of all time and lamenting the lack of weather-related drama in modern championship games. But the Ice Bowl was hardly the kind of game that football lovers craved to see in person, and Green Bay isn't a usual first choice for a midwinter getaway.

So when faced with the political issue of deciding where to hold the first Super Bowl, the founders were faced with an intractable problem. Neither league's champion would be satisfied by awarding home-field advantage to the team with the better record when those records were

compiled against wholly different competition. So they struck an obvious but fortuitous compromise: play the game at a neutral site.

Rozelle's vision for the new championship game was simple: a large
stadium, a warm-weather city, and a big crowd. The Los Angeles Coliseum met the first two criteria.

The last requirement—a big crowd—proved more problematic.
When the NFL championship game was played in the hometown of
one of the teams, a sellout was assured. And the organizers of college
bowl games generally knew which teams were going to play on New
Year's Day by the time Thanksgiving rolled around. That first NFL-AFL
Championship Game had neither advantage. The crowd of 61,946 was
respectable, but it was about 30,000 short of filling the huge stadium.
"We got a bunch of tickets for NFL Films," recalls Steve Sabol, president of NFL Films. "And before the game at our cameramen's meeting,
my dad came to me and said, 'I don't want to get back into the elevator.
Here are twelve tickets, if you can get rid of them.' So I stood there, and
I had twelve tickets, and never sold one of them. I saved three or four of
them. They're worth something now."

And while modern Super Bowls enjoy at least the appearance of
clockwork precision, the first Super Bowl had anything but. For example, Dallas GM Tex Schramm suggested using a state-of-the-art remote-
control system for the scoreboard clock that the team had tested during
the season. The primitive remote was attached to the large wrought-iron
hands of the Coliseum clock, and during the week before the game the
system was checked and checked again, with the referee starting and
stopping the clock over and over again and the inventor of the system
showing off by firing the remote from between his legs.

However, on the opening kickoff, one of the clock's hands simply
fell off, plummeting like a javelin more than fifty feet to the stands—
fortunately empty—below.

"What the hell happened to the goddamn clock?" bellowed Rozelle.

What had happened was simple. They had tested the old clock so much that the metal fatigued and the hand fell off.

The beginning of the second half didn't go much better. The game was being televised by both NBC and CBS, and the NFL crew in the booth was monitoring the CBS broadcast. The NBC broadcast was running a few seconds behind schedule, so while CBS viewers saw the kick-off, NBC was still in commercial. The referee saw the problem and whistled the play dead while the ball was in the air, and the ball was teed up again for the do-over to end all do-overs.

And it wasn't much smoother during play. For its official ball, the NFL used a Wilson model called the Duke, which was optimized for kicking. The AFL used a slimmer Spalding ball, similar to the ball used in college football, that was better for passing. The question remained: Which ball would be used for the first world championship game? An unwieldy compromise was reached. Each team would snap the ball used in its league while on offense, and throughout the game there were several instances in which the wrong ball was put into play and a center stopped play and told the officials, "Hey, this isn't our ball."

How much has the Super Bowl changed over the years? Steve Sabol has a unique perspective on the subject. He is one of only a handful of people who have attended every Super Bowl. Indeed, in many ways, NFL Films has grown with the game. Founded in 1962 by Sabol's father, Ed, who was an overcoat salesman, NFL Films started small, but the rich colors, the tight head shots, the poetic slow-motion action, and the dramatic narration by John "Voice of God" Facenda soon helped to establish the image of professional football during the period of the league's fastest growth. Now NFL Films is a subsidiary of the league, generating $50 million in annual revenue and substantial promotional value. And while its operations are totally separate from the broadcasts—indeed,

NFL Films' footage is shot on film rather than videotape—the NFL Films style has also been an undeniable influence on the game that's seen in America's living rooms. Those in-the-face-mask close-ups and reverse-angle replays that define the best broadcasts are straight out of the NFL Films playbook.

"I was an art major in college, and I studied Picasso and Braque," Sabol explains. "And I always thought that what Picasso did with a bowl of fruit was to look at a single image from multiple perspectives and from separate moments in time. So I try to do the same thing in football, except that what Picasso did with a woman's head, I'm doing with a draw play or a power sweep."

Sabol is also a master storyteller, and this yarn about Super Bowl IV in New Orleans illustrates just how far the game has come.

"We booked like twenty rooms at the Bienville House five months before. So we get down there on a Thursday, and we go to check in, and they only have ten rooms for us. So my father says, 'What do you mean, ten rooms? I've got forty people here!' And it was, 'Oh, Mr. Sabol, we got a dry cleaners' convention that came here, and they paid more money, and . . .' I mean, can you imagine? In the public's mind, the NFL wasn't that big a deal. The official camera crew came in, and we got kicked out of our hotel rooms for a dry cleaners' convention. In my mind, that just said everything about the Super Bowl back then."

Enter Plan B. One of the part-time assistant cameramen was a doctor, and he managed to find a block of rooms at the charity hospital in New Orleans.

"It was a funny expression: ten patients under 'limited observation,'" Sabol recalls. "And three of our guys actually were in rooms with other patients. The awful part of the story was that our main cameraman, Morris Kellman, shared a room with a guy who died in the middle of the night on the Saturday before the game. He had a heart attack or something, and a siren went off and they had the defibrillators in there. He was a World War II veteran, and his wife was there. Morris had had a chance to talk to them a little bit about football. Morris was so shaken the next day, he just felt he couldn't shoot."

As Sabol's story illustrates, the Super Bowl wasn't an overnight success. Soon enough, the technical glitches, low attendance, and hotel rooms given away to dry cleaners would be a thing of the past. But one number from Super Bowl I proved to be prophetic: More than 50 million television viewers tuned in to watch that inaugural Super Bowl, a taste of things to come.

8

THE SHOW

No Direction Home

It's one of those scenes that gets sports fans all warm and fuzzy. It was a couple of hours before Super Bowl XXXIX in Jacksonville, and New England Patriots linebacker Tedy Bruschi took his two kids out onto the field. He ran into FOX sideline reporter Brian Baldinger. After a little casual conversation, Baldinger figured that the quickest way to any parent's heart is to entertain his kids.

"Guys, c'mon over here and see this," said Baldinger. "They put a camera inside the pylon."

Baldinger turned back to Bruschi. The kids turned their attention to the end zone pylon. To ripping the pylon out of the ground, more accurately.

"Get those kids out of there!" shouted Artie Kempner, the director of the Super Bowl for FOX. The problem, of course, was that Kempner was watching this transpire on a monitor in the FOX truck a quarter mile from the field. And the camera operator in position was high in the stands, hundreds of feet away from the disaster in progress. Baldinger wasn't wearing his earpiece. So Kempner was as helpless as someone listening to a friend choke on a chicken bone over the phone. He shouted, he cursed, all to no avail. In the truck, no one can hear you scream.

Kempner watched in disbelief as the kids played with the pylon, knowing that if they managed to disconnect the wire buried under the turf, there'd be no way to fix it only hours before game time. Just a couple of days earlier, Kempner and his FOX network colleagues had talked up the pylon cam as the network's biggest Big Game innovation in front of a roomful of reporters. Now two unattended children were about to torpedo the biggest broadcast of the year—and, perhaps more relevant, Artie Kempner's first Super Bowl.

But then, like two adolescent grizzly bears who get bored while mauling a hiker, Bruschi's kids abandoned the pylon just as suddenly as they'd attacked it, and Artie Kempner's blood pressure began falling back toward normal.

As for the pylon cam? "We ended up using it twice," Kempner recalls.

Kempner is the director on FOX Sports' A-Team. While you've probably never heard of him unless you're one of those read-the-credits types, you've certainly seen his work. Every week, he and his crew are at the weekend's biggest NFC game.

What exactly does the director of a sports broadcast do? He's in charge of deciding what live pictures you'll see. On Sunday, Kempner sits in front of a bank of monitors in the truck and tells the technical director which camera to switch to—getting the red light, it's called in the business. It's a straightforward job with a multitude of complexities, a bit like saying that a head coach's job is to win football games. And right now, Kempner, who'll sit on the hot seat in the FOX truck at the Super Bowl, is the best in the business.

He has eight Emmys to his credit, but he also owns an even more rarified distinction. When he's not directing football, he also directs FOX's NASCAR telecasts. So when Pixar needed to translate the excitement of racing to the screen for the movie *Cars*, director John Lasseter sought out Kempner. They discussed the camera positions and how they're used in a broadcast. Then Lasseter tossed the question open: Where would Kempner put the cameras if budget and safety and sheer physics weren't an issue? So the animated racing sequences in the film feature cameras hovering between cars and buried in the track (an innovation that FOX has subsequently adopted for its broadcasts).

To repay that contribution, Kempner was not only named as a technical consultant in the credits but also got a cameo of sorts. In the big race at the end of the film, there's a quick scene in the television truck, with a purple car wearing headphones barking instructions to a pickup truck. That first car was Kempner. Because each screen on the monitor bank was playing live video, it was also the most complicated shot in the history of Pixar Films.

And in a way, that's what Kempner and his crew are up against. This is an age when viewers in every medium are inundated with dazzling images courtesy of computer-generated graphics. They're led into every sports broadcast with highly polished and slickly produced pregame, postgame, and halftime shows that sometimes command more attention—and draw higher ratings—than the game itself. And on Super Bowl Sunday, even the commercials provide competition. Amid this barrage, Kempner and company have a straightforward but not-so-simple task: to keep the game relevant.

Kempner is sitting on a high stool at a table in the photographers' lounge in Arthur Ashe Stadium, site of the U.S. Open tennis tournament. It's still almost a week before the beginning of football season, but his summer vacation is rapidly coming to a close. His wife, Marcy, who has seven Emmys of her own, is working the CBS broadcast, and he's come to watch a little tennis and, when she's done in the broadcast truck, steal a quick date with his wife while his three teenage boys are occupied elsewhere. But even here, even now, it doesn't take much nudging to shift Kempner's focus to Glendale in February.

"There's a tremendous amount of temptation in the Super Bowl. It's South Beach, and we're loaded with money," he says, reflecting on the lessons of the pylon cam. "You've just got to be careful that you don't misuse that money, or misuse that time, and make yourself look like a jackass on America's biggest stage. All games are important, but this game is way too important to be messing around."

The challenge for a Super Bowl production team is striking a balance. The first fear is the obvious one, the one where you look like a jackass by missing a clean angle on a crucial play. Kempner recalls a Broncos-Patriots playoff game on another network the previous winter where Denver defensive back Champ Bailey made what appeared to be an interception. The question was whether he'd had possession of the ball. Based on the angles that CBS had, it was impossible to tell. "I would have had the same angles if I were doing that game," says Kempner.

As bad as a moment like that is in a playoff game, it becomes a disaster of major proportions on Super Sunday. Keep in mind that in the modern NFL, with instant replay, the lack of a definitive angle could affect not only the broadcast but also the outcome of the game itself. With the advent of the current instant replay system in 1999, officials use the broadcast video feed to make decisions on challenges of the game's most controversial calls. Up until now the outcome of a Super

Bowl had never been decided by the lack of a clear replay, but the prospect chilled Kempner to his very core.

"The worst thing that could happen in your whole life as a production person in the Super Bowl is that somebody from some pool feed has the definitive look that you don't have. They happen to be standing in the right place at the right time. And there was a play that was overruled, a touchdown that wasn't a touchdown."

Kempner catches his breath. "Those are the kind of things you have nightmares about." He stops and edits himself. "I don't have *nightmares*. Those are the kinds of things I *think* about."

The obvious solution to that problem is to add cameras. Kempner gets out a piece of paper and begins to diagram camera angles like a coach drawing a play. In a typical football game, there are high cameras at each team's 25-yard line and at the 50. In the Super Bowl, FOX will add cameras looking down each goal line.

Plus, he says, "we'll have cameras looking down each sideline. That's their job. Feet. Ball. Hands. Possession. To give us as much chance to capture that moment and be definitive."

The temptation, of course, is to assume that if a few extra cameras are good, then lots more are better. But that's not always the case. During most of the year, budgetary constraints get in the way of putting these ideas into practice. But not on Super Bowl Sunday.

"They've done Super Bowls with fifty cameras," he recalls. "Back in the day they just kept on adding cameras all over the place. They had four in each end zone. They had two carts rolling up and down the field. They had *eight* handhelds. I don't know how you control that." He shakes his head at the prospect and laughs. "You're not herding cats. You're herding *tigers*. You're gonna get hurt."

Kempner is old-school in the very best sense of the term. He watches game tapes like a coach watches film, and internalizes all of it. Kempner can watch a random clip and tell you not only which network did it but also which *director* was at the controls. He's seen how the very best production teams—and after all, it's only a network's best crew that works the season's final game—have gone astray in covering the Super Bowl: In an attempt to avoid looking like the proverbial jackass, they've gone into broadcasting's equivalent of the prevent defense and risked the integrity of the broadcast in an attempt to stave off an embarrassing mistake.

And for the guy who'll be sitting in the hot seat next, that realization—that the best in the business have taken on this challenge and fallen short—is more than a little daunting.

"If you go back and look at Super Bowls and you look at the first quarter, they're all very, very choppy," Kempner explains. "Some of them, the second quarter is very, very choppy. For some of them, even the third quarter is very, very choppy. For some, the whole game is choppy. Because it's the Super Bowl, they changed everything they did, and all of a sudden their core cameras are not their core cameras anymore."

As is his wont, Kempner pulls out a football analogy. "It's not like Bill Belichick says, 'It's the Super Bowl, so we're going to play with fifteen guys.'" Kempner reveals his deceptively simple strategy: Approach the Super Bowl like it's any other game. Add only a few cameras to the mix, rely on the same camera angles that worked in the NFC Championship Game, and use those extra cameras largely as a safety net.

"You have to go in there with a logical plan," says Kempner. "You can't get caught up in the fact that you've got a little more money to spend."

It all sounds so straightforward, sitting in a tennis stadium at the end of August. But Kempner's done this before. He understands how big this game is and how much can happen between now and February.

"I know it's a football game. I know I can cover a football game," he says, smiling a slightly worried smile. "But it's the Super Bowl. This is history. And there's a big difference."

9

THE SHOW

The Men Upstairs

"One of these days my response is going to be that we're going to do it in black and white with only five cameras," says Ed Goren.

At the network's Rockefeller Center offices, Goren, the president of FOX Sports, was responding to one of those softball questions that top execs usually love: What sort of new and exciting innovations are planned for the upcoming Super Bowl? Many suits would have taken this as the opportunity to launch into the broadcasting equivalent of the presidential candidate's stump speech, a thirty-second house ad for the upcoming Super Bowl specifically and FOX Sports in general.

But Goren doesn't take the bait. Instead, this grizzled thirty-year veteran of the tough world of sports broadcasting steers the conversation in an entirely different direction. Innovation, he has learned, can be a double-edged sword.

"It's like the national budget. Every year, for whatever reason, it expands. Super Bowl production has always been 'How many more cameras do you add this year?'"

Goren's boss, FOX Sports chairman David Hill, looks up from his cell phone and chimes in.

"It's like the height of the Cold War," he bellows, his jovial Australian accent tempering the sheer volume.

"'We've got eight cameras.'

"'We've got 10.'

"'We've got 12.'

"'We've got 24.'

"'We've got *three hundred*.'

"'We've got *seven thousand* miles of cable.'"

The message in all this is clear: Sometimes more is less. A live television broadcast isn't like a feature film. Here, time is the enemy, especially when there's only thirty seconds between plays.

"For every camera you have to add a tape machine," Goren explains. "If you have ten videotape machines for replay and you expand it to twenty tape machines, it's going to take you longer to find the definitive replay on twenty machines than on ten. We found that you get to a point where you have so much equipment that it actually slows down the broadcast."

Why the extra equipment? At some level, it's about wanting one more toy and having the money to get it. On the other hand, it's all about the fear of the worst-case scenario that Kempner outlined earlier. "Every game has, in effect, a defining moment, a controversial moment where the viewer is relying on television—and, in this case, the NFL is relying on television for their review procedures," says Goren, echoing his top director, or perhaps vice versa. "Did you fumble the ball or not? There are times during the regular season where we don't have the definitive angle. That's not acceptable in a game like this. There should be no *question* what the proper call should be."

But for everything else that it is, the Super Bowl is still a game, not unlike a conference championship, which gets the network's best team and most equipment, but nothing truly out of the ordinary. And this has been the mantra around FOX Sports all season long. Goren trots out his own football analogy, remarkably similar to what Artie Kempner said a few weeks earlier. It turns out that the brash director does pay attention in meetings.

"It would be as if the New England Patriots go undefeated in the regular season, undefeated in the playoffs. And now they're in the Super Bowl, and Belichick throws out half his game plan and puts in stuff they haven't used all year," says Goren. "You stay with what works."

"All this stuff is really the meringue," says Hill. "We need to make sure the pie is right, and the pie is a production of the game where everyone can see what goes on and knows what the hell just happened." He pauses for a moment. "I'm sorry for switching metaphors," he laughs, and goes back to his phone.

Hill and Goren not only sit at the top of the food chain at FOX Sports, they've been at the network since its very inception. Hill came from an unusual background—equal parts television news and television sports—and was hired by Rupert Murdoch's fledgling Sky Sports in Great Britain in 1988. When Murdoch launched FOX Sports in 1994, the brash and energetic Hill seemed like the perfect choice to bring the network's edgy, upstart style to the world of sports. He's always been the guy with one more idea. For example, during those early days, he had his staffers play video games for a half hour a day so that they could get into the mind-set of younger viewers. And he's nothing if not hands-on.

When FOX first won the rights to NASCAR racing, he walked out to the edge of the track with a camcorder, scouting camera angles. He was quickly hustled away from this dangerous vantage point by security guards, just before three cars crashed violently and came to rest in the very spot where Hill had been standing only moments before.

FOX's move into the NFL shook up the tight little world of sports broadcasting. Industry insiders thought there was little chance that CBS would get bumped out of the NFL rights club that then also included NBC, then broadcasting AFC games, and ABC, doing Monday Night Football. But money talks, and FOX committed $1.58 billion over four years to snare the rights to NFC games away from CBS. While the package included a doubleheader for each weekend of the seventeen-week season along with the playoffs, the biggest prize was the right to broadcast every third Super Bowl. When FOX signed a six-year extension of its NFL deal in 2004, the price tag had increased to a cool $4 billion.

Still, Hill was enough of a pragmatist to know that radical ideas and mind-boggling investment would only go so far in creating a sports division from the ground up. So one of Hill's first moves was to hire Goren. Working at CBS Sports, Goren had collected a shelf's worth of Emmys and wide respect throughout the industry. His presence gave the network the instant credibility it needed to hire on-screen talent such as John Madden and Pat Summerall as well as top technical staff like Kempner and his producer Richie Zyontz.

Hill and Goren complemented each other, with Hill as the big-picture guy providing the creative spark—always asking "Why not?"—and Goren handling the nuts and bolts, figuring out how to implement the ideas they'd come up with. It's a classic fire-and-ice kind of partnership, and one that's worked out well for both parties.

"It's like a marriage," Hill says, only half jokingly.

All of this back-to-basics talk from Hill and Goren would sound very strange to the network's detractors. One of FOX Sports' first innovations was the FOX Box, a graphic that would display both the score and the time remaining in the game. Hill had used a similar graphic device in soccer broadcasts in England, and in his first collaboration with Goren, who had come over from CBS, they did the same for NFL football.

It was a controversial concept, to say the least.

"The reaction was unbelievable, like it was the end of motherhood and religion and the sun wouldn't come up tomorrow," Hill recalls. "We got *death threats*."

"Mine was from San Francisco," says Goren.

"Mine was from Texas," chuckles Hill. "And now every sport in the world has stolen the idea."

While some have accused FOX of pursuing technological razzle-dazzle above all else, Hill and Goren contend that it's the ideas that drive the technology, not the other way around.

"We have never stumbled across something," says Hill. "We will go to someone and say, 'This is what we want to do. Can you build it for us?'"

Take the case of the glowing hockey puck. When FOX won the broadcast rights to the NHL, the first thing they discovered was the fact that casual viewers had trouble following the puck. So they created FOX Trax.

As Hill begins his explanation, Lou D'Ermilio, the network's senior VP of media relations, hands me something that looks like a piece of modern art. It's half a hockey puck, with a gold battery in the middle atop a green circuit board with a dozen infrared sensors radiating toward the edge like a robotic snowflake. In use, all this technology would be covered by a layer of epoxy and the other half of the puck. In conjunction with this space-age puck, the network installed twenty infrared sensors and ten infrared cameras around the arena, which would detect the pulses emitted by the puck. This information would be sent back to a dedicated trailer—the Puck Truck—which would translate it into computer graphics. The result? A puck that glowed blue on-screen and grew a cometlike tail when a shot was particularly hard.

Did FOX Trax revolutionize the sport and capture record ratings? No. It was used for two years, and while some hockey purists hated it, casual viewers seemed to like it, but not enough to make them watch hockey in greatly increased numbers. But Goren and Hill are quick to point out that this technology was quickly adapted for other sports, notably NASCAR, where it allowed producers to generate graphics that could be tagged to cars moving in a pack, and in the NFL, where it was used to give a visual representation of the first-down marker. "It sounded simple and we tried to do it with the equipment we had, but we couldn't," says Hill. "We had to get the technology."

Just as important, FOX Trax was a harbinger of the approach the network would bring to its biggest events, including the Super Bowl. On one hand, no idea was too far-fetched. On the other hand, innovation didn't mean much if it didn't deliver.

"Before we do anything, Ed and I spend endless hours playing devil's advocate," Hill continues. "We go round and around, and then when we decide we're going to do it, we do it." These meetings take place via cell phone, on the golf course, or, as Hill explains, over an adult beverage.

"Everything that we've done since, we've done with the belief that there's a solid editorial rationale," Goren agrees. "When it doesn't work it's because it's gimmicky."

In the television world, the Super Bowl is, well, a freak show. It's totally unlike any other program. For example, since the game is rotated among the NFL's rights holders, it puts networks in the unusual position of rooting for their rivals.

Indeed, entering the 2008 game, three networks could claim a piece of Super Bowl supremacy. The highest ratings in terms of number of viewers was NBC's broadcast of the 1996 game between Dallas and Pittsburgh, with 94.1 million. ABC could lay claim to the largest number of homes, 45.9 million in the 2006 Pittsburgh-Seattle game. To find the highest rating, you have to go back to 1982, when the 49ers, playing in their first Super Bowl, took on the Bengals, drawing a 49.1 rating for CBS. Interestingly, the viewership has little to do with the teams involved or the quality of the game. Pittsburgh and Dallas have strong national followings, but Super Bowl XXX was rather one-sided. The 49ers' big rating came very early in their dynasty, before Joe Montana became a household name.

But these are just minor blips in the ratings. The real story is the year-to-year consistency of these numbers. The 1991 and 2006 Super Bowls posted nearly identical ratings (41.9 and 41.6, respectively), and for all the years in between the ratings stayed between 40.4 and 46.0. In a world where narrowcasting is increasingly a fact of life, the Super Bowl is one of the last remaining bastions of good old-fashioned broadcasting.

"Super Bowl ratings are as consistent as anything," Goren explains. "You've seen dramatic erosion on any other TV show, but you can go back ten years and every year the Super Bowl is in the low forties."

Despite the year-to-year consistency in viewership, there's an even more dramatic countertrend: the increase in the price of ad time. The price of a Super Bowl commercial in 1991 was $800,000, compared to $2.7 million in 2008. Even adjusting for inflation, as calculated by *Ad Week* magazine, that 1991 spot still cost only $1,198,515, or less than half as much as a 2008 spot. There are roughly sixty 30-second spots available per game; that means that ad revenue for the entire Super Bowl increased from roughly $71.9 million, inflation-adjusted, in 1991 to $162 million in 2006. (This figure is an average because advertisers who buy multiple spots or lock in ads in advance, as Anheuser-Busch does, may pay less than the going rate.) Approaching the 2008 game, FOX reported that some advertisers that bought their spots late paid as much as $3 million. Entering the 2009 game, NBC expects to average $3 million for Super Bowl XLIII spots, up from $2.7 million in 2008.

These advertisers—and the viewers they're trying to attract—clearly see the Super Bowl as something more than a football game.

"There are going to be people on Tuesday who say, 'Did you see that commercial?'" says Hill. "On what other TV shows do they talk about the commercials two days later?"

As a native Australian who's worked in Great Britain, Hill has a special appreciation of just how strange it is for a single football game to command a country's undivided attention. World Cup soccer may be huge, but it's also played between nations every four years, a format more akin to the Olympics. As an intranational contest, played annually, the Super Bowl stands alone.

"It's a remarkable worldwide phenomenon that a football game has become an unofficial national holiday," he says. "It defies all common sense, all common logic. It fulfills the need for human beings to be in the loop."

And that's where the Super Bowl broadcast has to walk a fine line. On one hand, it's the championship game of what can arguably be called America's national sport. On the other hand, the Super Bowl attracts casual fans who wouldn't even think about watching a conference championship game. So the goal for FOX is to make sure these once-a-year fans understand what's happening without dumbing down the broadcast for the hardcore fans who are second-guessing the coach's use of the cover-two defensive scheme.

Toward that end, Hill reimagined the Super Bowl's pregame festivities. He was perusing some notes in the imported black leather-bound datebook he carries with him in lieu of a laptop, and found a common thread. Since the casual fans are the ones that need to be cajoled to come to the television before the game starts, why not shift the focus away from matchups and coaching strategies and create a chance for viewers to see the celebrites who flock to the game? *American Idol* host Ryan Seacrest would host the red carpet ceremonies, and, of course, many of the celebrities he'd interview would have shows on FOX. Can you say *synergy*?

As for the game itself, Hill suggests that the key to pleasing everyone is the two guys in the booth, Joe Buck and Troy Aikman.

"Probably of everything, the most important part of our business is the announcers," says Hill. "At the base of our business it's a human being talking to another human being. A very knowledgeable, warm, close friend who's sitting on the sofa next to you," explaining what you've just seen. That's the key. Everything else comes from there. We're very fortunate with Joe and Troy that they're both intuitive teachers. They explain the inner workings of the game. We don't want anyone to sit on the sofa and say, 'What happened? Why did that happen? I don't understand it.' That would be a total failure."

Hill loves outrageous analogies, and he shifts forward on the sofa as he's about to launch into another one. He draws a parallel between the genial Buck and Howard Cosell, the *Monday Night Football* legend, who was in equal parts brilliant and abrasive.

"This is going to sound absolutely ridiculous, but I'm going to say it anyway—the thing that Cosell brought to sports broadcasting is that he went outside the narrow realm of sports. And he would use allegories and similes to describe a sporting situation using entertainment stuff. Joe does exactly the same thing. Now, how that would look in print? Joe Buck is like Howard Cosell? No, that's not what I'm saying. He uses his whole life experience as a palette from which to draw when he does his commentary. Most commentators use only their sport." In other words, Buck is the guy who can make those once-a-year television viewers feel at home—say, by dropping references to Green Day—while not losing the diehard.

Then, in a way, Goren circles back to my original question, of what FOX plans to add to the year's biggest game. "If you have the right announcing team, you can cover it with three cameras," he says. "And the viewing experience is going to be fantastic."

It seems that the mavericks of television sports, who have computerized hockey pucks and dodged death threats, have come full circle. The innovation for FOX Sports' exclusive coverage of Super Bowl XLII will be . . . drumroll, please . . . *a football game*. Now it's up to Artie Kempner and Company to deliver.

10

THE SHOW

Kicked Off

"You need a credential and a parking pass," says the security guard at the gate at Giants Stadium.

"But my credential and parking pass are at the gate," I explain.

"Well, that's not my problem," she says without a trace of sympathy. She turns away, walks back into the little hut, and motions me to turn my car around.

It is eight o'clock in the morning at Giants Stadium, five hours before kickoff of the first home game of the season, and even the hardiest tailgaters are nestled all snug in their beds. I have no choice but to head to the auxiliary parking lots, made necessary by the construction of the Xanadu shopping complex near the Meadowlands Arena—now called the Izod Arena.

I follow the signs to a parking lot at an office building across the road. Parking aplenty, and someone there to take my $20. However, there is no way to get back to Giants Stadium. I wander from attendant to attendant looking for information on the shuttle buses and discover they're only slightly more cooperative than the attendant at the stadium gates, lacking only a little hut to retreat to.

And then a cop comes over. Not just any cop, but the Lyndhurst police chief.

"I'm going over to the stadium to meet the FOX television crew and I'm late already," I implore.

He takes pity on me and tells me to hop into his black SUV. We take the two-minute drive over to the stadium and approach the same attendant who turned me away half an hour before. She's not impressed by the police car or his uniform. The chief actually has to flash his badge to gain access. I guess the next step would have been unholstering his Glock.

The chief drops me off near the TV compound, and Artie Kempner walks out with a small round TV compound credential. "Any trouble finding the place?" he asks.

I consider retelling the story about my police escort, but instead I just smile and shake my head. An attendant makes a quick check of my backpack and that's it. Artie and I stroll past the state police SWAT team and the German shepherds of the K-9 squad. I'm in.

While the FOX marketing guys will talk about the metaphorical road to the Super Bowl, this is its literal manifestation. FOX has a clear pecking order among its production teams, and the A-Team, led by Kempner, producer Richie Zyontz, and on-air talent Joe Buck and Troy Aikman, is at the top of that order. Every week they get the marquee matchup in the NFC, not knowing from week to week where that's going to take them. But one thing they do know—come the first week in February, they'll be in Glendale, Arizona.

Choosing the week's top game is a little bit art and a little bit science. Normally, the A-Team will be covering a game with "playoff implications." Translation: At least one of the teams involved has a good chance of representing the NFC in Super Bowl·XLII. But right now parity reigns supreme in the NFC, and there's no clear-cut powerhouse like the Dallas and San Francisco teams of a decade earlier.

It's only the second week of the season, and the contenders haven't yet been separated from the pretenders. Which is why Kempner and company are at Giants Stadium in East Rutherford, New Jersey, to bring you the Green Bay Packers and the New York Giants. Neither of these teams figures to be a real powerhouse this season. The Packers have Brett Favre, the last major holdover from their Super Bowl team, but otherwise seem to be in a rebuilding mode. A last-second win against Philadelphia in their opening game warmed more than a few hearts but changed few minds. The Giants started strong last year but stumbled through the end of the season and just barely made the playoffs. Despite that, the callers on WFAN, the local sports talk station, have been getting restless, calling for the head of coach Tom Coughlin, along with the scalp of disappointing young quarterback Eli Manning, who also suffered a worrisome shoulder injury in the opening game. A lopsided loss to the Cowboys last week did nothing to quell the growing dissatisfaction. But the Giants represent the NFC's largest market and the Packers have national appeal; in September that's enough to earn them the network's top spot.

The A-Team's traveling circus is housed in a dozen white trailers— with little extensions that can be cranked out for a couple of feet of extra elbow room—that are hauled from stadium to stadium. Today they're parked in strict alignment in a lot just west of the stadium. Kempner and I enter the trailer via an aluminum staircase that creaks like an extension ladder as Kempner bounds from tread to tread. Just inside the door is a small flag about the size of a bandanna: "The Beatings Will Continue Until Morale Improves." It's clearly a relic of Kempner at his we-kid-because-we-care best. Jokes aside, the FOX truck has been custom-fitted, but it still features a utilitarian look. The ceiling is lined with acoustic tile; the floors are laminate, as are the oak-trimmed counter-tops. In the back is a bevy of tape machines, which handle the nuts and bolts of the game's replays.

The central focus of the place is clear. In the front, there are three rows of desks facing a giant wall of monitors, mission control style. There are 108 monitors in all, each one sporting a different image. It's like an electronics store display on steroids. To the right is the control board, a giant Grass Valley console with a dizzying array of switches and sliders that allows them to jump among the thirteen cameras. "It's a giant remote control," explains technical director Colby Bourgeois, with a certain calculated modesty. The technical director's job is a bit like a coordinator's position in the NFL: a stepping-stone. A good one on a good team doesn't stay around very long, and this is Bourgeois' first season on the FOX first squad.

Kempner dumps his backpack at his desk at the front and hustles up to the press lounge, where he's called a camera meeting. While there's no actual rehearsal for the game—just a few minutes of camera checks on Friday to make sure everything's working as it should—there's plenty of homework. Kempner hands out a face book so that the crew can identify every coach on the sidelines, and he goes over their responsibilities and their likely locations. He also reviews situational responsibilities for each camera operator, no matter how obscure the situation. Game-winning field goal? Check. Hail Mary? Check. On-side kick? Check.

"I try to make everything as black and white as possible," he explains.

Then he starts analyzing the important players on each team the same way a coach might.

"Green Bay running game. Numbers 32 and 42, they have had seventeen carries combined in their career. The Green Bay offense is really boring except for number 4 [Brett Favre]. [Donald] Driver's his only go-to receiver as of now. . . .

"Giants defensively. Last week they got the shit kicked out of them by the Cowboys' offensive line. Andre Gurode had an absolute highlight day. That'll be his next contract tape. They really struggled against the run. . . .

"Giants offensively. How long can [Eli] Manning stay in the game? [Amani] Toomer being back is the biggest difference for Manning. That's his security blanket. He looked like a different guy against Dallas than he did all of last year. His confidence is high. [Jeremy] Shockey hasn't had a big play since . . . he didn't have one in 2006 . . . it's been a long time. Let's not everybody run to [head coach Tom] Coughlin after every play. Let me call you in . . .

"Green Bay has been excellent on defense. They have a really good defensive line, their corners are really aggressive. Al Harris has a bad elbow; let's keep an eye on how much he can do on the line of scrimmage. . . .

"For the Giants, their snappers are different for kicks and punts. They're both rookies. Number 93, Jay, what's his name?"

"Alford," replies one of the cameramen.

"Jay Alford is the short snapper and Zak DeOssie, Steve DeOssie's son, is the long snapper for punts," Kempner explains with mock gravitas. "The interesting thing is DeOssie's not the backup kick snapper and Alford's not the backup punt snapper. I think this is a situation fraught with peril."

The room erupts with laughter.

"Play-by-play framing. Any questions? John, your play-by-play framing is dictated by the outside linebacker and defensive ends. Are you a Giants fan?"

John nods.

"Remember a guy named Lawrence Taylor? Think of every outside linebacker and defensive end as Lawrence Taylor. Make sure he's included in the frame. That guy can shake up the game. . . .

"The only time we're going to use a pure Bobby Orr is if they're in the red zone and they put everybody in. No Marshall Plan this week."

Bobby Orr? That's the camera coverage in a four-wide-receiver set. What does the Bruins Hall of Fame defenseman (and Kempner's favorite hockey player) have to do with any of this? Four is Orr's number. This started when Kempner called for "four-wide" and instead found camera four pulling back from the action. In this sports-crazed world, it's a perfect solution. The Marshall Plan? A similar nod to Rams running back Marshall Faulk, who lined up in the backfield but often functioned as a receiver.

The tone of the meeting is jocular yet serious. A core group of cameramen travel with the A-Team, and in New York it's no real problem to cover the few open slots with seasoned pros. These guys know how to do their jobs. Kempner is updating them about the likely scenarios within the game and reminding them how they're going to fit into the A-Team's system.

"There's more selecting than directing now," he explains as the crew filters toward the brunch buffet. "Fifteen years ago, this meeting was a lot longer and a lot more serious. I had six cameras and four guys who I just met that day."

After the main meeting, he pulls one of the new guys aside. He's a pickup guy, not part of the traveling core group, and while he's experienced, he's manning a camera position he's never worked for Kempner before.

They talk about framing, with Kempner reminding him that with the A-Team the key is to follow his assignment, safe in the knowledge that everyone else is doing their job too. Talented camera operators on less-than-stellar crews will sometimes "chase the red light," deviating from the director's plan, hoping to get the shot that's likely to be chosen to go on the air. As much as any NFL coach, Kempner preaches that there's no *I* in *team*. Or in *Emmy*.

This camera op is moving to a position where he'll see less play-by-play action but still have important responsibilities for replays.

"So I'm basically like a safety?" he asks.

Bingo.

"Your job is to cover my ass," says Kempner.

"We don't have as many guys shooting play-by-play," Kempner explains as we walk back to the truck. "In another truck, with a big game like ours, you'll see ten guys following the ball. We don't understand why people do that. You lose out on a lot of elements of the game."

As game time approaches, the atmosphere doesn't change much. Back in the truck Kempner pours a glass from a big pitcher of iced tea and rips open a couple of packets of Sweet'N Low. Seated to his right, producer Richie Zyontz picks absently at a lean corned beef sandwich. Over the talkback, Joe Buck mimics boxing announcer Michael Buffer doing a prefight announcement. "Ladies and gentlemen, let's get ready toooooooo . . . draw on the Telestrator."

It's the looseness that comes when everyone's at the top of their game.

When Packers kicker Mason Crosby boots the ball, I remember what Kempner told me.

"Camera two does the kickoff, and as soon as the guy's tackled I'm looking at five and twelve, which are the two carts. I'll bring the quarterback on with either camera five or camera twelve." It made sense at the time.

This is what actually transpired in the seconds before, during, and after the kickoff, all rattled off at a pace that would make an auctioneer envious.

"Gilbride. Camera three. Gilbride please. Dissolve seventeen. Dissolve ten. Ball's on the tee. Change. Pictures, people. Set 'em up, set 'em up, set 'em up. Work the picture. Wide, fifteen. Come back. Dissolve seven. Quick. What the hell happened there? I got a whole big fucking duck. Eli coming out?"

As I would later discover, the profanity wasn't standard procedure for Kempner when addressing the crew, and it wasn't a good omen. As the game starts in earnest, a certain controlled frenzy permeates the truck, and I feel like I'm half a step behind, like I'm watching a complex video game where everything moves at lightning speed and I don't quite understand the rules. After a quarter or so a pattern begins to emerge.

Monitors one, two, and three, situated at eye level, are Kempner's main cameras for live play-by-play. "Those cameras are located in the grandstand high enough that you can see the play clearly, but not so high that it looks like ants on television," Kempner explains later. "Camera one is at the left 20, and I'm going to use that anytime the team is snapping the ball from the left goal line to the 35. Camera three does the same thing as camera one at the opposite end of the field. Camera two is directly at the 50, so I'm going to use him between the 40s or the 35s."

"Seven, my low end-zone camera, is below camera one. Five, my near-side cart camera, is below camera two. And nine, my right low end-zone camera, is below three. With those six cameras I could do the whole game and make it look really good," Kempner explains. "The rest are just, in my mind, ancillary. I have the two handhelds. They give me great color shots. Cameras ten and four are in the end zone for field goals, extra points, and isos." *Isos* is an abbreviation for one-on-one isolation framing, which is the bread and butter of replays.

One of the tangible perks of working on the A-Team is having access to a second sideline cart camera, the so-called reverse cart, which provides pictures of the near sideline. Kempner is the only FOX director who plays with this toy on a regular basis, and it's similarly exclusive at the other networks.

"It gives me an *entirely* different look at the same game," Kempner enthuses. "He's going to shoot play-by-play, give us that different angle. But after that play, he's headhunting guys on the near sideline, where I'd normally only get the back of their heads."

Kempner's got three play-by-play cameras—when you include the cable cam suspended over the field, there are eight different choices immediately after the play. Indeed, it's between plays that Kempner shows his signature style—in a word, aggressive. It means eschewing the safe shots of a guy walking back to the huddle and looking instead for a coach chewing a player out or a close-up so tight that it shows the confusion in a quarterback's eyes. It's in-your-face television, an NFL Films view of the world, but in real time. Kempner's lofty goal is to let the viewer see things that are invisible even from the best 50-yard-line seat. Better than being there.

"My wife said the Sunday night and Monday night games were more aggressive than we were," he told the crew before the game, throwing down the gauntlet.

"I think I have ADD," Kempner will confess. "I don't have the patience to watch one picture." Indeed, part of his evolution as a director has come from resisting these instincts just a little. "Good directors learn that sometimes the best picture is the one that's on. I try to be a little more patient, to hold the shot for just a second longer. When you cut right on the ball, it's jarring for the viewer and they don't even really know why."

Still, as this game moves on, I get the sense that things are just a little more frenetic than usual.

"Eight seconds," shouts the young guy sitting next to me.

There's one job in the truck that's the equivalent of playing the triangle in a symphony orchestra. Seated to my right, behind Bourgeois, is the eight-second guy. In front of him is a monitor with a split screen. On one side is the basic high-angle feed of the game. On the other is an isolation of the play clock.

When the play clock gets down to eight seconds, his job is to yell— you guessed it—"Eight seconds." It's not a complex job, and later in the season Kempner's thirteen-year-old-son, Jack, will hold down the job for a game.

But the eight-second guy is particularly busy today. When the Giants have the ball, he is getting hoarse.

And that's when I realize: As much as they prepare, the FOX A-Team is very much at the mercy of the teams on the field. "Offensive formation dictates defensive alignment," Kempner explained earlier. "Defensive alignment dictates camera framing. We come out, we see what the offense does and we adjust. We see what the defense does. We adjust again."

All the things that a modern offense does—quick counts, no huddles, hurry-ups—to try to keep the defense off balance serve to throw the television crew off as well. "They're doing it to try to keep the other team from making defensive substitutions, right?" He laughs, trying not to take it personally. "But they're also keeping us from running a replay."

What's even harder to deal with is when the offense is truly out of sync, the way the Giants are this afternoon. On most plays, Eli Manning is slow getting to the line of scrimmage, as if he's dreading what he might find there, and on several occasions he lets the clock run down so far that he incurs a delay-of-game penalty. And after a close call on the play clock, he compensates by rushing to the line on the next play.

The Giants' offense is running with a herky-jerky rhythm—or lack thereof—like a teenager trying to learn how to drive a stick shift. The Packers are a little more efficient, a young team run by a veteran quarterback, but they aren't exactly poetry in motion either. That same choppiness is apparent in the telecast and in Kempner's growing annoyance.

Giants kicker Lawrence Tynes misses a short field goal because of a bad snap by Jay Alford. But the crew doesn't have the shot. "C'mon, guys, what did I say in the meeting? Throw's got the cover, you morons." They had committed the cardinal sin of chasing the light, and because everyone was looking for the make, nobody got the miss. The viewers saw that the field goal was missed, but the blown assignments didn't allow the production team to show *why*. Producer Richie Zyontz simply purses his lips and rolls his eyes, but his displeasure is just as obvious.

As the Giants founder and the Packers lengthen their lead, the FOX crew channels the Giants. The framing is a little bit off, and Kempner sometimes looks for a shot only to find it isn't there. These aren't glaring mistakes—even the most attentive viewer at home isn't likely to catch them. But the A-Team didn't bring its A-game today. Kempner says his quick good-byes and plans his getaway, He stuffs his laptop in his bag, along with a DVD of the game. He normally watches a replay of the game on the train ride home. But not this time.

"Awful," he says, walking briskly through the parking lot, as if trying to escape. "Just awful."

11

THE SHOW

Rashomon
of the Red Zone

Fate. It's daunting to consider the role of chance in a career, or even in a life. A random decision made by a personnel office or a whim when you're twenty-three years old can shape the future in a way so profound that it's scary.

Such was the case with Artie Kempner and Richie Zyontz, the producer on FOX Sports' A-Team. What has evolved into a forged-in-battle friendship between two pros at the very top of their game, ready to work the biggest show in sports, started off as a rivalry between two young bucks each trying to find his way in the broadcasting business. It was the early 1980s, CBS Sports was the epicenter of the sports broadcasting universe, and both Kempner and Zyontz were broadcast assistants only a couple of years out of college. Zyontz had been on the road with the

Pat Summerall/John Madden crew and needed to get some studio experience if he was going to take the next step.

Did they hit it off?

"Not at all," says Kempner. "First of all, we're incredibly different. He's quiet and I couldn't be louder. He doesn't want anybody to know he's at the game doing it, and I want the whole world to know I'm doing the game. So our egos are 180-degree opposites."

And, at least in Kempner's eyes, they were competitors in a zero-sum game, fighting for the same starting spot in a lineup. "I had done the studio the year before, so I was like, 'Why is *he* the lead guy? He doesn't know shit about the studio. *I* should be the lead guy here.'"

What confused Kempner at first was that his rival wasn't interested in fighting back. With the impetuousness of youth, Kempner mistook Zyontz's reserve for weakness. "I was kind of going around him a little bit, because I just didn't think he got it. But I just didn't read him well, because he did get it—he got *everything*."

This minor-league turf war could have played out any number of ways, and most of them wouldn't have led to the Super Bowl for either Richie or Artie. But in the third week of that season, Zyontz calmly went to Kempner with a proposition.

"Listen," Zyontz said to Kempner. "We're really different. I know that. I know you like yourself to be out there, and that's fine. I don't care, I don't want to be out there. But we will do a lot better if we work as a team. If I have a great idea, we present it together. If you have a great idea, we present it together, you know. And if something bad happens, we take it together."

Zyontz pushed exactly the right button in his would-be rival. As a former college athlete, just a few years removed from the football field, having played special teams at the University of Florida. Kempner still viewed the world in sports metaphors. Zyontz had said, in essence, "Let's be teammates."

"Knowing him the way I do now, he probably thought about this a thousand times and ran every scenario through his head before he actually made the decision to talk to me about it," says Kempner. "He was 100 percent right. He straightened me out."

"Yeah, I do overthink things a little bit, as opposed to Artie, who kind of reacts before he thinks," says Zyontz. "We're a good team. The same dynamics exist today. Personalitywise, it hasn't changed a lot. Just the responsibilities have. We must have done something right, because I think we did okay. I know that I wouldn't be where I was today if I didn't have him as a partner all these years." And one more thing: "Believe me, he drives me crazy too sometimes."

The Zyontz-Kempner marriage, which seems surprisingly similar to the dynamic between their bosses, the loquacious David Hill and the more reserved Ed Goren, is a prime example of how opposites attract. It's even obvious in the FOX truck during the game. Zyontz is quiet and economical in his movements. He sits tucked in the left corner of the truck, while Kempner is positioned front and center, the proverbial bull in the china shop. While Zyontz is waiting—and there's plenty of that during a game weekend—he'll sit quietly reading or maybe doing a crossword puzzle. Whereas Kempner is all about perpetual motion and volume cranked to 10, Zyontz is reserved to the extreme, the quiet guy who waits and watches and then waits some more. He listens rather than waiting to talk. And despite Kempner's force of personality, it's really Zytonz who leads by example—his placid demeanor is the calming influence in a chaotic environment.

"There's no junk that goes on, there's no animosity anywhere—and that really comes from Richie," says Joe Buck. "Richie is a very low-key producer. He sets the tone: Everybody's responsible for their own job, and we all go do it, and we're proud of the end result."

Before he was a sports producer charged with televising the world's biggest sporting event, Zyontz was a sports-crazed kid from Queens with a particular passion for New York teams. His father took him to Madison Square Garden for that iconic game seven when Willis Reed limped out onto the hardwood floor against the Los Angeles Lakers in 1970. He still has a Willis Reed throwback jersey that he only takes out for special occasions. "That's a memory that's etched forever," he recalls. "Indelible."

And the sports jones continues, in slightly altered form, even today. "My greatest joy in life is shooting baskets," he says. Zyontz is a little taller than average, with a build that's evolved from downright skinny to merely thin. Just the sort of body that can give a kid basketball dreams. "I have a hoop in my backyard and I always have a basketball with me when I travel. I'll find a schoolyard and that's how I unwind, how I get the stress out. I'll be Earl Monroe or Cazzie Russell firing up a line drive from the baseline."

Zyontz's apprenticeship in the broadcasting business was again the result of a series of happy accidents. It was the late 1970s, and he was working his way through Boston University doing temp jobs during the summer. One of those jobs was at Black Rock, the iconic headquarters of the CBS network, on 52nd Street at Sixth Avenue in Manhattan. Zyontz made friends with someone in personnel, and when an entry-level job opened up shortly after graduation, he pounced on it. "I squeezed all 140 pounds of me into a white shirt and a uniform and a clip-on tie, and I became a security guard," he recalls.

This undersized, introverted keeper of the peace forged an unlikely connection with Van Gordon Sauter, then president of CBS Sports, and suddenly a career was on its way. "He was a very gregarious, friendly guy who took the time to get to know me," Zyontz recalls. "He sent me for some interviews with a little note attached to it: 'Pay attention to this kid.' And luckily they did."

One of his first assignments was with John Madden, just as the former Raiders coach was coming into his own as the premier color guy in the game. Madden, who traveled the country on a bus because of his fear of flying, was revolutionizing the world of color commentary, bringing viewers a coach's detailed and nuanced understanding of the increasingly complex world of pro football.

"We were sort of like an odd couple. He kind of got a kick out of my city background," Zyontz recalled. "I couldn't drive a car. And I used to travel with a stickball bat."

Zyontz learned the game from Madden and has internalized his unique worldview. The legendary Raiders coach views the game from the inside out, grounded in the belief that games are won and lost at the line of scrimmage. On the other hand, Zyontz's current analyst, Troy Aikman, watches the game the way a quarterback might, focusing on the wide receivers and the activity on the perimeter of the field. It's this synergy that helps make Zyontz—and his broadcasts—so good.

"I think it's my job to make sure that the broadcast tells the story of what's going on in the game." That's Richie Zyontz's modest explanation of his mind-bogglingly complex job.

The producer's job on a live sports broadcast is at once ill-defined and all-important. It's actually more like that of a director on a film set. At its most basic level, Zytonz is responsible for everything that goes on the air, from the basic story line of the broadcast to a graphic that's flashed up on the screen for three seconds. He also needs to make sure that the commercials and network promos get aired. Every Sunday, Zyontz makes thousands of decisions large and small, one after the other.

"The hardest thing is you have all this input coming, and it's almost like you have this . . ." Zyontz pauses, searching for just the right metaphor. "This bicycle wheel, and you're sitting in the middle of it, and you have all these spokes poking out in different directions. You're filtering all the input you're getting, making sure that you're listening to the right person, talking to the right person, making the right decision at the right time. It's like a moving target that you're constantly trying to stay in front of. It's not hard to do—it's hard to do well."

Zyontz is a perfectionist, which makes him very, very good at his job. And also doomed to eternal frustration. In a business where every broadcast will have at least a few inevitable glitches, he dwells on his own small mistakes. He doesn't need Hill and Goren at FOX headquarters, or even his partner Kempner, to tell him when there's a problem. Zyontz would make a fabulous media critic.

"If you're on your couch at home, it just looks so simple," he explains. "But boy, I tell you, if I feel like I made a mistake, even something that you at home would never even notice—maybe I brought up the wrong replay angle—I'll just beat myself up mercilessly over it. We don't have a lot of margin for error. We have to be damn near perfect all the time, and I never forget that."

Does this preternatural ability to make decisions extend to other parts of Zyontz's life? Not a chance, he assures me. "I am fairly incompetent in virtually every part of my life. Ask my wife. All it takes is coming home on a Monday and her marveling at how I can do my job on the weekend when I can't seem to get anything done at home during the week."

While Zyontz spends most of the week fretting about ways to close that tantalizing gap between the real and the ideal, when he's in the chair in the corner to the left of Kempner on Sunday, Zyontz works with an almost Zen-like composure. He enters every game with a plan, an expectation about how a game is going to play out, but then has to be willing to abandon it if the game doesn't unfold as he predicted.

"Producers have some ideas going into a broadcast, stories and elements they'd like to try and get on the air. But you can't get too fixated on these preconceived things. You can't let your ego get in the way of the game. You need to make sure that stuff fits around the action, not try to fit the action around your own material," he says.

"You want to make sure you were patient, you didn't force things on the screen that didn't belong—that's usually one of the first mistakes that people make in their eagerness to contribute. You have to flow with the game. Be patient. Don't force stuff. Let the broadcast breathe a little bit sometimes. I'll watch a tape of a game we did and I'll get angry with myself for trying to do too much. Don't fill up the screen with graphics or constant, meaningless replays. Let it breathe. Let it breathe." Zyontz pauses for a long beat as his self-editor kicks in. "Does that make sense?"

He's the Gretzky of our business, a guy who sees things that the other guys don't see," says Kempner, again slipping into sports metaphor mode, as he explains his partner's subtle greatness. "He doesn't have great speed, he doesn't impress the hell out of you, except that every time there's a play to be made, Richie makes it. If he says we need to do something, we do it. Because 99 percent of the time he's making the right call—and that's a pretty high percentage for live television."

Kempner is not only a professional but a student of the craft. He rates broadcast teams the way other people rate football dynasties, rattling off the names the way a hard-core fan might list the defensive backfield of the "Steel Curtain" Steelers or Joe Montana's secondary receivers. And he's been lucky enough to have worked with many of the greats, first at CBS Sports during the network's heyday and then at FOX. They may be anonymous to viewers, but to a fellow broadcaster, they are like Montana and Jordan and Mays. And he puts Zyontz up with any of them. "These were the top people in the business. Nobody was better than them. And I've never seen anybody make decisions as quickly and effectively as Richie does. Nobody. It's not even close."

While the live game shots make viewers tune in, the heart of the broadcast, the place where the production team can make a difference, lies in those stolen seconds while a team is in the huddle. The thing that separates Zyontz from a producer who's merely good is his replays. A competent producer gives another view of what happened. Zyontz tells *how* and *why*. On a play where New York Giants pass rusher Michael Strahan sacks Cowboys quarterback Tony Romo, a lesser producer might show another angle of Michael Strahan beating offensive lineman Flozell Adams, and then follow that up with a reaction shot from the photogenic Strahan or perhaps cut to Tom Coughlin, the demonstrative Giants head coach. Zyontz will take the viewer inside the play in a wholly different way. He will start by showing Strahan's reaction, then switch to tape machine F, the coverage of the far-side receiver, next cut to tape machine N, the route run by the near-side receiver, and finally go to machine A, the inside receiver.

Armed with these replays, color commentator Troy Aikman will tell the viewers what Coughlin and defensive coordinator Steve Spagnuolo already know: This was a coverage sack. The stat sheet gives Strahan credit for the sack, but the lion's share of the credit for the big play has to go to the Giants' much-maligned defensive secondary. Romo, the FOX replay reveals, had more than enough time to throw the ball, but every available receiver was covered. The Cowboy QB stayed in the pocket hoping someone would slip free, but it never happened. This lockdown pass coverage gave Strahan and company enough time to eventually shake their blockers and finally take down the Cowboy quarterback.

It's the Sunday afternoon answer to *Rashomon*, the Akira Kurosawa film that parses reality by showing the same event from different points of view. Alone, these isolated shots of a well-covered receiver who never sees the ball signify little. Together, they tell the story of the game in a way that only football insiders get to see. The story of a football game often lies in what *didn't* happen, and Zyontz finds a way to show that to the viewer.

"It's documenting the stuff away from the ball that really gives me satisfaction," says Zyontz with typical modesty.

Zyontz's tendency to go away from the action places huge demands on the rest of the crew. Most camera operators are trained to follow the ball and instinctively relax a bit when they realize that the play isn't going toward them. That's a big mistake on the FOX A-Team. Zyontz is like a law professor utilizing the Socratic method—you never know when you're going to get called on. Kempner makes sure to warn the camera crew and the replay tape operators: "You've got to concentrate the whole time because you're gonna get called on for a replay in situations that you'd never even consider," he explains. "Because the way Richie does things is different. And it's better."

And so thanks to a few smart decisions and a few lucky breaks, Artie and Richie are going back to the Super Bowl. Typically, Zyontz offers mixed reviews of that first game. He thought the crew's back-to-basics game plan was solid enough. "We wanted to basically do the same game we had done all year, and whatever equipment we had added for the Super Bowl, we brought extra people in to help us with that," he explains. "And I never did feel overwhelmed. I never was lost. I never was looking around, like, 'Where is that shot, where is this, who's got it?' The first one, you sort of just want to get through it, you know? I think I'll be able to enjoy this one more."

On the other hand, even the best producer has to make do with the game he's been given. Super Bowl XXXIX wasn't a 51–7, over-in-the-second-quarter blowout the way that some Super Bowls have been. But despite the quality of the matchup between the Patriots and the Eagles, the game wasn't quite as good as Zyontz had hoped it would be.

"Even though the score was 24–21—on paper, it seemed like a close game—that Super Bowl lacked moments. It lacked drama. And, really through no fault of our own, I just don't remember a memorable moment, a turning point, a big play, a picture that people remember," he explains. "So I'm just sort of hoping we get a little more to work with in terms of drama this time."

12

THE GAME

An Extreme Makeover

Turn off I-10 West onto 101 North and you can't miss it. Looming in the distance, the University of Phoenix Stadium is at once organic and alien. Its sheer size and mass channel the mountains in the background. But where those peaks are craggy and rough-hewn, the stadium itself seems as smooth as a surf-washed pebble. A seven-year-old might say that it looks like a flying saucer come to earth, and in a way, it does. If some buildings have a solidity that suggests that they grew up from the ground, the product of some seismic event rather than of human intervention, the University of Phoenix Stadium looks as though it could have hovered for a bit and then touched down for a soft landing, a close encounter of the domed kind.

When you're making this sharp turn on the highway, the building appears on the horizon with the enticing suddenness of a surprise party.

It's the best reveal in sports, and it's never going to be better than it is at this moment. Right now the stadium sits there, largely alone and slightly alien. But make no mistake. This giant $455 million building is not only a landmark, it's a cornerstone. Soon the landscape around Eisenman's creation will fill up, mostly with architecture that's far less original and only unintentionally provocative, stores and restaurants and hotels largely drawn by the promise of the stadium and the Westgate development that's already growing up around it.

The stadium is particularly attractive in the early-morning light, taking on a slightly golden hue, but the traffic gets the blame, or the credit, for me being here just past 7:00 A.M. When I asked at my downtown hotel how long it would take for me to get to the stadium, I got a cryptic answer. "Depends," said the clerk. "It should take about forty-five minutes, maybe a little less. But I was headed out that way during rush hour last month and it took two and a half hours."

A little more interrogation led me to believe that this delay wasn't caused by a thirty-seven-car pileup, a toxic waste spill, or an in-store appearance by Miley Cyrus. This was a routine volume delay, the by-product of the continuing population boom in greater Phoenix, which has resulted in more people driving farther to work. I didn't want to miss the beginning of the FOX production meetings, so I left in plenty of time.

You can just barely catch a glimpse of the University of Phoenix Stadium out the front door of the It's a Grind coffee shop in the Peoria Crossing strip mall in Glendale. But make no mistake. Without the stadium, this shop or the Verizon Wireless shop next door or the Kohl's across the parking lot wouldn't be here. Call it a Super Bowl by-product. The shop itself exudes a certain calculated hipness. The furniture here is deliberately mismatched, with Warhol-inspired prints hanging on the walls.

It could be the set for a *Friends* spin-off. But as I pecked at my iBook, I could divine a real sense of community here.

"Tea this morning?" asks Alycia the barista. "Or maybe that banana split?"

"Just tea," says the older woman who's just walked in with her granddaughter.

Alycia the barista is slim and attractive and her demeanor lies just on the tolerable side of perky, her long hair splitting the difference between blond and brunette, a few stray strands from her ponytail brushing her left cheek. This morning she's proudly wearing a Cardinals jersey bearing quarterback Matt Leinart's number, although when push comes to shove she admits she's more of a Seattle Seahawks fan.

"How about those Cardinals?" Alycia asks the lady.

Yesterday the Cardinals beat the mighty Pittsburgh Steelers at home. It was one of the biggest wins in recent Cardinals history—not that that's saying much—and the biggest W to date at the University of Phoenix Stadium.

"It was just too frustrating," says Janelle Hockenberry, picking her tea off the counter. She recounts how she turned the game off as the score seesawed in the third quarter, with the Cardinals inching ahead and then surrendering the lead. She abandoned hope, flipping instead to a different brand of uncertainty on a rain-delayed NASCAR race. "Then my granddaughter says that they're ahead."

Like a lot of the morning's other customers at the Daily Grind, Hockenberry is a regular, stopping in most mornings as she takes her granddaughter to school. This morning she's wearing a pink blouse and slacks. Seven-year-old Ashley wears an orange T-shirt and is carrying around a small stuffed brown dog. "It was my dad's but he couldn't take care of it, so it's mine now," she tells me with the sort of innocent seriousness that only small children can muster.

When I head over to talk football, Hockenberry is quick to set me straight.

"I'm not a Cardinals fan," she says. "I hate Bidwill. But I want the stadium to do well because if the stadium does well, the area does well."

Hockenberry has been here for twenty-one years, and she's seen Glendale transformed in the last few years. She moved here with her husband from a military base in Germany, and when she arrived she was unhappy, to say the least. "I went into therapy," she reports without a trace of self-consciousness. "It was a hellhole."

In the mid-1980s, Glendale was mostly farms—cotton farms, alfalfa farms, and feed lots for cattle. "There was dust everywhere," she says, describing the gritty detail of the less-than-idyllic western vista where the stadium now stands. The western side of Phoenix was very much the wrong side of the tracks. "Scottsdale?" she says, all but spitting the name of the tony suburb located to the east of downtown. "We used to call that *Snobbs*dale," she says.

Hockenberry recalls the first day that the I-10 was open. She entered the freeway and there wasn't a single car in sight. She wondered if someone hadn't knocked down a barricade by accident and she had driven onto a still-closed stretch of roadway. But no, it was open, just empty.

And even now, downtown Glendale, located about five miles to the east of Westgate, has a vibe that can be best described as shabby chic. On one block of Glendale Avenue, you can find Smilin' Jim's Pedal Cars, where you can buy antique toys. Next door sits an appliance repair shop. Farther down the block are a bail bondsman (1-800-FOR-BAIL) and a tattoo parlor. The ubiquitous "Restrooms for Customers Only" signs say a mouthful, but the unrepentant authenticity is endearing all the same. While *USA Today* gave Glendale a shout-out for its antique shops, don't expect to find Martha Stewart here searching for hidden treasure. Even the visitors' center exudes this slightly rough-and-ready attitude: "We'd Like to Tell You Where to Go" is their motto. Except for a lone Subway,

Glendale is devoid of chain stores, not so much as a Starbucks. It's sort of charming, in a way. For the moment at least, downtown Glendale seems protected, buffered from the head-spinning changes that are happening only five miles away. But perhaps not for long.

Up close, the University of Phoenix stadium feels very different. Standing in its imposing shadow, the smooth, almost monolithic surface is anything but. Those seemingly ornamental vertical slots are wide enough to drive a truck through. The sandwich panels on the outside skin wouldn't fit into a typical New York City apartment. Its profoundly two-layered form looks like a giant robot's wedding cake.

The most prominent embellishment on the stadium's sleek skin is the giant red lettering that reads: The University of Phoenix Stadium. But even this is not what it seems. The Cardinals aren't sharing this stadium with a college team, as they had for so many years. The University of Phoenix doesn't even *have* a football team. The for-profit institution is the nation's largest private university, but virtually all of its 323,000 students commute to class or are enrolled in on-line courses. The Apollo Group, the school's parent company, reported revenues of $2.3 billion in 2005. In 2006, the school, looking to enhance its national profile, signed a naming rights deal with the Cardinals for $154.5 million over twenty years. That total will cover about a third of the construction costs of the stadium. According to *Forbes*, it's the sixth largest naming rights deal in the history of sports, and the third largest in the NFL behind Reliant Stadium ($300 million over thirty years) and Washington's FedEx Field ($207 over twenty-seven years).

I negotiate my entrance—Artie Kempner has invited me for FOX's pre–Super Bowl production meetings—and walk toward the field. What's most striking is what's missing: the *Field of Dreams* moment. It's a staple of every nostalgic sports essay. Walk down the dark corridor with a light literally at the end of the tunnel. Move along and the darkness fades, the brightness intensifies. As you reach the end, the payoff approaches: One more step and the darkness is in the past, replaced by the emerald-green turf of Yankee Stadium gleaming in the bright sunshine.

There's none of that here. I look past the security gate, and there's the field, plain as day, end zone to end zone in a VistaVision panorama. It's more like the Grand Canyon. Walk up, and *boom*—it's there. They claim that the seats of the stadium, if removed and set end to end, would stretch eighteen miles. From this vantage point, it's easy to believe that.

And it's bright, too. Despite the fact that the roof is closed and the lights are off, it feels airy, more like an outdoor stadium than a dome, thanks to the translucent roof panels made of Birdair fabric that's so tough a grown man can run across it like a giant Moon Walk.

"The quality of the light is stunning," say Eisenman proudly. "If the NFL would allow it, you could play a game with the lights off."

While this open-plan layout may be less dramatic, in Eisenman's mind the practical considerations more than compensate. The tunnels that lead from the concourse to the seating bowl—called vomitoria in the architectural lexicon—hark back to the days of the Roman Colosseum. Vomitoria are nothing if not functional. Besides the big reveal, they allow for an orderly flow of spectators in and out of the stadium. It is estimated that the Colosseum, which seated about 50,000, could be filled and emptied in fifteen minutes through its seventy-six public passageways.

But the problem with vomitoria is that they separate the concourse from the seating area of the stadium. And for a football fan like Eisenman, who can't bear to miss a moment, that's a huge problem. "That's what I don't like about Giants Stadium," he explains to me. "You want to pee, you want to get a hot dog, you have to go out through a vomitorium," he says, relishing the word more than a little. And the places where he has watched games during his fan's life—the Yale Bowl, Giants Stadium—have all been built in the classical style, with this fatal flaw.

A single moment sealed the deal for Eisenman. "I missed a great play in the Rose Bowl," he recalls with true regret. The game was the 1997 Rose Bowl, where Jake Plummer and his underdog Arizona State Sun Devils were giving favored Ohio State everything they could handle, and took the lead with a little over a minute left. Eisenman's then-young son had other things on his mind. "My son had to go to pee," Eisenman recalls. "He's a little kid, and I said, 'Sam, for chrissake.'"

But like a good father, Eisenman heeded the call, and while they were in the men's room, he missed the winning touchdown, with OSU's backup quarterback Joe Germaine hitting David Boston for a touchdown catch with only twenty seconds left. To hear Eisenman tell it, that day he made sure that Cardinals fans—and ultimately Super Bowl fans—wouldn't be faced with such a Hobson's choice. The food lines and the path to the restrooms all have sight lines to the field, as well as video monitors to catch the instant replay. If Eisenman could have gotten away with it, the urinals in his signature stadium might have been al fresco as well.

On this Monday morning, eighteen hours after the Cardinals and the Steelers played, the stadium itself is all but empty, but abuzz with activity at the same time. The NFL is holding another in a long series of Super Bowl prep meetings, and the FOX A-Team has flown in from Dallas to figure out how the telecast is going to come together.

While the University of Phoenix stadium was built with the idea of hosting a Super Bowl, it wasn't necessarily constructed with the idea of televising one. The movable field, for example, created challenges aplenty for the FOX crew. At the most obvious level, since much of the many miles of cable runs the length and width of the field, the crew won't be able to finish plugging in until the field is moved in for the last time a few days before the Super Bowl. Then there are the little things. Though the platforms that border the field on the sidelines seem rock solid while you're standing on them, it's a different story when footfalls and other vibrations are magnified by the kind of long telephoto lens used by the A-Team. So at this point, the crew is working below field level, avoiding the black widow spiders that sometimes lurk there, and using jacks, plywood, and drywall screws to brace the platform for the sideline camera carts.

Most of the meeting is about nuts and bolts of this kind. Additional camera positions must be negotiated and then reviewed, because the additional equipment will block the view of at least a few fans on site.

But there are at least a couple of big ideas in play. The biggest is sitting along the sidelines. It's a Panavision camera that's a virtual reinvention of the camera cart. In most cart cams, the operator is actually raised or lowered in a small hoist. In this new Panavision setup, the operator stays at ground level, but a sophisticated monitoring system, coupled with a precise remote control, allows him to move the camera over an even greater range.

Kempner watches the demo and nods in approval. The advantages are obvious. Without the weight of the operator, the crane can be moved over a greater range more quickly. The downsides? One is that the greater height and range of the camera mean that some very expensive seats could become partially blocked by the camera. The other is that it's never been used in a big game before. In an industry as hidebound as this one—not to mention in a game where a technical glitch would be visible to 100 million viewers—that's a major factor.

Later in the morning, audio engineer Fred Aldous raises the prospect of an even more outrageous new toy. A Norwegian company is introducing a digitally controlled audio array. It features over a hundred shotgun mikes suspended above the field, each targeting a tiny area of the field and synched with a bank of digital recorders that archive the sound. Essentially, it allows the audio engineers to zero in on a target the way that a camera with a telephoto lens can. The price is $210,000, and while that would take up a huge portion of FOX's production budget, it's not a total deal breaker. One option: An equipment rental company might purchase the piece and rent it back to FOX for the week for a more reasonable slice of the budget. Or the manufacturer might be willing to loan the piece to FOX in exchange for promotional consideration. Being able to brag that a new piece of equipment was used at the Super Bowl is not without value.

After the meeting, Aldous, Kempner, and Colby Bourgeois drive over to Westgate, just outside the stadium, for lunch. Kempner has to catch a 2:00 P.M. flight back to the East Coast, so it'll be a quick bite. In less than two months, Glendale, Arizona, will get its close-up, ready or not. But even with the stadium completed, it's still very much a work in progress. Even as we walk toward the restaurant, curbs are still being built, trees are being planted, and everywhere you turn there's a temporary chain-link fence.

As we make our way across the freshly paved parking lot, Kempner tells a story. The FOX sports crew working yesterday's Cardinals-Steelers game had booked a block of rooms at the Renaissance Hotel near the stadium a few weeks before the game. One of the veterans on the crew tried to change his reservation to visit with his son, who is going to school in the area. "So he calls the hotel and gets the central reservations desk and explains this to the guy. The guy just stammers for a second and he says, 'Um, sir, that hotel doesn't open for another month.'"

Located in an office park on the other side of Phoenix, next to the headquarters of the Cold Stone Creamery ice cream chain, the Arizona Super Bowl host committee is trying to anticipate these little disasters. What is a host committee? It's an ad hoc group that puts on a Super Bowl and disbands once the game is over. I met Susan Sherer, the executive director of Detroit's host committee, the day before Super Bowl XL, and she was surprisingly calm. With the game still twenty-four hours away, her work was all but done. "I guess come Monday I'm looking for a job," she joked.

That's not the case in Arizona, where the stakes are higher than for any Super Bowl in recent memory. Chalk it up to the NFL's unofficial Super Bowl rotation. A cold-weather city like Detroit understands that no matter how well the Super Bowl festivities come off, the NFL is not going to return to the city anytime soon. Indeed, a Super Bowl in a northern city seems to be roughly a once-in-a-decade event, with the previous cold-weather venues being Pontiac, Michigan, in 1982 and Minneapolis in 1992.

Miami, which hosted Super Bowl XLI in 2007, faces exactly the opposite situation. South Florida has hosted the game a record nine times and will get the game again in 2010. Why? If you were to design a city to host a Super Bowl, it might look a lot like Miami. It starts with great winter weather and adds both the sizzle (world-class nightlife) and the steak (the availability of hotel rooms, transportation, and other tourist-related infrastructure), not to mention the intangible but very real benefit of having done the game before. They've also got a substantially remodeled stadium. Three of the cities that would have been mentioned in the same breath as Miami a decade ago—San Diego, Pasadena, and New Orleans—won't see the game again unless (or until) new stadiums are built. So while Super Bowl XLI was perhaps not the smoothest game on record, with a transient shortage of rooms that came from a few big hotels not being completed on schedule and uncharacteristic game-day rain, the bottom line is that Miami is in the Super Bowl business to stay.

The closest recent parallel to Phoenix's current situation was Jacksonville. The city had the first prerequisite for cracking the unofficial Super Bowl rotation: potentially spectacular weather. Alltel Stadium was also largely up to the task, having recently undergone a $135 million renovation. But during Super Bowl week, things didn't go as planned. The weather was cold and damp, the events were too spread out, and the host committee's $11 million solution to a dearth of hotel rooms—it rented five cruise ships—was a memorable flop. Jacksonville won't get another Super Bowl anytime soon.

So Arizona knows that it has the chance to crack the rotation, but as Jacksonville learned, when the stakes are this high a return engagement is hardly a lock. Because of this, the host committee staffers are being pulled in several directions. Their primary focus is, of course, the herculean task facing them four months down the road—pulling off the upcoming Super Bowl. "The last four or five months we've staffed up for the operational side, and we're starting to really tighten things up and finalize plans for February," says local attorney Michael Kennedy. With a casual backslapping charm that complements his rugged good looks, and a Rolodex filled with the names of the city's movers and shakers, Kennedy is the public face of the Arizona Super Bowl as the host committee chairman. And while the host committee's specific responsibilities range from securing hotel rooms to negotiating with Arizona's twenty-two sovereign Indian tribes, the real mandate is diplomacy.

"We work peace between all the different governmental factions," Kennedy explains. "You saw that in Miami the sweeter they talked about how they were getting along, the more you knew that they weren't. That's what we do here. We need the right hotel rooms, the venues, the hospitality, to make sure we have 10,000 volunteers."

But at the same time, part of the host committee's attention is focused four years down the road on future Super Bowls. Super Bowls are awarded generally four years in advance by a vote of the NFL owners. A franchise—or, more accurately, a host committee representing the franchise—must prepare a bid package, not dissimilar to a bid for the Olympic Games. The presentation must include both style and substance, according to host committee president Bob Sullivan. While the bid routinely includes dazzling graphics and glowing testimonials from local celebrities, it also has to address the most minute details ranging from security to garbage collection—every concern raised in 200 pages of bid specs. And as the game grows, those bid specs are a moving target. For example, in their bid for the 2009 game, the Tampa host committee offered to pay for all the tenting for the NFL Experience fanfest.

"That's like a million dollars," explains Sullivan, who was an award-winning television news producer before signing on at the host committee. "Now when you see the bid specs for future games, it's Velcroed on."

In an attempt to display its seriousness about cracking the Super Bowl rotation, the Arizona host committee made the bold move of bidding for the 2011 game even before the 2008 game was played.

"We decided we wanted to get right in the game and show them we wanted to play, so there was no question in their minds that we wanted them to come back," explains Kennedy. "And we also wanted to show them that we understand that every time we throw our hat in the ring, we're not gonna get yes as an answer—nobody does."

And that was the case for 2011. The owners awarded that game to north Texas, a bid spearheaded by the Dallas Cowboys. This was no surprise: Dallas owner Jerry Jones is influential if not always popular, the Cowboys will be unveiling a new stadium, and this is the city's first-ever Super Bowl. But by simply declaring their intention, the Arizona host committee was sending a message. And, on balance, it worked.

"They did more than send a message," says Frank Supovitz, the NFL's Super Bowl point man. "They said, 'We'd like you to consider us to always be here for you.' That was their message. They said, 'Even if we don't get the Super Bowl in 2011, you can count on us being there on into the future as an interested and active host—and we want you back.' And in fact everything they offered for the 2011 bid, in terms of additional enhancements to their bid—extra service, extra attention, extra facilities—they retroactively offered for the 2008 Super Bowl. So they didn't just send a message—they actually said, 'We want you to feel like the Super Bowl can be at home here.'"

With the 2008 game still several months away, the host committee has shifted its attention to 2012. Their major competition will come from Indianapolis, which will also open a new stadium but because of its winter climate doesn't have a real shot at the Super Bowl rotation, and from Houston, which hosted the game to mixed reviews in 2004. The fact that a potential player's strike or lockout during the 2011 season puts that game very much in doubt doesn't deter the Arizona host committee.

"We are in the Super Bowl hosting business," says Kennedy, with more than a little pride.

13

High Tide,
Green Grass

"It's high tide at the ranch," says Alison Kostas as she disembarks from the rental Escalade and catches a whiff of the Old West. An uncharacteristic rainy spell in the Phoenix area, which has caused landslides in other parts of the region, has left sloggy yellow puddles on the clay-colored soil and the distinct aroma of livestock in the air. She is the creative director of Relevent, the party-planning firm responsible for taking the Playboy Super Bowl party from conception to reality. Her boss, Relevent president Tony Berger, and the Playboy Party Team have assembled on this December morning for a site survey at Wild Horse Pass.

Located about twenty miles to the southeast of Phoenix, Wild Horse Pass sits on the tribal lands of the Gila River Indian Community. The development features a remarkable range of attractions, from a luxury hotel and spa to a thirty-six-hole championship golf course and a casino.

We've come to Rawhide, a kind of Disneyesque re-creation of an 1880s Wild West town, complete with tumbleweeds and faux gunslingers. But our focus this morning is the 52,000-square-foot pavilion. It's a hangar-sized building, plenty big enough for a football game as long as you don't mind restricting the spectators to a few close friends. In terms of usable square footage, it dwarfs the American Airlines Arena, where Playboy's Miami Super Bowl party was held last year. Space is indeed the final frontier here, because the building offers little more than that. It's minimalist at best, with a metal exoskeleton, vinyl tarps over the sides in lieu of actual walls, and a cold, hard concrete floor atop that red clay.

For the moment at least, it's mostly empty, with a small Christmas scene on one side dwarfed by the sheer size of the building. Clearly someone spent plenty of time and thought on the display, but despite a patina of kitschy charm, it isn't exactly Macy's windows. In less than eight weeks, this enormous, slightly strange building will be the site of what's supposed to be the hottest party on the planet.

Make no mistake, this is a huge gamble. The Playboy team has looked at dozens of sites around Phoenix, most of which were much closer to downtown Phoenix or to Scottsdale, where most of the other parties are taking place. And while there are dozens of other Party Teams making the same kinds of decisions, none of them is facing the same kind of pressure as Team Playboy. Last year's Playboy party was a disappointment—to the Party Team, at least, if not to the partygoers—and Donna Tavoso and company understand that the timing problems could have turned into a disaster. They can't make the same mistakes twice.

Wild Horse Pass is in the middle of nowhere, fifteen miles from downtown Phoenix. (How far out of the way is it? The NFL selected a hotel on the property as the official NFC team hotel, thinking that the location is so far afield that it would keep players from temptation.) This is in rather stark contrast to last year, when the American Airlines Arena was just a quick cab ride from party central on South Beach. After much careful deliberation—and visits to nearly a hundred sites in and around Phoenix—the Party Team decided that they would trade location for more than enough space to create the party of their dreams. They're hoping that the Playboy name and reputation will be enough to make this a destination party where guests commit to making it their only stop on Super Bowl Eve. It's hardly a given.

The second part of the equation is finding a way to use all this space to maximum effect. That's where Relevent comes in. Berger unrolls blueprints that explain how he plans to slice and dice the space. The near end of the tent will become the reception area—coat check, registration, and the red carpet, a function that was situated outdoors in Miami last year. And while the Playboy team dodged a bullet last year—the rains that soaked that game didn't start until dawn—everyone will sleep better if they're not at the whim of the elements, even in the desert.

A couple more condominium-size chunks are earmarked at the opposite end for back-of-house operations—catering, changing areas for the Playmates, and the like. But that still leaves plenty of pavilion for the party. And a key is finding just the right amount of it for the party proper. Too small and guests are crammed elbow to elbow. Too big and the space can seem empty, even with almost 1,500 people.

See, I'm color-coordinated," says Berger. He's wearing an orange Nike fleece, somewhere between Syracuse University orange and the color of a traffic cone. He's also carrying a smartphone that has a rubber bumper around the outside edge, and the orange phone matches the fleece to a T.

He laughs about it when Lisa Natale, Playboy's senior vice president of marketing and promotions, notices this, but it's not an accident. Tony Berger lives by the Mies van der Rohe warhorse "God is in the details," and he very much wants his clients to know he knows it.

Berger doesn't fit the stereotype of the typical party planner. While he can talk about party motifs and color palettes, he leaves most of this to Kostas. And as he surveys the building, he seems more at home working with a laser level than a swatch book. His color coordination notwithstanding, he's not particularly fabulous.

It turns out that in some slightly alternative universe, Tony Berger would be spending this morning making motions or taking depositions. Before starting Relevent, he was a lawyer by trade working for a prestigious New York firm.

"My mother had been an event planner, and she did this event with the Philadelphia Flyers and I thought it was the coolest thing in the world," Berger explains. "But I always thought, 'I'm supposed to be a lawyer.'"

Still, when he was in college he took charge of his frat's spring formal at American University, and at a time when a hotel in Reston, Virginia, might have been considered an exotic location, he sent them on a road trip to Atlantic City. As the last bus pulled away for the return trip to Washington, D.C., he said to himself, "Hey, I pulled this off." Indeed, that's the thrill of this business: raising the bar, just barely clearing it, and then sitting back for a moment and admiring how you pulled it off. And the bar is never higher than it is during Super Bowl week.

In the party-planning business, pulling it off can mean any number of things at any given moment. For example, at a recent event at the Sundance Film Festival in Park City, Berger had to negotiate with the owner of an old lumberyard to use the site for a major party. Next he had to negotiate permits not only with the city but with the Sundance Institute as well. He secured their support by offering them 100 parking spaces for out-of-town volunteers out of the 400 he'd created on the site.

"I think that's sort of an example of where experience of seeing the big picture, working with both political and governmental entities, really paid off for us," he explains.

Then, only hours before the event, a local building-code official decided to scrutinize some of the decorative lighting fixtures. They'd been assembled in Relevent's Los Angeles shop, so they lacked the little Underwriters Laboratories sticker that the official insisted on. So with only a few hours before the guests started to arrive, Berger had to hunt down a licensed local electrician. The electrician chuckled as he ripped up and replaced this perfectly good wiring, but it wasn't a laughing matter to Berger. "Besides the fact that we were sweating getting it done, it cost us thousands of dollars at the last minute that we didn't anticipate having to spend."

Still, in a project like the Super Bowl, Murphy's Law is a constant companion. "Problems are going to happen. It's how you deal with them that separates you," he says philosophically.

Indeed, Berger is a reflection of an event industry that has grown and evolved at a dizzying pace. When Berger's mother was doing decor, her objective was simple: to make the room look pretty. Berger's clients, including Playboy, with their seven-figure party budgets, demand much more. It starts with the concept, making sure that the theme fits the needs of both the client and any subsidiary sponsors. Then it's all about the implementation, from securing permits to a building process that resembles an industrial construction project. And it all has to be done on deadlines with little or no wiggle room. If the invite says that the party starts at nine-thirty on Saturday, the doors had better be ready to open or heads will roll.

Still, Berger knows that in the big picture sometimes it's the little things that make a difference, like a car designer being judged by his cup holders. So he's included a changing area for the Playboy team in case they can't get back to the hotel before the party. He's included task lighting for Lauren Melone's PR team so they can read guest lists as they check in partygoers. And he'll supply space heaters aplenty in case it's unseasonably cold.

"It's a collective, collaborative approach, as opposed to 'God, we just need to make the room look pretty,'" he says. "How can we figure out what our client's objectives are? What they're trying to achieve? How we're going to be measured? And then creating and programming events that meet those objectives, so that at the end of the day we can go back to them and say, 'Hey, here's the money you spent. Here's what we did. And this is why it made sense.'"

After the walk-through, the Playboy Party Team huddles up, and there's an undercurrent of urgency. While there's some discussion about the overall theme—Rawhide will be transformed into Playboy's Desert Oasis—at this point the discussion centers on more practical issues. A party this big needs its own infrastructure.

Which is why they spend half an hour talking about toilets. The problem? Acquiring private facilities for the VIP area. It's no problem to find attractive executive-style portable bathrooms. But they're only good for about 1,000 flushes. The high-capacity units suited to the kind of traffic that a party requires look more like Porta-Johns, not exactly the kind of thing that's likely to work for Usher or Alyssa Milano.

The macro issue is flow of a different kind. Donna Tavoso is concerned about the proximity of the sunken dance floor to the DJ booth. The elevated cabanas for VIPs represent another balancing act—they're debating between a narrow passageway, which could create bottlenecks, and a wider passage, which might encourage revelers to congregate on the platform, creating another traffic problem. In Detroit in 2006, the VIP lounge was a huge hit. In Miami, they replicated it, but it remained all but empty. It's prominent on the plans this time, but the Playboy team is looking at it with a slightly jaundiced eye.

They know that they're facing a delicate balancing act, and any stumble on the night before the Super Bowl couldn't be more public. They want to replicate the success of Detroit, but they also know that each venue is different, and shoehorning the ideas that worked in one space into another is a recipe for disappointment.

"In Miami, everyone had a good time," says Lisa Natale, senior vice president of corporate marketing. "In Detroit, it was electric. It was a snowy, cold, terrible night—"

"It was a *blizzard,* and everybody had the best time," adds Lauren Melone.

"People had a good time in Miami," says Natale. "It just wasn't that wow!"

Dana Rosenthal is sitting at the table, calmly looking around. She makes eye contact with Donna Tavoso. They've done the heavy lifting so far, having looked at dozens of properties a day in Arizona's searing summer desert heat. Rosenthal has done this so often, she only needs to squint a little in order to see the building not as it is but as it will be on party night. She's calm because she just knows Rawhide is going to work. "I can walk into a place and in five minutes I know 'It'll never work here' or 'This is the perfect place for our party.'" She is quick to point out that this skill doesn't transfer into other aspects of her life. "In my own apartment I can't hang anything on the walls because I never know if it should stay there," she laughs. "I've been living there for three years and I still move my furniture around constantly."

Lisa Natale's phone rings and a hip-hop tune emanates from her cell. Her teenage son has pranked her ring tone, and she laughs it off with the cool-mom vibe that serves her well on her job. When she gets off the phone, she pulls up the "Soulja Boy" video he downloaded onto her phone and does a few playful dance steps with an expertise that suggests she might have practiced just a bit. Natale is on site at the Rawhide Pavilion for the first time, and while she's been involved in the negotiations, this is her first real look at the cavernous space where they've laid down their chips.

She watches Tavoso and Berger hash out the details of the floor plan, wondering again about the cabanas. "We all want to Monday-morning quarterback," says Berger reassuringly. "We want to take some solace, have some comfort level that we've got a good grasp on this."

"I think I can see it," says Natale as she peers around the cold, cavernous room. "But I thought I could see it before, and obviously I didn't." She looks back to the cabana negotiations, heartened, it seems, by the sound of details being hammered out. "My job is to worry," she says as she fields another phone call.

14
THE GAME

The Point Man

"Communicate or die," says Frank Supovitz, the NFL's senior vice president of events, with a smile that belies the urgency of his message. "That is *truly* our mantra this year. There will be no excuses for not sharing information with us and vice versa. Remember that everything that you do will be affected by the things going on around it. So make sure you stay in touch with the people who interface with your areas. Any decision you make will have ripple effects."

Supovitz is big on mantras. Last year's was "Stop and double-check everything," and he's quick to point out that it has been supplemented, not supplanted.

It's December 10, and the Super Bowl countdown clock sits at fifty-five days and counting. Supovitz has brought 230 people from all over the country to this darkened, double-width conference room at the

Phoenix Convention Center. This will be the last of a series of planning meetings that have spanned more than four years. In some ways the planning for Super Bowl XLII is all but over, and in others it's barely begun.

In front of this group, Supovitz's job is a bit like that of a head coach—part tactical, part administrative, and part inspirational. He may be talking about deadlines, but his message is much bigger than that.

"There are 230 people in the room, and you are the most important of about 20,000 people who are working on the Super Bowl," he says. "If everyone needs a little bit of easement on a deadline and you multiply it by 20,000, you can see how we would be tearing our hair out by the end of the event."

This very large room is filled almost to overflowing, and yet these are the Super Bowl's VIPs, ranging from key NFL staff to gun-toting representatives of local police departments. They are, by design, the tip of the iceberg, with each attendee representing perhaps fifty staffers, and in many cases hundreds or even thousands, who aren't at the meeting. They are the apostles of Super Bowl week, charged with not only performing the tasks but also spreading the word and, when necessary, cracking the whip.

With the mantras out of the way, Supovitz goes over some ground rules for the meeting. To accommodate the sheer amount of communication that will take place this afternoon, there'll be no scheduled rest breaks. Just find a soft spot on the agenda and create your own, he suggests. He's done this before.

"Have a spectacular meeting," he says with a smile bordering on a grin, and then walks away from the podium.

I have the greatest job in the world," writes Frank Supovitz in the introduction to his book *The Sports Event Managing and Marketing Play-*

book. But he follows that up with a reality check. "Brian Burke, an NHL general manager, thinks it's the worst." Burke goes on to liken Supovitz's job—then vice president of special events for the NHL—to "navigating through a thorny patch of briars anchored in quicksand."

Since he wrote that in 1999, Supovitz has gotten a job that's even better or even worse, depending on your point of view. His business card reads "Senior Vice President of Events for the National Football League." You could call him something overblown, like the czar of the Super Bowl, but that wouldn't be quite the truth, either. In reality, his job is more subtle than that, more Tom Hagen than Michael Corleone. He's a backroom consensus builder with a vague but immense responsibility: making sure that the biggest game in sports goes off without a hitch.

"I guess my micro job description is to be an air traffic controller for all of the NFL's events and to keep everything landing one at a time, safely," he says a couple of weeks before the Phoenix meeting in his modest and slightly cluttered office in the NFL's headquarters on Park Avenue in New York. "You're not just taking out the plan from last year, dusting it off, and starting on February 5 to worry about what's going to happen the following year at the Super Bowl. You're thinking about what you're gonna change four years from now," he says. "So I kind of see events at the NFL as all the airplanes in various stages of their journey, and you're landing them one at a time. Trying to keep them from crashing into each other. It's high-stress fun."

It's a very apt description. Supovitz bears a huge amount of responsibility, but he'll also remain largely invisible unless something goes very wrong. It's a job with no margin for error, a job that requires a certain facade of calmness in the face of inevitable and even potentially catastrophic problems. Yes, Frank Supovitz is an air traffic controller—at O'Hare, on the Wednesday before Thanksgiving, with a blizzard coming in. It might be the most challenging job in sports. And he might be the most powerful man you've never heard of.

Only three men have held this position in the forty-two-year history of the Super Bowl. The first was the late Don Weiss, who slid over from public relations during the game's formative years. The next was Jim Steeg, now the president of the San Diego Chargers. He left the NFL just after the Janet Jackson wardrobe malfunction; infer what you will from the timing of his departure. Now Supovitz wears the big shoes.

Frank Supovitz isn't a commanding figure. He's five foot nine or so, straddling the line between small and medium in height, with a build that's a bit soft but not exactly pudgy. He's comfortable wearing a suit—NFL central is a jacket-and-tie kind of place—but he's hardly a clotheshorse, as evidenced by the fact that he'll wear a Super Bowl commemorative tie to the office. While beauty shots of various Super Bowls adorn the walls of his office, pride of place is given to a blowup of Jets wide receiver Justin McCareins hanging on for a touchdown catch.

On the shelf above the sofa near the door is a bobblehead doll of racing legend Roger Penske holding a tiny snow shovel. Penske was the chairman of the host committee for Super Bowl XL in Detroit, and during a downtown winter festival that was planned as a dry run for the Super Bowl festivities a year later, the city was buried in a blizzard. "Roger was out shoveling with everyone else," recalls Supovitz approvingly.

He takes this as an opportunity to explain the impact that the game has on the host cities.

"One of the most exciting parts about hosting a Super Bowl that cities are only starting to understand is that it provides a deadline for major infrastructure projects. You've got four years," he explains. "I think Detroit probably took the best advantage of a Super Bowl that I've ever seen. They said, 'We need to improve our highways. We need to improve our downtown area. We need to make it look better. We need to make it feel better. We need to have wayfinding signage. We need to fix up building facades. Abandoned buildings need to look better, so it doesn't feel like a ghost town.' And they did all of that. So when you go from the airport today to downtown Detroit, I defy you to find a pothole."

While Supovitz has literally written the book about his job for college students who might want to follow in his footsteps, his career path has been anything but linear. He grew up in Queens and went to public school and then to Queens College, where he got his bachelor's degree in biology. During college, he got a job as an usher at Radio City Music Hall, ultimately being promoted to usher captain. "Which is a big deal," he recalls. "I think your salary went from two bucks to two eighty-five." Around this time, Radio City began changing its focus, moving from the Rockettes and the Christmas show to putting on special events outside of Rockefeller Center. Supovitz worked on the giant funeral for Dr. Edwin Land, founder of Polaroid, which was so crowded they had to do two seatings.

"In the 1980s, events were not an industry yet," he explains. "Now there are people who do this for a living, and who get trained to do it, who go to college for it—none of that existed then. People either came from the PR world to do it, or they came from the not-for-profit world to do it, or they came from the theatrical world to do it, but there was no discipline, there was no industry called the event industry to speak of, back then."

His first Super Bowl was 1988, when the game hadn't yet morphed into the entertainment extravaganza that it's become. "There were eighty-eight grand pianos and all this crazy stuff back when halftime shows were all about tonnage and pageantry and all of that, and there wasn't really a star. It was a big field show. I really, really enjoyed doing that, and I wanted to learn as much as I could about producing those kinds of things, not just selling that business but actually working on the crew."

One of Supovitz's secret weapons is his remarkable people skills. Julie Frisoni, the marketing director for the City of Glendale, recalls the first time that she and Supovitz were in the same room for a preliminary Super Bowl meeting. She had met him only once, years before, when he was working at the NHL and the league was considering holding its All-Star Game at the Phoenix Coyotes' home arena in Glendale. "Hi, Julie, how are you?" he said. "It's been a long time." Supovitz made a point to seek out Frisoni and made sure she knew he remembered her. It's a small thing, yes, but as essential to this job as a coach coming up to a player and asking about his pregnant wife or his brother who's about to graduate. This tip, to treat total strangers like friends, isn't in Supovitz's book, probably because you can't teach it. But when you rely upon the cooperation of hundreds of people, each with differing agendas, the ability to make each of them feel like an individual rather than a cog in a machine can be a huge asset when it comes time to ask for one of the concessions that are part and parcel of an endeavor as big as the Super Bowl.

So what does the general manager of the Super Bowl actually do? On game day, at least, as little as possible. He camps out in a specially designed control center in the stadium, where he's got access to a representative from virtually every important constituency, from the television networks to league officials to Homeland Security.

"In general, my job is to catch the passes as they come toward me," he explains. "I try not to have a specific function at that point because my hands are tied to whatever the issues are, and my job is to deal with those issues as they come up, and they come up pretty fast."

He does have one responsibility: keeping the event clock. "During the halftime show for the Rolling Stones, I actually stopped the clock during the halftime countdown at a certain point." He calculated in his head how long it would take for the stage to be dismantled and moved so that the players weren't running out when the stage was leaving. "I stopped it for about a minute and a half," he continues, "with six and a half left on the clock in halftime. While ninety seconds doesn't sound like a lot, it is, especially if there are 350-pound players heading down when 2,250-pound stage units are being pulled out, with Mick and Keith inside. Having been to the rehearsals, and knowing how long it took then, and knowing that it never is going to go as smoothly as that, we hit it within five seconds."

In preparing for the game, Supovitz has an almost preposterously wide variety of responsibilities. "I'm dangerous because I know a little about a lot," he explains.

Take the Saga of the Sideways Turf at Super Bowl XLI in Miami. Unknown to most fans, the Super Bowl is always played on a fresh field, on turf grown off-site and installed at the venue sometime between the team's last home game and the Super Bowl. The sod that was supposed to replace the grass at Dolphin Stadium was grown near Orlando. For all the attention lavished on it, a drought made the roots of the turf grow sideways instead of down.

Less than two weeks before the game, the grounds crew chief took Supovitz down on the field, handed him a three-pronged spadelike device, and told him to twist it. Up came a clump of turf. Then another. "We were just pulling out pieces of ground constantly," he explains. The alternative? Rip up the field and lay down the backup field, which had been grown in Georgia.

The wisdom of that decision was made clear on game day, when the heavens opened for what would become the first-ever wet Super Bowl. "When the new turf came in and we tested it, you couldn't move it. So we knew it was gonna be tight," he says. "In the fourth quarter of the game you still didn't see mud on any of the players."

Once the agenda at the Phoenix planning meeting begins, it becomes clear that Supovitz has got this down to an art. When environmental coordinator Jack Groh tells a long but interesting story about how his program is helping Native American families finance traditional woman-hood ceremonies, Supovitz chides him gently for his time-wasting tangent. "Have we solved global warming yet?" he wonders.

The transportation team's presentation leavens the afternoon's festivities. Last year they brought a marching band into the meeting. This year they provide a video with a western theme, starting off with an Ennio Morricone spaghetti-Western sound track before morphing into a Roy Rogers and Dale Evans romp. Two lovely blondes in Cardinals jerseys try without success to pronounce Supovitz's last name.

But even the levity is calculated. The traffic team had given a pre-screening copy to Joan Ryan-Canu, Supovitz's longtime executive assistant, to ensure that no one would get offended. "I'm afraid to think about next year," the secretary says, wondering what the transportation guys might be plotting for the Super Bowl XLIII planning meetings.

Supovitz and company run through a three-page agenda with shocking precision, and they actually wrap up this monster of a meeting early.

The Super Bowl's point man gets the afternoon's last word, and he makes the most of the opportunity.

"All of you in this room, whether you're a vendor, a partner, or an NFL staff person, the reason why you're here working on the greatest annual American event is because you're the very best at what you do."

He pauses for a long second to let the audience members pat themselves on the back. "Keep investing in the thinking required to execute this very best event. Not just the things you can do in your sleep, but all the things you don't see coming around the corner. All the what-ifs.

"The ball is going to get kicked at 6:28 whether you're ready or not. What if the lights don't go on after the halftime show? What if a team bus gets a flat tire? How are you going to deal with it? I sleep better at night knowing you're the guys thinking about it. I'm going to leave you with an unofficial mantra: Surprises suck."

Supovitz gets not only the last word but the last laugh.

"With that, I wish you a spectacular rest of the week. Let's go Super Bowl XLII." And with that, the meeting is adjourned.

15

THE GAME

Twelve Minutes
of Terror

Carol Channing.

Those two words describe just how far the Super Bowl halftime show, and for that matter the Super Bowl, has come.

Need a few more?

Up with People.

The *Hello Dolly* star was the first solo performer to play the Super Bowl halftime show, in Super Bowl IV, as a step up from the Florida A&M marching band the previous year. And Up with People, that irrepressibly cheerful ensemble, has entertained at four Super Bowl intermissions, more than any other act.

But in 1992, FOX changed all that with one bold move. The network, which was not an NFL rights holder at that point, performed a counterprogramming masterstroke. They created a special episode of *In*

Living Color to go head-to-head with the official Super Bowl halftime show, which that year featured Gloria Estefan and figure skaters Brian Boitano and Dorothy Hamill. As usual, the Super Bowl audience represented one of the year's biggest collections of eyeballs, and between the gun at the end of the first half and the second-half kickoff, FOX saw them as fair game. *In Living Color* even featured a countdown clock so that Super Bowl refugees knew how long it'd be until the end of the figure skating and the beginning of the second half.

The edgy "Men on Football" sketch, featuring young comedians Damon Wayans and David Alan Grier pushing the boundaries of good taste, provided a stark contrast to the pabulum programming on CBS.

"Tonight, we are live and uncensored," said Wayans, introducing a sketch featuring two flamboyantly gay movie critics weighing in on football.

"Naked to the world," replied Grier.

"What other game boasts such great names like *Dick Butkus*?" Grier continued.

"Or my favorite, *Bob Griese*."

"Isn't he a tight end?"

"He was."

It worked perfectly. Frito-Lay bought all the advertising for the *In Living Color* special, spending roughly what they might have for a single $850,000 Super Bowl spot. That episode of *In Living Color* drew as many as 28.6 million viewers away from the Super Bowl, and in some cities it approached the ratings of the official Super Bowl halftime show. It launched the upstart comedy into seventh place in the week's ratings, close to hits like *Roseanne* and *Murphy Brown* and ahead of *Full House*.

(The third-ranked show that week made history of a different kind. With his campaign reeling from allegations about an extramarital affair made by actress Gennifer Flowers, presidential candidate Bill Clinton and his wife, Hillary, agreed to do a *60 Minutes* interview that would air immediately after the Super Bowl. Interviewer Steve Kroft said, "One of your campaign advisers told us the other day, 'Bill Clinton has got to level with the American people tonight, otherwise his candidacy is dead.' Do you feel like you've leveled with the American people?" To which Clinton exclaimed, "I have absolutely leveled with the American people!" The Kroft Q-and-A was a defining moment of the Clinton campaign, and it was made possible by the 34 million people who stayed in front of their televisions after the Redskins beat up on the Bills.)

Sensing a very real threat, the NFL fought back in 1993 with a vengeance. The halftime talent the next year was Michael Jackson, who was then the most popular solo artist on the planet. Instant relevance. And since then the Super Bowl halftime show has become all about creating the world's biggest televised popular music show.

Charles Coplin can breathe a little easier. The NFL has just signed Tom Petty and the Heartbreakers to play the halftime show. Unlike other aspects of the Super Bowl, which are planned years in advance, the halftime show isn't usually nailed down until after the start of the football season. Even recording artists of Petty's stature make big decisions only months in advance.

"Tom was late for us," Coplin explains, referring to the late-October signing and early December announcement. "And he sort of fell into our laps, which was great." Here's how the pieces fell into place: Coplin went to see Petty at Madison Square Garden during his last tour and was introduced to Petty's manager, Tony Dimitriades. "I just said, 'Hey, would Tom ever do this?' And Tony said, 'No, Tom would never be the second part of an event. He would never be comfortable with that.' And so he tried to pitch me on some of his other acts."

A few weeks later, Coplin got a call saying that the agent had talked to Petty again and Mr. Damn-the-Torpedoes was now willing to do it. "I was like, 'That's great.' Because there are certain artists you feel would be great, and he was on that list."

Just how big is the NFL's short list? Coplin pauses for a second or two, re-creating the list in his head.

"The fingers on two hands, I think," he says.

While Coplin won't rattle off the names, looking at some of the recent acts—U2, Paul McCartney, the Rolling Stones, and now Tom Petty—you can get a feel as to what the list might look like. Bruce Springsteen, for example, would clearly be at the very top of the list. Radiohead? Maybe not. One thing is certain: The short list doesn't seem to be growing. "I think the music industry is changing rapidly," says Coplin. "I wonder, twenty years from now, who the next U2 is. Look at Radiohead. They're about the only band now that seems to be carrying that torch of megastar. I think they would do a phenomenal show—but I don't think they're quite right for us. Their music isn't that accessible to a lot of people. So it's going to be interesting to see how things evolve, whether there's going to be anybody else."

How does the list get made? It is, like so many other aspects of the Super Bowl, art masquerading as science. While sales data and popularity polling are reviewed in advance and later marshaled in support of every choice, Coplin suggests that it's more about feel than about an artist's recent record sales, digital downloads, or radio airplay. And, of course, the short list looks quite different than it did before Janet Jackson's "wardrobe malfunction" and the fallout associated with it.

"I remember having an argument with an executive with one of the networks last year about Prince. He just felt like we should have gone in a different direction," Coplin explains. "This was a gentleman who spends his whole year trying to do a number in a universe where ratings are eroding. With Super Bowl halftime, we don't have those concerns. We know they're going to be in front of their televisions."

In this way, the Super Bowl halftime show is truly unique. There's that giant built-in audience, nearly 100 million strong. So unlike any-one else in television, and indeed in the entire entertainment business, Coplin doesn't necessarily need an act that's going to draw people to the screen. The game itself accomplishes that. And most of America will stay to watch at least some of the halftime show. What Coplin needs is an act that will keep people from turning back to the bean dip after the first song.

Enter the Hummability Factor.

"They have to have a catalog that's accessible and familiar and rec-ognizable," he explains. "When songs like 'Hey, Jude' or 'Purple Rain' are played, the world sort of comes together for a moment and sings the song. And when you see 80,000 people in a stadium singing, it provides an energy that's really unique. And I know that sounds sort of esoteric, but that's really a key. Because I think if everybody is singing along, then you've got everybody."

While popular music is more and more about narrowcasting, the game remains the ultimate broadcasting event. And on Super Bowl Sun-day, nothing else will do.

While it represents twelve minutes of entertainment for an individual football fan, the stakes of the Super Bowl halftime show are much bigger for the artist. On one hand, the vast audience, America's largest collec-tion of eyeballs and eardrums, represents an unprecedented opportu-nity. Even for Paul McCartney, who performed at the halftime show in 2002, it was the biggest show he'd ever done and likely ever will do. While the Beatles' appearance on the *Ed Sullivan Show* may have been more of an iconic moment for Sir Paul, the Super Bowl represented an even larger audience (86 million in the United States, compared to about 70 million for the Beatles' first Sunday night appearance). And that ex-posure has an immediate impact on the bottom line. The week after the

Super Bowl performance, McCartney's sales on Amazon went up 350 percent. Prince after Super Bowl XLI? Seven hundred percent.

"They get a much better deal than we do. We get twelve minutes; they get their careers," says Coplin.

On the other hand, on Super Bowl Sunday, even Sir Paul isn't the main event. The twelve-minute-long show represents just a snippet of a regular concert. And while it's not a real issue for anyone big enough to make the NFL's short list, artists don't get paid for the appearance; the NFL does cover their expenses, which often run into seven figures. But the biggest concern on Super Bowl Sunday is this: The artist cedes control of a potentially defining moment to an outsider.

Forget the it's-only-rock-and-roll attitude. Rock-and-roll stars are really the entertainment world's ultimate control freaks. From banning brown M&Ms from the dressing room to deciding what songs to play and how to play them, the biggest stars in the music business get their way in almost every situation for one simple reason: because they can. Superstar athletes listen to their coaches. Even the biggest movie stars do what the director says. But rock stars, on the other hand, call their own shots from beginning to end. And when push comes to shove, even the biggest record company or the most influential promoter will allow their top-selling artists to do pretty much what they want. They don't mind ceding creative control. At least as long as everyone continues to make money.

Not so the NFL. The league has ultimate creative control over its talent, imposing yardage penalties and sometimes fines on players who go overboard with their sack dances and touchdown celebrations. In 2002, the NFL went so far as to threaten to fine Colts quarterback Peyton Manning as much as $25,000 if he violated the league's dress code by wearing black cleats in a game in honor of the recently departed Johnny Unitas. And the league has always been especially proprietary about its marquee event. Commissioner Pete Rozelle, the most powerful figure in sports and the man most responsible for the league's remarkable growth in the 1960s and 1970s, used to get involved in choosing balloons and floral arrangement for Super Bowl week events.

So that's where the pas de deux between the 800-pound gorilla of the NFL and the biggest prima donnas in the entertainment business begins. And Charles Coplin is the one in charge of the choreography.

"How do you get them, creatively, to think your way?" says Coplin, distilling the problem into a single question. "To them you're a suit from New York City. They're placing their careers in your hands."

This dance has led Coplin to some interesting places, such as Paul McCartney's office in London. The meeting included a few Beatle-maniac-gone-to-heaven moments like Paul singing a impromptu snippet of "Hey Jude," but mostly there was a show to plan and work to be done. Producer Don Mischer broached the possibility of Paul playing a white piano and was politely shut down.

"White's a little too Vegas-y, and John [Lennon] played a white piano, so I don't really think that's right," McCartney countered.

"I just remember thinking, 'This is the way a producer and an artist talk. The producer sort of takes a shot, sees if there's a receptivity, and if there's not, he pulls back,'" says Coplin. The next idea is better received: distributing audience cards that have some of the lyrics to "Hey, Jude" on them.

Coplin recalls that at one point McCartney excused himself to take a call from his then-wife Heather ("Hold there, the boss is on the phone, got to go"). "And as soon as he walked out, his guys made sure he was out of the room, and they said, 'Is "Na" spelled N-A or N-A-H?' I was the one in the meeting who went, 'No! It's an 'A'!' And they were like, 'Right—because N-A-H would be "Nah"—and this is not New Zealand!' And I was like, 'This is the *Spinal Tap* moment of the meeting.'"

Still, with McCartney, the big-picture stuff went pretty smoothly, and the details were hammered out quickly enough. "It's very clear when you meet Paul McCartney—he gets showbiz, he gets TV."

This wasn't quite the case with the Rolling Stones. There were serious disagreements about what to play—Coplin and company wanted the Stones to dig deeper into their rich back catalog for familiar hits, while the band wanted to highlight fresh material from their new album. Above all the NFL, wanting to avoid another controversy, expressed concern about some of the language in the lyrics as well as what Jagger might improvise into an open mic.

"They're always worried about how many times we're going to say 'Fuck' on the air," the lead singer half jokingly told a documentary crew. Indeed, the strained marriage between the NFL and rock's ultimate rebels almost fell apart at the very last minute. The band insisted on playing "Start Me Up" and a new one called "Rough Justice," both of which contained language that wouldn't pass muster with the FCC. The league resisted, and the impasse continued as the rehearsals continued Thursday evening.

As late as Friday morning before the game, Roger Goodell, then the league's chief operating officer, was prepared to pull the plug and find a last-minute replacement for the Stones. Ultimately, an uneasy compromise was reached and the songs were performed with the offending words "muted" for both the home and stadium audiences.

Still, it's not the artistic politics that give Coplin nightmares. It's the nuts and bolts of putting on such a huge show under such immense time pressure. A rock band playing a stadium-size show will take a day or more to set up the staging and the sound system at a football stadium. Super Bowl Halftime? Six minutes to set up, and six minutes to break it down and get it off the field. And the timing is such that anything more than the smallest delay will be on display for the whole world to see.

"It's the sheer terror of the six minutes on and the six minutes off the stage," says Coplin. "There's just no way to describe that other than sheer terror."

But the timing is only the first of the challenges. The show is happening on the playing surface of the biggest football game of the year. A section of sod torn up by a broken wheel on a piece of staging isn't a problem, it's a disaster. Every piece of equipment has to be moved in with near-surgical delicacy, and that means no motor vehicles. Everything must be pushed or pulled by hand, often through the most precarious openings.

"They don't spec stadiums for Super Bowl halftimes," Coplin explains. "In Detroit, for example, you're walking through this tunnel which almost does like a complete turn, uphill."

This is all fraught with peril under normal circumstances. For Prince's performance in Miami, the torrential downpour added a whole new level of uncertainty. "I remember walking into the truck and hearing one of our producers saying, 'What do you mean, you have no power?' And when you see the terror in the eyes of the people who you pay to know what they're doing, it's sort of like looking at a pilot saying, 'What do you mean we have no landing gear?' That was terrifying." It turned out that when the stage was brought out, a cable was cut. An act of death-defying improvisation was the only reason the show was able to go on at all. "One of the stagehands took two leads and went like this for twelve minutes." Coplin moves his fists together as if splicing a giant wire. "That's a true story."

Ultimately, Coplin's biggest fear isn't rebellious rock stars or last-minute power shortages. It's more ephemeral than that: Will the show be a flop? "We can't control the quality of the teams on Super Bowl Sunday. They'll either play well or they won't. We will not be criticized for that. But the show is our construct, it's our creation. So you're also just scared to death that people won't like it."

As he prepares to present Tom Petty to the world, Coplin understands the ground rules. If the show is a smashing success, he'll get a few attaboys while the artist basks in the glory and watches the cash register ring. But if something as small as a tank top strap goes awry, Congress could get involved. It's not a job for the faint of heart.

"How many times you go to work and you say, 'What I do today, everybody's gonna see it'?" says Charles Coplin, preparing to pull out the T-word one last time. "It's terrifying."

16

THE GAME

The Toughest Ticket

"Richard Branson is on the phone," says Joan, Frank Supovitz's assistant.

"Richard Branson or Richard Branson's assistant?" asks Supovitz.

"Richard Branson."

Even before he picks up the phone, Supovitz has some idea of how this conversation is going to go.

It's the beginning of the week before Super Bowl XLI in Miami, and Richard Branson, the Virgin records media mogul, has called Supovitz and wants Super Bowl tickets for his girlfriend, who's on vacation in Florida.

"I'm sure you can appreciate that you don't know me and I don't know you," says Supovitz, with the utmost in diplomacy. "If you can validate your identity, we can continue to talk."

"But of course," says Branson. The billionaire mogul and adventurer proceeds to reveal to Supovitz a wide variety of intimate details: how much money he makes, how many jets he owns, and where his houses are. Supovitz isn't sure, but he thinks he hears Richard Branson typing just before every answer. While he's listening to the billionaire prattle on, Supovitz turns to his computer and opens Branson's Wikipedia page. Sure enough, all of this "personal" information—quoted verbatim—is just sitting out there on the Web, ready for the plucking.

"Why don't you fax me over something on your letterhead?" says Supovitz to the Richard Branson wanna-be, stifling a laugh. Needless to say, the fax never comes.

A few minutes later, another NFL staffer pops into Supovitz's office. "You'll never guess what happened," he exclaims. "I just got a call from Sir Richard Branson."

While there are any number of answers to the question "What's a Super Bowl ticket worth?" a story like that one provides as good an answer as any. A Super Bowl ticket is the most desirable ticket in the world of sports. Sure, there are some insiders who quibble and cite tickets that are even harder to come by. A ticket to the Masters golf tournament in Augusta is generally considered an even tougher get, with an inner-circle waiting list that has been closed for thirty years. ESPN's Darren Rovell argues that a Duke-North Carolina college basketball game at tiny Cameron Indoor Stadium when both teams are in national championship contention can be even tougher. The difficulty in getting those tickets is based on the very small number of tickets in circulation, the supply side of the equation. But when it comes to sheer demand, there isn't a ticket that's more coveted than a Super Bowl ticket.

And that demand translates into dollars. The Super Bowl capacity of the University of Phoenix Stadium is 73,000 and Super Bowl tickets carry an average face value of $800. That's a total of almost $60 million. But it certainly doesn't stop there.

The market for Super Bowl tickets is unique in that virtually every ticket is at least theoretically up for grabs. Here's how the tickets are distributed. The NFL keeps 25 percent of the tickets for distribution to sponsors and other VIPs. Each of the teams playing in the game gets 17.5 percent. The host team gets 5 percent. And the other 29 teams each receive a 1.2 percent allotment.

Several things make the Super Bowl market unique. Unlike, say, a World Series or an NBA Finals, most season ticket-holders for the teams playing won't get tickets through the team—in Phoenix each participating team gets only 13,000 tickets—so that creates an instant audience of tens of thousands of fans seeking alternative means of securing a ticket.

The answer to that demand comes from those tickets distributed by the other teams and the NFL itself. Each of the noncompeting teams has a 900-ticket allotment, and each player and assistant coach has the right to buy two tickets at face value. The league requires coaches, players, and team officials to sign a release that they won't resell their tickets (purchased at face value of $700–$900) at a profit. But that doesn't mean it doesn't happen.

In 2005, then–Vikings coach Mike Tice was fined $100,000 by the league for his part in scalping Super Bowl tickets, while his assistants Dean Dalton and Rusty Tillman were fined $10,000 each. A *Sports Illustrated* report suggested that players received $1,900 each for tickets with a face value of $500–$600 at the time. *SI* also reported that when a veteran player tried to buy tickets from Vikings teammates for family members, Tice became enraged. "Tice, one source said, accused the player of trying to 'backdoor the head coach.' Tice then successfully pressured some players to renege on their commitment and sell their tickets through him, the player said, even though Tice was offering slightly less money per ticket." The story further contended that this practice was widespread throughout the league—although no other teams were implicated and no other sanctions levied—and that Tice was singled out because a former player with a grudge dropped a dime on him. In the wake of the scandal—and a less-than-stellar season—Tice was fired by the Vikings after the 2005 regular season.

While the four-figure profits on these tickets may seem like pocket change to an NFL player with a multimillion-dollar contract, it all adds up. Even at a conservative estimate of $2,000 per ticket, that puts the total potential "wholesale" market for Super Bowl tickets at almost $150 million.

Those who are neither rich nor well-connected can try for the handful of "general public" tickets available through the NFL's little-publicized ticket lottery. Every year 500 pairs of tickets are up for grabs through a random drawing. All entries must be sent through registered or certified mail and must be received by June 1; duplicate entries are discarded. The lottery typically receives over 35,000 entries for the 500 available pairs.

Ram Silverman had a good weekend. The vice president of Golden Tickets, a Plano, Texas–based ticket broker, couldn't have been happier with the results of the NFC divisional games. As a football fan, he's a little disappointed that his hometown Cowboys lost. But from a business point of view, he's much happier that the Green Bay Packers and the New York Giants both emerged victorious.

"It was a win-win situation," he explains.

Golden Tickets began as a conventional brick-and-mortar ticket agency, but they've flourished in the age of the Internet, where better information makes for a broader market. While some would call them scalpers, they refer to themselves as ticket brokers, and look upon the tickets that they sell as being like any other high-demand, low-supply item. Golden Tickets is a legitimate business, and they're careful to avoid violating the antiscalping laws that govern ticket resale in various jurisdictions, although increasingly those laws have been softened or repealed.

In Silverman's world, Super Bowl tickets are a little like lobsters at a restaurant. Regular-season tickets, like steak and pasta entrées, have a firm price attached to them. But like a lobster on a menu in Chicago, Super Bowl tickets are sold for market price, which is subject to change on a daily basis.

The day after the NFC divisional games, the market for Super Bowl tickets breaks down as follows. A ticket that gets you in the game, high behind an end zone, is $3,250. An upper-level seat near the middle of the field will cost you $4,250. Lower-level tickets range from $3,500 to $7,500. A club-level ticket in the middle of the field costs a cool $8,950. That represents a modest increase from Miami. "Last year it was $2,850 up to about $8,500," Silverman says. "It was always around that price."

And, Silverman explains, there's always a market within the market. "Last year it started at about $3,000 to about $7,500. The cheaper seats went down in price to about $2,200. The more expensive seats went up to about $8,500 to $9,000." Silverman thinks this could be the year that those really good (but not awesome) 50-yard-line Super Bowl tickets crack the five-figure plateau.

"There seem to be quite a few upper end zones and upper corners around," he explains. "The demand for good seats is much greater than most people expected. It's supply and demand."

Indeed, the soft demand for the less expensive tickets may be a harbinger of the recession that will take hold by the middle of 2008. Those tickets are generally bought by regular fans who crack open the piggy bank when their team makes it to the big game, and as such there's a degree of price sensitivity built into them. Pricewise, a $3,000 in-the-door ticket competes with a big-screen TV or a cruise or a Disney World vacation—or even a couple of months of mortgage payments.

Silverman notes that the prices of the least-expensive tickets have stabilized and even receded a bit in recent years. The peak for nose-bleed seats came in Tampa in 2001. "It was about a $3,500 ticket to get in," he recalls.

The more expensive seats, on the other hand, seem immune to the vagaries of the economy. Even in the toughest times, there will always be people rich enough that even $10,000 for a football ticket is pocket change. And for them, the difference between $8,500 and $10,000 is essentially negligible.

One of the factors that does change from year to year and dramatically affects the market for tickets is the matchup. Last year, Bears fans—who are loyal and seeking an excuse to get out of Chicago in the middle of winter—helped drive up prices. The Colts aren't a great traveling team, but Peyton Manning's national profile, coupled with the fact that they hadn't been in the Super Bowl for more than thirty-five years, helped boost prices.

On the basis of the past weekend's games, Silverman is bullish. "The Packers have a really good traveling fan base, and the Giants too," he says, handicapping this year's market. On the other hand, the Dallas Cowboys, America's Team or not, don't seem to inspire quite the same level of fanaticism. That's why, team loyalty aside, Silverman is happy that it will be the Packers or the Giants in the big game.

On the AFC side, Silverman lost his top choice during the wild-card weekend. The Pittsburgh faithful are legendary for their loyalty and willingness to follow the Men of Steel virtually anywhere. Even though the Patriots have been to the Big Game often in recent years, the quest for the perfect season helps stir national interest on the AFC side.

"I think that if it was the Patriots and the Cowboys, the market would have been a lot softer," says Silverman. "They just don't travel. Steelers fans and Packers fans just seem to be a lot more passionate about it."

Interestingly, the location of the game seems to have little or no impact on the price of tickets. Two years ago, Steelers fans proved just as happy to flock from cold and gray Pittsburgh to equally cold and gray Detroit as they would have been to head to a warm-weather locale like Miami.

But it's not only about the football either. Tickets for the year's second-biggest games—an AFC or NFC Championship Game—generally run from $300 and top out at about $1,000, roughly 10 cents on the dollar compared to a Super Bowl ticket.

Given the single-conference dominance in the modern NFL, pundits have often argued that a Patriots-Colts AFC playoff game, like a Dallas–San Francisco NFL matchup a decade ago, is "the real Super Bowl." That may be true to the fans watching at home, but no matter how lopsided the actual Super Bowl matchup may appear, fans voting with their wallets argue otherwise.

What will happen to Super Bowl ticket prices between now and game time? That depends on the outcome of the NFC Championship Game. Rank-and-file Packers fans are among the hardiest in all of football, ready to follow their team almost anywhere, and would be especially motivated now because they understand that the Brett Favre era is drawing to a close. They're likely to bolster demand for those lower-priced, get-in-the-door tickets. Giants fans may not be quite the fanatic pilgrims the Packers faithful are, but whatever they lack in conviction, they make up for in sheer numbers. And there's likely to be additional corporate buyers for those prime seats. Either way, this will be a good matchup if you've got tickets to sell.

Just do the math: At an average "retail" cost of around $7,000 a ticket, the value of a stadium full of Super Bowl tickets is $511 million, or just over half a billion dollars.

When it comes to understanding the value of a Super Bowl ticket, Hagos Mehreteab and Gerry Wilson, the principals of Yoonew in New

York City, have a unique insight: They run a stock market for sports tickets.

Spurred on by Wilson's futile quest to score tickets for the 2003 World Series, the two MIT Sloan Business School students started this venture as a class project. While there has been a thriving secondary market for tickets, it wasn't a free market as economists understand the term. It was more like a supermarket. Sellers like Silverman attached a price to the ticket and you either paid it or not.

The Yoonew model created a more sophisticated market that allowed for real-time fluctuations in ticket prices, just like on Wall Street. The real fun came in the form of derivatives. Derivatives are a hot item on the stock market. For example, instead of buying a stock outright, you can buy the right to buy or sell it under a specific set of circumstances, all for a fraction of the cost of buying the stock outright. If you're right, you stand to make a huge profit.

But instead of shares of Google or pork belly futures, Yoonew applied this concept to sports tickets. Unlike a conventional ticket broker, or an exchange like eBay or Craigslist, where fans can buy and sell only whole tickets directly, Yoonew sold not only whole tickets but also ticket derivatives, called "fantasy seats." You could buy a fantasy seat—the right to buy a ticket if a certain team or pairing of teams made the Super Bowl—for a fraction of the price of a whole ticket. If your team made the Super Bowl, you could convert that fantasy ticket into a real ticket (which you could then, if you so chose, convert into cash). If your chosen team didn't make the Big Game, the fantasy ticket was worth nothing.

The market for fantasy tickets was like a stock market, but with one key difference: Virtually all the players had a full understanding of the market. While plenty of investors simply put their money into Google because their neighbor did, and couldn't tell you the fifty-two-week high price, much less the stock's profit-to-earnings ratio, sports fans buying fantasy seats on Yoonew knew every intimate detail of the teams they were following, parsing immediately how an injury or even a change in the weather would affect a team's chances of making it to Phoenix.

On Yoonew's database, the prices for Super Bowl fantasy seats can be tracked in real time, so it's possible to monitor the price fluctuations not only day-to-day but minute-to-minute. This volatility peaks, of course, during a late-season game involving two playoff-bound teams. A touchdown results in an instantaneous price spike for the scoring team and a corresponding dip for the team scored upon.

Yoonew began selling Super Bowl fantasy seats early last season, and it's fascinating to watch the fluctuation in the price of New England derivatives, the most stable of any team's, and Giants derivatives, the team with the biggest price fluctuations, as that movement literally graphed the hopes and dreams of the team's fans.

When the market opened on October 21, the price of a fantasy ticket for the undefeated Patriots opened at a strong $3,320, a little less than half of what a Super Bowl ticket might cost the week before the game. As the wins piled up, the price only increased. With the Pats having beaten the defending champion Indianapolis Colts to go 9–0, the price crossed the $4,000 barrier on November 8. It dipped momentarily to $3,647 on November 13, during the team's bye week, but on December 22, when the team went 14–0 to equal the 1972 Dolphins, the price topped $5,000. On January 14, after the Colts lost to the Chargers in the divisional round, the price leaped from $5,892 to $7,029.

The Giants ticket market was much more volatile, like a tech stock being buffeted by promising product news followed by a disappointing earnings report.

With the team on a five-game winning streak following an 0–2 start but the NFC still considered to be wide open, a Giants fantasy ticket opened at $723.80, less than a quarter of the price of a Patriots fantasy ticket. It topped $1,000—hitting $1,067, to be exact—on October 29, after another win against Miami. The price reached a regular-season high of $1,121.76 on November 5 during the team's bye week, as the sports radio buzz focused on the Giants' success, and then began a slow and steady shedding of value. After the Giants got thumped by their division rivals the Cowboys, the price dipped below $500 on November 13. A month later, it had plummeted to $280.53. And on December 19, with the Giants having just barely clinched a playoff spot with a win over Buffalo but having lost star tight end Jeremy Shockey for the season with a broken leg, you could buy a Giants Super Bowl fantasy ticket for only $167.97. A little more than a month later, on January 21, the day after the NFC Championship Game, a Giants fantasy seat reached its final price of $7,378.34.

On the subject of tickets, Frank Supovitz tells one more story about the Miami Super Bowl.

He was sitting upstairs in mission control a couple of hours before game time when he got a call from one of the entrance gates. "There were 125 foreign fans who were standing there with their tickets and they weren't scanning," Supovitz recalls. "Their tickets were dead. There was something wrong with the bar codes."

"What do you want us to do with them?" asked the gate supervisor.

"The tour guide speaks a little English," explains Supovitz. "The other 125 do not. They don't understand what's happening. It's pouring rain. And we had a very impatient group leader."

Through the group leader's broken English, this story was pieced together. The groups claimed they'd entered the stadium at around ten-thirty through the NFL Experience. Then they left and got on their bus to go out to lunch. While there are signs that say "No Readmission" very clearly in English, there were no signs in the foreign language spoken by the tourists. (In an effort to be politically correct, Supovitz declines to name the language.)

"Should I let them in?" asked the supervisor.

"No, you don't just let 125 people in," replied Supovitz.

It was already a hectic moment in mission control, with players arriving and a group of owners not able to get where they needed to be, and the soggy and annoyed tourists were only adding to Supovitz's aggravation.

Was this a large group of customers caught up in a legitimate misunderstanding? Or was this a remarkably well-planned and well-executed scheme to sneak into the Super Bowl, one that depended on the flurry of game day activity—as well as the sheer scope and audacity of the plan—to overwhelm the NFL's checks and balances?

"Have them wait a little longer," said Supovitz.

Supovitz looked toward the transportation coordinator to find out if any buses had left the stadium. No, came the answer. And then he asked around to see if 125 people had wandered out through one of the gates without somebody stopping them. No again.

"It's now starting to stink a little fishy," explains Supovitz. "But it's forty-five minutes into this and people are literally starting to scream at me. 'These people are standing in the rain. How come we're not helping them out?'"

"I'd like to see five tickets," Supovitz asked as calmly as possible, assuming that a random sample of the tickets would prove pretty quickly if they were legitimate or fakes.

How do you make 125 wet, complaining foreign tourists disappear from the stadium on Super Bowl Sunday?

You just ask for their tickets.

17

THE SHOW

Fist Bump

Robert Lachky is sitting in the conference room in Atlanta with his face pressed up against the two-way glass. He's looking at the eyes, because the eyes, he has learned, always tell the story.

On the other side of the glass are about fifty calculatedly average consumers, mostly young, the median age between twenty and twenty-five, a proportionate mix of men and women. The attempt is to replicate the environment of a Super Bowl party. They've been paid only a few dollars each for their time, but their task is anything but trivial. They'll watch commercials that are candidates to be aired in the upcoming Super Bowl and be asked to decide which ones are worthy of being aired on advertising's biggest day.

Lachky is Anheuser-Busch's executive vice president of creative development, and he's more than a little bit worried right now. Anheuser-

Busch, maker of Budweiser, is the exclusive beer advertiser for the Super Bowl and has bought eight 30-second spots, the maximum allotment available. The brewing giant won't reveal exactly what they've paid, except to note that companies that buy multiple spots the way Anheuser-Busch does can negotiate more favorable rates. Still, the average rate for a thirty-second Super Bowl spot is $2.7 million, so those spots represent almost $22 million worth of ad time.

The next spot to be shown to the focus group—known internally as "Fist Bump," officially as "Clydesdale Team"—is one of the finalists. And Lachky knows that it had better be good.

"When you get to the final round of focus groups, say in mid-January, and the consumer says, 'That's not a very good spot. I don't like it,' you go, 'Oh my God, what are we going to do now?'"

The process of assembling the company's Super Bowl spots started back in July and August. Anheuser-Busch solicited pitches from four different advertising agencies for both Bud and Bud Light spots. A collection of thirty-five initial concepts was winnowed down to about two dozen that were actually put into production. The spots were then shot in two waves in late summer and mid-autumn.

Lachky's problem is straightforward. For the brewing giant, Super Bowl advertising doesn't exist in a vacuum anymore. Two of the summer spots in particular had Super Bowl written all over them. One featured two guys at the opera house, holding bottles of Bud Light. The soprano hits a high note and the bottles shatter. "First time at the opera?" asks a guy next to them, holding a *can* of Bud Light.

The other spot featured an actual gridiron theme.

The defense is huddling up, and one of the players says to his teammates, "Anybody who stops this guy, the Bud Light is on me," while the referee eavesdrops.

So on the snap of the ball, the referee flies in and makes a bone-crushing tackle, much to the amazement of players on both sides.

In the last scene, with his fellow refs looking on, the official says, "What? It was a clean hit."

The good news is that the spots were clever, funny, and a little bit edgy. The bad news? Anheuser-Busch sells beer all year long, and it was decided that these two commercials were too good to sit on the shelf for months. A-B decided to run the spots in the fall as part of their massive ad buys during regular-season NFL football, which took them out of the potential Super Bowl rotation.

"We went out with a pretty healthy dose of creative," Lachky explains. "We did it in two waves. Our first wave was awesome, but we wanted to use it for the fall and it got chewed up. And we just don't run creative in the Super Bowl that's run before. You get penalized by the consumer for doing that."

Once upon a time, this would not have been a consideration. In 1989, Anheuser-Busch created the so-called Bud Bowl, in which bottles of Bud and bottles of Bud Light would battle in a mock football game, and an era of Super Bowl–specific advertising was born. Up until that point, advertisers created ads for the Super Bowl, but most of them could be— and often were—aired on other programs. The Bud Bowl took that concept to another level. The Bud Bowl spots weren't ads so much as between-play programming. They told a story, and the element of surprise was so important that the D'Arcy, Masius, Benton & Bowles agency filmed two endings to prevent news leaks about Bud's last-second "win." No expense was spared on production—the $5 million spots were made using expensive, labor-intensive stop-motion animation, where filming two seconds of film could take a whole ten-hour working day—but it was the concept that revolutionized Super Bowl advertising.

The spots accomplished what they set out to do—to get attention at a time when Miller was the "official" beer sponsor of the Super Bowl. And, of course, to sell beer. The company's sales increased by 17 percent, which translates to 200 million bottles and cans of Bud and Bud Light bought that January. The next January, Bud Bowl II featured announcer Brent Musburger and Steelers great Terry Bradshaw in a story line that mimicked the actual game and prompted an even bigger 19 percent increase in sales.

But after running the Bud Bowl spots for nine years, Lachky decided that a change was needed, and the approach was back-to-basics. Super Bowl spots would be more like the spots that were run during the year, commercials that tied in to the messages of the campaign as a whole. Most of the time, this made things easier for Lachky. But not this year.

With the opera spot and the referee spot out of the mix, the emphasis fell squarely on "Fist Bump." This DDB Chicago ad was pretty simple—a young Clydesdale is the last cut for the team to pull the Budweiser wagon. But instead of just going back to the feedbag, he hooks up with a Dalmatian who pushes him through his paces. The music from *Rocky* kicks in as they begin their training. It ends with the young horse making the team and the dog and the horse doing an interspecies fist bump.

The spot was definitely old-school, which, ironically, made it risky. It was also sixty seconds long, so it demanded twice as much viewer attention. And its humor was subtle, rather than the broad comedy that characterizes most Super Bowl spots.

"The concern I had was that it might be too typical," says Lachky. "It might not be remarkable enough."

This spot would live or die in the execution. If not pulled off just right, it could be slow or sappy. So when it came time to film "Fist Bump," A-B and its ad agencies did what they do best: They hired a legendary director, in this case Joe Pytka, and asked him to make a little film. "Great advertising is really art," explains Lachky.

A Super Bowl is unique among television shows. It's the one day of the year where the commercials are just as important as the programming. During the rest of the year, commercials have always been a reason to go to the fridge to get another beer—or to the bathroom to make room for another one. And with the rise of DVDs, video on demand, TiVo, and the ubiquitous remote control, the simple act of sitting through a commercial is an inconvenience that few viewers have to endure.

But not on Super Sunday. The Super Bowl broadcast has turned into the world's largest festival of short films. It all began in 1984 with a commercial that ran exactly once and never even showed the product being advertised. With Ronald Reagan in the White House and the Cold War in full swing, George Orwell's political novel *1984* was very much on people's minds. And one Super Bowl ad struck a chord.

The sixty-second-long spot, created by Chiat/Day, depicted a line of workers, heads shaven, clad in gray coveralls, marching toward a giant screen on which a man is declaring, "We have created a garden of pure ideology where every worker may bloom free of the pests of contradictory thoughts." This image of Orwellian conformity played right into the fears of the day: War is peace, freedom is slavery, and Big Brother is definitely watching.

Enter the possibility of an alternative scenario—a woman with bleached blond hair, dressed in a white top and red shorts, sprints through the crowd, with the Thought Police in hot pursuit. She hurls a sledgehammer, Olympic style, at the screen and shatters it. The voiceover said simply, "On January 24, Apple Computer will introduce Macintosh. And you'll see why 1984 won't be like '1984.'" It was the ultimate home run.

While it never showed the keyboard or the monitor, it communicated the compelling idea that the Apple Macintosh computer represented *possibilities.* It was also stirring television, done by Ridley Scott, who'd brought a similarly bleak vision of the future to life in the seminal *Blade Runner* only a couple of years earlier.

The irony is that this commercial seemed destined for failure. It tested poorly both in focus groups and internally. Second-guessers abounded, with Apple president Steve Jobs wondering if computer buyers—remember that the original Macintosh was a $2,500 cutting-edge product at this point—were actually watching the game, and agency president Jay Chiat worrying that some other Super Bowl advertiser might beat Apple to the punch with a similar *1984*-themed spot. The reaction from Apple's board was so lukewarm that Chiat/Day actually dumped one commercial block to McDonald's and another to United Airlines. The agency kept a single sixty-second spot that they claimed they couldn't get rid of.

In the minutes after that ad aired, this potential debacle became the biggest coup in advertising history. The spot was aired over and over again by news outlets. The company sold $4.6 million worth of the computers within the first six hours alone and 72,000 Macs in the first 100 days, a 50 percent increase over even the most optimistic sales projections.

Why doesn't every advertiser swing for the fences with this kind of statement spot? In a word: "Lemmings." The next year, Apple tried to go right back to the "1984" well. They hired Ridley Scott's brother Tony to shoot a similar spot. It featured a line of blindfolded clones wearing business suits and carrying briefcases, marching in lockstep to the tune of "Heigh ho, heigh ho, it's off to work we go." They marched toward a cliff and then blithely continued off the edge. At the end of the spot, a single nonconformist removed his blindfold, stopped just before the abyss, and turned back toward the camera. Then came the voice-over: "On January 23, Apple Computer will announce the Macintosh Office. You can look into it . . . or you can go on with business as usual." The problem with that high-concept spot, which was filmed at the same EMI studios where *Star Wars* was shot, is that it parodied the very same corporate managers who were supposed to buy the product. The fact that the Apple software itself wasn't quite ready for prime time didn't help the situation either. The spot hit many of the same artistic notes as the "1984" Apple ad did, but the results couldn't have been more different. Macintosh Office was a nonstarter; within a year, Apple had closed three of its six plants and laid off 20 percent of its employees. The "Lemmings" ad was an abject failure.

And a cautionary lesson.

Fist Bump" was a controversial spot even within Anheuser-Busch. Lachky drew some internal criticism for running a sixty-second spot from the year before, which featured a young Dalmatian in a similar situation. Although the ad ultimately tested and aired well, if not remarkably, there was concern that the spot was overly long and not quite edgy enough, and the same things might apply to "Fist Bump." "Are we going to have a problem telling the story and keeping people engaged?" Lachky wondered.

Those concerns abated when Pytka cued up the theme from *Rocky* at the transition point in the spot as they were reviewing the day's footage. They hadn't yet secured the right to the music, but Lachky knew that if they could, it would address any questions about the length of the minute-long spot. "We were hoping to find some magic along the way," said Lachky. "Joe can usually take an idea and plus it up, and he did."

Then there was the question of the ending. Aiming for a big laugh, DDB posited an alternative ending. In the second version, one of the Clydesdale trainers says to the other, "Wow, Rusty sure is a great trainer," and then looks at his partner's paunch and says, "Looks like you could use one too." That version of the spot ends with a cutaway to the dog and the chubby trainer wearing a sweatsuit, running together.

Lachky's reaction was vehement. "That's too sarcastic. Who the hell is Rusty? And I think you're getting into a negative space. This is a warmhearted story. We can end it a better way."

He thought a softer ending—the fist bump—was the way to go.

"The agency did not want to do the fist bump," he recalls. "They were intent on doing the second ending. We fought them and fought them and fought them."

With so much on the line, a compromise was brokered. Pytka filmed both endings, and it would be up to the test audience to decide not only which ending was better but whether either was good enough to crack the Super Bowl rotation.

As the season's test marketing began, Lachky got a rude awakening as he moved from focus group to focus group. "The thing that hit me between the eyes is that it's getting harder and harder to surprise and entertain people because they're entertained and surprised every day on YouTube." A kid with a camcorder in Omaha can get away with things that multinational corporations and Madison Avenue agencies cannot. And these edgy, shocking little films have had the effect of raising the bar for the big guys. "It's simply harder to surprise people than it was only a couple of years ago. We started to realize that our pretesting scores were harder to come by," Lachky explains. "You don't have the luxury of keeping them for thirty seconds."

How does Anheuser-Busch measure success on game day? Through the Ad Meter. For the last twenty years, *USA Today* has been doing a morning-after poll about Super Bowl ads. This is the unofficial scorecard of Madison Avenue's biggest day, but a very real one nonetheless. Anheuser-Busch has won it nine years in a row and is gunning for number ten with "Fist Bump."

Many other Super Bowl advertisers push the envelope with controversial commercials, such as the sexy spots for Internet provider Go Daddy. They reason that an ad that becomes a news item is just as good as an ad that draws high audience scores.

Budweiser, on the other hand, is in it to win it.

"It's not about winning awards," Lachky says. "It's about having the greatest performance on Super Bowl Sunday so that the consumer, the people who sell your product, and the distributors all feel you're the market leader and that nobody can top you. It's very important to look like a winner on that day."

Budweiser also caught a huge break with the "Fist Bump" story line. The Clydesdale tapped into the real-life story line of the Super Bowl, with the wild-card Giants acting as a huge underdog against the undefeated Patriots. The young horse was the equine equivalent of Eli Manning's crew. It seemed like it was perfectly tailored to the zeitgeist, except, of course, that when it was filmed, the Giants hadn't yet qualified for the playoffs. Sometimes it's better to be lucky than good.

So as "Fist Bump" comes up on the monitor in front of the focus group, Lachky understands how much is at stake here. He has already committed to the ad buy, and if he's wrong about this spot, there's really not enough time to reshoot it. If Budweiser's spots disappoint, *that* could easily be the breakout news story of Super Bowl Sunday.

And so Lachky peers through the glass, waiting and watching for the decisive moment. He doesn't need to see the cards the focus group members will fill out—with the highest scores ever for a Clydesdale spot. Lachky simply hears the *Rocky* music kick in and looks at their eyes. What he sees is proof that the biggest commercial of the year from the game's biggest advertiser is a winner.

18

THE SHOW

The Buck Starts Here

"Should I stay or should I go now? If I go there will be trouble. If I stay it will be double."

That old Joe Strummer chestnut neatly sums up the conundrum that Joe Buck is facing right now. It's plenty cold in the car outside the Green Bay restaurant where he'll be eating lunch on the eve of the NFC Championship Game, as the heater struggles gamely, but ultimately in vain. Outside, it's five degrees below zero and the windchill is thirty below, frigid enough to tempt frostbite on the way from the passenger seat to the dining room.

But in a strange way, this visit to the frozen tundra is a homecoming. The play-by-play man on FOX's A-Team, Buck is the son of the late Jack Buck, a Hall of Fame broadcaster. Buck the Elder worked the epically frigid 1967 NFL Championship Game between the Cowboys and the

Packers, which has since been dubbed simply the Ice Bowl. And while Buck the Younger wasn't yet born when his dad made the call of Bart Starr's quarterback sneak, he can revisit that broadcast through the magic of videotape.

"Here I sit, forty-one years later, in the same town, about to be in the same stadium," he says. "They did their on-camera from the middle of the field at the Ice Bowl, which I can't imagine. But he and Ray Scott are down there, and Ray Scott says, 'Well, Jack, what do you think about today's game?' And my dad's comment is, 'Well, Ray, I think it's cold.' That was his first on-air utterance at the Ice Bowl. And it's just so simple and so great." There's a short pause as Buck the Younger mulls this over. "I don't know. Maybe I can find a way to get that in this weekend. It will definitely apply, I know that."

At the age of forty, Joe Buck is sports broadcasting royalty, chosen for his network's biggest assignments, calling both the World Series and the Super Bowl. And yet for a figure whose appeal is supposed to be universal, there's surprisingly little middle ground when it comes to Joe Buck.

On the Internet, for example, 1,092 people "disgusted . . . with his awful commentary and 'so-called' premier play calling" have signed a petition flatly calling upon Buck to "resign from broadcasting." Others, however, are more flattering. "Joe Buck drinking a tallboy is the definition of America," argues a poster on YouTube.

Of course, this difference of opinion breeds a complete cycle of metacriticism. The fans who don't like Buck, of course, criticize him for being on too much, bouncing back and forth between baseball coverage and his NFL duties. The ones who do like him criticize him for being on too little, such as in the fall of 2007, when he cut short his regular-season baseball work.

But this kind of split decision is part and parcel of the sometimes unenviable task of dragging television play-by-play into the twenty-first century. If Pat Summerall is Jock Nation's answer to Johnny Carson, then Joe Buck is Conan O'Brien. Modern television lives in the land of irony, and so does Buck. And some old-school fans have been slow to come around to his pop culture references, his slightly snarky take, and his wry, often self-referential humor.

During an appearance on *Late Night with Conan O'Brien*, Buck mentioned how his friends will sometimes challenge him to work obscure words into his telecasts—a word like *wasabi*, for example. Hearing this, O'Brien promptly bet Buck $1,000—with the proceeds to go to the winner's favorite charity—that he couldn't work the name *Jub-Jub* into a World Series telecast. Jub-Jub, of course, is Aunt Selma's pet iguana on *The Simpsons*, the FOX hit where O'Brien had once worked as a producer. Buck took the bait early in the game, introducing his sideline reporter as "our own little Jub-Jub, Chris Myers."

It was at once too much and not enough. "What surprises me is that Buck didn't milk this thing," wrote blogger Richie Rich on the Home-RunDerby.com site. "I would have kept the untold legions of Conan fans who were watching the World Series just to hear me say 'Jub-Jub' dangling night after night. . . . Think of the extra boost in ratings. Instead, those Jub-Jub watchers are now gone. After a mere 3-plus innings of baseball. And now I can go back to muting Joe Buck and the World Series play-by-play."

Cruel. But true. But cruel.

It's good that Buck applies his sense of humor to himself first and foremost. During those same 2007 baseball playoffs, Buck and his baseball broadcast partner Tim McCarver were making an appearance on the ESPN talking heads show *Pardon the Interruption*. By way of introduction, host Michael Wilbon launched into a diatribe about the drawn-out scheduling of the baseball playoffs, largely to accommodate television, and how a possible seventh game could stretch on into November.

"We could be waiting and waiting and waiting," Wilbon argued.

"It's TV. It's FOX. It's FOX's fault," replied Buck in perfect deadpan. "You know this, Michael and Tony. We're actually responsible for Iran's nuclear program. Global warming. Please. Any complaints? Send them to FOX."

By leaning into the punch, he won Wilbon over in a second.

But love him or hate him, Buck was born to sit behind the microphone. His father was not only a baseball legend but also a prolific football announcer, having worked the very first televised AFL game and later doing the radio broadcasts for *Monday Night Football*, with young Buck often tagging along. "He was a better radio football play-by-play guy than anything else he did or anybody else I've ever heard," says Buck. "And to listen to him do it just makes me appreciate how great he was."

His dad also did play-by-play on Super Bowl IV, and that game between the Cowboys and the Colts, decided on a last-minute field goal, was the most exciting, if not most significant, Super Bowl to date. Jack Buck's color guy (along with Frank Gifford) for that game was the Giants placekicker Pat Summerall, who had also worked the first Super Bowl as a sideline reporter.

While Jack Buck never worked another Super Bowl, Summerall moved from doing color to becoming one of the most respected play-by-play guys in the business. He did his first championship game in that capacity in Super Bowl X. He went on to do play-by-play on eleven Super Bowls, first on CBS and later on FOX, more than any other broadcaster. (Dick Enberg did eight for NBC.) And when his partner John Madden left FOX, Joe Buck replaced Summerall as the play-by-play guy on the Super Bowl broadcast, one short degree of separation between father and son.

Despite Buck's pedigree, there's still something about the Super Bowl that can get inside any broadcaster's head. Part of it is the legacy. When Joe Buck did the play-by-play at his first Super Bowl in 2005 in Jacksonville, he joined a select club, still only ten strong. The list of names—Ray Scott, Jack Whitaker, Curt Gowdy, Jack Buck, Pat Summerall, Dick Enberg, Al Michaels, Greg Gumbel, and Jim Nantz, in addition to Buck—reads like a who's who of sports broadcasting. Those are big shoes to fill.

"It's so trite and almost stupid to say, but you have to realize that it's just a game," Buck confesses. In that first Super Bowl, Buck noticed that he got out of his weekly rhythm and spent the extra time doing research, cramming for the game like an honors student taking one more practice test the night before the SATs. "You just get overwhelmed by the detail. And by the time the game starts it's like, wait a minute. They're still kicking the thing, they're still throwing it and trying to catch it, and you have to remember that you shouldn't really try to do anything different than you've been doing all year."

What exactly is it that Buck does the rest of the season? He prepares. And then hopes he doesn't have to use it. His preparation begins with reading everything he can get his hands on during the course of the week, from the local papers to national magazines, watching game tapes from the teams' contests earlier in the season, and talking to players and coaches. While he's been using his new MacBook more and grabbing more of his information from the Internet, when it comes to putting that research to work in the booth, Buck's methods are strictly old-school. Using a system he learned from his partner Troy Aikman, he puts a player's vital stats—number, height, weight, alma mater—on grid squares on a board. "I have pretty good handwriting, I can write small, so instead of trying to do all of this through a computer program, I just get out a multicolored pen and put different points in different colors to try to have them stand out to me when I'm looking for it on game day."

Buck realizes that the only thing that's worse than not having enough information is having too much. And vice versa. "I don't act as if I'm an accountant the first two weeks of April, going nonstop all day, all night," he explains. "But when you've got a New York-Green Bay game, you've got two whole markets that crank out a lot of information. And I feel compelled to read it all, because I'm always scared of missing that one detail that could make the difference."

He pauses for a moment.

"It's like being back in school, you know? There's nothing better than going into a test when you know you studied it and you know it front and back. You can go in and almost enjoy taking the test. And that's what this is. It's a test every Sunday."

At the same time, it's also a disaster drill, the play-by-play announcer's answer to stockpiling bottled water, flashlight batteries, and canned food. The week's homework is a safety net for those Sundays when it's 21–3 in the second quarter and the game hasn't been as close as the score indicates. So Buck works all week to uncover that great little story about the third-string cornerback's mother, then spends Sunday morning praying he doesn't have to use it.

"The good games are the ones where 88 percent of the stuff that I've prepared doesn't even come out of my mouth," Buck explains. "We can watch film all we want, and I can read all the articles and talk to as many players as I can, but that's all based on what's already happened. The good games are the ones where you're covering what's going on in front of you. So when you're diving into page three of your information and looking at the smallest bit of your chicken scratch, you have exhausted all your options."

The game. That's the X factor in any broadcast. If the game is good, then the play-by-play guy can almost sit back and watch. If the game is bad, even the best anecdotes can't keep most fans from reaching for the remote. Last weekend in Dallas, Buck looked like a genius. A 21–17 war between two division rivals that remains in doubt until the very last play will do that for you.

While Buck's first Super Bowl—New England topping Philadelphia on a fourth-quarter field goal—wasn't quite a classic, it was competitive. But with the undefeated New England Patriots likely waiting for the survivor of the NFC Championship Game, there's no guarantee that Buck's second Super Bowl won't send him combing his game notes to tell the world that Tedy Bruschi was the valedictorian of his high school class.

"The scary thing is to have an audience of that size and to have some dog game where there's really nothing to talk about, and you feel compelled to entertain millions of people with show tunes," says Buck. "I pride myself on trying to make those games fun and entertaining and informative. That's definitely where you earn your money. And if you do that at the level of a Super Bowl, I guess you're doing it two times over."

Buck is quick to tell you that talking is only part of his job. The difference between a competent play-by-play guy and the guy who broadcasts the Super Bowl before his fortieth birthday is this: listening. This is a skill that Buck cites as one of the keys behind his father's deceptively easygoing style. "He really listened," says Buck. "He wasn't so overly prepared that he wasn't able to react off of what somebody said, whether he was doing an interview or working with his analyst."

It wasn't something that always came easy to Buck the Younger, especially during his first Super Bowl run. FOX was then experimenting with a three-man booth, with Buck playing traffic cop with Chris Collinsworth and his current partner, Troy Aikman. The three-voice concept has been successful at times, most notably during *Monday Night Football*, but often the broadcasters end up competing for the opportunity to talk. "I think if you really pay attention to broadcasting today, very few on-air partners listen to one another," Buck admits. "When you have three in a booth, which is what we had when we had Collinsworth with us, nobody's really listening to each other. You're only thinking about what you want to say."

Since the departure of Collinsworth, Buck and Aikman have emerged as a surprisingly good team. The reason is chemistry. This factor is perpetually overrated in assessing a football team's on-field performance—disruptive players like Terrell Owens may bounce from team to team, but they take the W's with them. But in broadcasting, chemistry *is* the product. Aikman lends a gravitas to the proceedings, while Buck helps the former quarterback to loosen up. Part of the reason is that, unlike so many other marriages of convenience in the media, the rapport between Buck and Aikman is real.

"We're contemporaries," Buck says. "We get along well, our families get along well, we've gone on vacations together. Not every production team has that."

Know this about Buck's partner Troy Aikman: He's one hell of a typist. When he was attending Henryetta High in Oklahoma, he found himself in a typing class with thirty-eight girls. As the school's star quarterback, he likely would have been excused if he merely went through the motions. Not Troy Aikman. He not only learned to type, he went with the best of the girls to a typing contest at Okmulgee State Tech. And he won. That's Troy Aikman in a nutshell.

At first glace, Aikman owns an impressive, even remarkable résumé. He was the first pick in the first round of the 1989 NFL draft. His Cowboys got to the Super Bowl three times, winning handily each time, with Aikman winning the MVP Award in the first victory against the Bills. And yet Aikman still seems to have something to prove. Despite having spent that top pick on Aikman, Jerry Jones selected another highly regarded quarterback, Steve Walsh, with a first-round pick in that year's supplemental draft. In his rookie year with the Cowboys, Aikman went

0–11 as a starter on a 1–15 team. Aikman was one of the architects of a remarkable reversal of fortune for a legendary franchise, but he gets little credit for it.

Despite winning three Super Bowls—only Terry Bradshaw and Joe Montana have more Super Bowl rings, with four each—Aikman is rarely mentioned in any conversation about the greatest quarterbacks of all time. Dan Marino, who never won the Super Bowl, is in the mix. So is Brett Favre, who won only one. But Aikman isn't. Even now, Aikman seems to have something to prove. Unlike Buck, who seems to shake off the criticism, Aikman seems to take it personally when media critics take him to task or fans accuse him—largely in equal numbers—of being biased for or against the Cowboys.

And perhaps because of that, he took the call in 2002, when Eagles coach Andy Reid, who had just lost Donovan McNabb to an injury, came looking for a quarterback. It was certainly a tempting offer—the Eagles were one of the elite teams in the NFC, with a legitimate chance at making it to the Super Bowl—and Aikman, who was in the middle of broadcasting another game, considered it seriously. Reid's call was followed by a soul-searching talk with his wife; ultimately, Aikman avoided the trap of "just one more season" that ensnared Michael Jordan and so many others. It was then that Troy Aikman decided that he was going to throw himself into being a broadcaster the same way he had thrown himself into being a quarterback. Or a typist.

More than anyone, Aikman knows what it is to do a Super Bowl from both sides. He's in a small fraternity, joining Collinsworth, Bob Griese, Phil Simms, and Boomer Esiason as the only players who have gone on to do the network broadcast of the game.

"Initially, there's a lot of adrenaline going on, but then you get settled into a normal game, just like you did as a player," Aikman explains. "Early in the game, it is a different game. You can't prepare yourself for the enormity of the event. When you hit the field, you realize, 'Wow—

this is different.' But then it settles in, like any other game. The same thing is true for the broadcast. When you get into it, early on you say, 'Man, this is great, this is the Super Bowl'—but then it's like . . . it's a game, you know?"

In the booth, Buck is charged with telling the audience what happened. Aikman has the harder job of explaining *why.* The language of contemporary professional football is astonishingly complex. To eavesdrop on a coach talking to his quarterback is almost like hearing an argument in a foreign language. Aikman is charged with translating that language into English for the lay viewer, to understand just how far the audience will follow, how much of Football 101 he can squeeze in between plays and during time-outs. And that tightrope is never more precarious than it is on Super Bowl Sunday. If his explanations are too simple, the hard-core fan will get frustrated. If they're too complex, the casual fan will zone out. When he's on his game, Aikman gives the viewer a glimpse of what goes on inside a quarterback's head.

"When I'm watching in real time, during the broadcast, I try to see who's on the field personnelwise. What's the defense doing? Are they playing man-to-man coverage? Are they singled outside? What's the offense? Do they have a spread set? Are they in a two-tight-end set? And then I start from the inside out and look at what's happening with the snap of the ball interiorwise, and then get a feel for what's unfolding on the outside. There's a lot to look at."

Keep in mind that this is all taking place within about ten seconds, and once the play concludes, Aikman has just a few moments to try to make sense of it, providing the voice-over to Richie Zyontz's artful replays.

"What I try to do is explain what just happened, in a way that's not so obvious to the viewers who are just watching it at home," Aikman explains. "If Randy Moss is not catching the ball, I think there's an interest there in knowing *why* he's not catching the ball."

In many ways, Buck functions as the class clown of the FOX honors class. On camera, he's Mr. Announcer Man, as he calls himself, where he may ad-lib a bit, but he never really breaks character. Off camera, Buck is like the smart kid cracking wise while the teacher's out of the room: a joke, a faux complaint, or just some kind of improbably goofy voice. It's all in a day's work.

"If you're in the truck and you hear me, I would probably come off like a goof. But I would say that the stuff I do off the air, whether it's on Friday and Saturday as we prepare as a group or during the commercial break, is as important as what I do on the air. Because I just try to establish a mood where we don't take everything so seriously."

Buck chuckles as he describes his interactions with his FOX baseball partner Tim McCarver. "Right before you see my face in a World Series game, I will turn to Tim and either mouth something that could never be repeated on television or make a gesture that would get me fired if it was ever seen on television. Just to get him laughing."

During their first Super Bowl together, Buck pulled the same thing on Aikman. As he was doing the introductions, he flashed Aikman a particularly goofy look, almost daring him not to laugh. "It's there on the tape," Buck says.

When did Buck realize he had turned the corner with Aikman? Earlier this season, when the former Cowboys star started giving it right back. The A-Team was in Chicago for a particularly frigid late-season game. The night before, *Saturday Night Live* had aired a rerun with Justin Timberlake hosting. "He did a skit, where he's got these big hands on, these big white hands, and he has this little dance and he was trying to get donations for a soup kitchen, and every song he sang, instead of 'Whoop, there it is' it was 'Soup, there it is.' So Troy was doing that, trying to make me laugh before we went on, as we're both shivering in the cold, and I thought, 'All right, now this thing's really come full circle, and we've got a chance of being really fun and really good.'"

As he contemplates leaving the relative warmth of his car for the frigid unknown in the restaurant parking lot, Buck turns his thoughts to Super Bowls past and future. In doing his homework for this Super Bowl, he found that old tape from his Super Sunday debut in Jacksonville and he's made his peace with it.

"I've seen enough of it to know that I sound like myself, I've seen enough of it to know that I didn't sound like I was nervous," says Buck with a shiver. "And you know, I really wasn't. But I think the second time around it'll be better, hopefully. Knock on wood. But a lot of times, you're held hostage to the game you get. If we get a good game, we'll do it justice."

19
THE SHOW

Homework Time

It's midwinter in Wilmington, and in the big house with the blue shutters and the basketball hoop at the end of the cul-de-sac, a Christmas tree is still sitting by the curb. But on this sunny January day, the mercury has climbed above 45 degrees, so Artie Kempner is pushing the seasons, the same way he pushes everything else. He's wearing a pair of cargo shorts topped with a red Tampa Bay Buccaneers shirt, not because of any team allegiance but because it's made of a performance fabric perfect for an outdoor workout.

"Shorts weather? Every day," he says by way of greeting as we walk through the garage. "We lucked out on this place. The developer was saving it for himself and then he and his wife got separated."

With Super Bowl XLII only ten days away, it's homework day for Kempner. He camps out on a massive tan sectional complete with cup holders, the large-screen television perched next to the fireplace, with more emphasis on the viewing angles than any aesthetic consideration. "It's a working house," Kempner says, his half apology containing more than a bit of pride.

Later in the morning, a crew from Best Buy will deliver two more televisions for an upstairs bedroom and a long-in-the-making finished basement.

When his niece stops over later before his son's high school basketball game, she notices the big boxes and teases Kempner. "How many televisions do you have?"

"What do I do for a living?" Kempner fires back with mock anger.

As he sits on the big sectional, Kempner is preparing for the biggest broadcast of his career. He's watching the weekend's AFC and NFC Championship Games, each with a different focus. Kempner's done a half dozen New York Giants games this year, so he understands their rhythms (or occasional lack thereof). The Patriots are a different story. The team's offense, efficient but hardly cutting-edge during the early part of their dynasty, has changed enormously.

Against the Chargers, the Patriots are using an innovative five-receiver set, a situation that gives nightmares to defenses and television directors alike. Offensive coordinator Josh McDaniels loves these complicated formations, and Tom Brady has operated this new offense with ruthless accuracy and efficiency, breaking Peyton Manning's single-season mark for touchdown passes, leading the Patriots to a record-breaking 589 points scored.

Even with the additional cameras that Kempner will have in the Super Bowl (but not the new Panavision cart camera or the Finnish mic array demonstrated in Phoenix, which were deemed not ready for primetime), the prospect gives him pause. Having an additional receiver on the field doesn't just add one more player but actually increases New

England's offensive options geometrically because of all the things the extra receiver can do on any given snap.

"I watch games like a defensive coordinator," Kempner says as the Chargers tackle Laurence Maroney. These undefeated Patriots have fooled defenses more effectively than any other team in football history. Kempner wants to make sure he doesn't get fooled as well.

Today, it's all about the details. He's happy that the usually efficient Patriots offense has stalled a little in the first half. A rare punt from the highest-scoring team in NFL history gives Kempner a chance to put Patriots punter Chris Hanson on the clock, and he's literally counting off seconds between the snap and when Hanson actually kicks the football.

He's taking nothing for granted. Kempner recalls a nightmarish college game early in his career. "It was the worst game I've ever directed— my worst personal experience," he says. Texas Christian University was a surprise contender that season and tried to keep opponents off balance with unorthodox special-teams play. "As soon as TCU didn't make a first down on third, the punt team would sprint onto the field and snap the ball. And that screwed us up more than anything. I must have missed the first three punt snaps. It just did not occur to me what was going on. The phone rang in the truck and I remember getting a call from Ted Shaker, the executive producer. He said, 'Artie? What the fuck happened?' And I said, 'Teddy—I have no idea. It's kind of all a blur right now.' I thought I was going to get fired."

He smiles at the memory of a storm weathered and a lesson learned.

"You have to be ready for the on-side kick," he says. "You have to be ready for *anything*."

The NFC Championship Game, by contrast, is an exercise in self-analysis for Kempner: *How am I doing?*

This kind of reflection is part and parcel of Kempner's week. Usually he's watching the game only minutes after it's over, popping a freshly burned DVD into his laptop at the airport, or, if he's in New York or Philadelphia, watching it on the train on the way home to Wilmington.

"I put it in right away," he says. "And, you know, I'm a little bit of a junkie in that way. I want to know how we did."

This review also serves to manage Kempner's own expectations. He had recently watched the tape of that first Giants-Packers regular-season game, and while it wasn't the crew's finest moment, it wasn't quite the unmitigated disaster that Kempner had thought it was at the time.

These reality checks cut both ways, of course. Kempner recalls a 49ers-Packers divisional playoff game that he did with producer Richie Zyontz several years ago. "It was phenomenal. And we really thought we killed it. There were no glitches at all," he recalls. "Not only was it an outstanding broadcast, it was a clean broadcast—nothing to make you cringe, even as a TV person. And I remember Richie saying to me, 'Let's not watch that game. Let's just leave it the way it is.'" So that's what Zyontz and Kempner did. But one day as he was organizing the library that contains every game that he's ever done at FOX, Kempner stumbled upon that game. Artie being Artie, he couldn't resist the temptation to pop in Pandora's tape. "I thought, 'Let me take a look at this game.' So I watched it, and it was good. But you know what? It wasn't perfect. Not remotely."

The Paley Center for Media in New York City keeps a most-wanted list. The list consists of televised events for which there are no known recorded copies. It begins with Franklin D. Roosevelt's appearance at the opening of the 1939 World's Fair, the very first commercial television broadcast. Also on that list is the very first NFL-AFL Championship Game. Hard though it may be to believe, while Artie Kempner has a personal library of every minute of every football game he's ever directed, there isn't a single known copy of the broadcast of Super Bowl I.

"But wait," you say, "I remember seeing that game." The images that are stuck in your head are probably from the NFL Films version of the game, which still endures. But the television broadcast has been lost to history. What happened to these now priceless tapes? Two factors: a lack of money and a lack of vision. While it's hard to imagine now, when a four-hour-long game can be taped using a $50 VCR and a 99-cent videotape or on any equally inexpensive digital medium, in the mid-1960s videotape was so expensive that even television networks were forced to erase tapes and record over them. Football games, even championship games, were candidates for erasure for a simple reason: In a day when there were no VCRs, no DVDs, and no cable channels, no one could imagine why anyone would want to watch a sporting event, even a championship game, a second time.

While this decision may seem ludicrous now, at the time it represented a consensus. That first Super Bowl was broadcast by both CBS and NBC, and the staff at both networks decided that the tapes were expendable.

During the Giants' half of Kempner's pre–Super Bowl homework session, Kempner is watching a dub with the sound from the broadcast truck, so he can hear his interplay with Zyontz and with Aikman and Buck in the booth as well as his instructions to his camera operators. Looking ahead to the Super Bowl, he's focusing not so much on the Giants as on the broadcast itself.

"We've done so many Giants games that there won't be a lot of surprises," he says. "I know their timing. I know they don't punt fast. I know that when Tynes has the ball teed up he's going to kick. He's not going to dilly-dally."

Kempner watches Eli Manning's snap count on the big screen. The tight shot shows the Giants' QB mouthing a big "O" sound and taking the snap.

"Whenever they say 'Omaha' it means they're gonna basically go on the next sound," Kempner explains matter-of-factly. "I asked Tiki Barber about that a couple years ago. So I know if I hear 'Omaha' from Eli, I'd better get the hell onto that, because he's gonna snap the ball, and I don't want to miss the snap."

The game-time temperature for the NFC Championship Game was one degree below zero, making it the third-coldest game in Lambeau Field history, rivaling the frigid 1967 NFL Championship Game, dubbed the Ice Bowl. And while FOX star Howie Long hammed it up by wearing his Elmer Fudd cap during his pregame show, no one had it harder than Kempner's camera crew. They stood outside for the better part of four hours, exposed to the cold and wind and snow, with cameras sometimes balking and the camera operators fighting to keep focus both literally and figuratively. In such extreme cold, Kempner explains, the combination of the long telephoto lenses used in sports photography and body heat rising from the crowd can cause the kind of shimmering waves that you usually find in a spaghetti Western.

This broadcast is chock-full of the kind of great pictures that Kempner always talks about, close-up shots of the players reacting to the cold and the pressure. He says that he runs down the roster to make sure he includes tight shots of all the big players—Snee, Strahan, Umenyiora, Manning. "We want to get those tight pictures to show, 'This is what this guy looks like. This is what he's facing. And these are his reactions after a bad pass,'" says Kempner. "Looking back at that game, Eli, at times, did not look confident. I don't know if the facial expression can really define somebody. People think he's emotionless. He's not. He's not Tom Coughlin either."

A high-angle isolation replay shows Packers wideout Donald Driver taking a Giants cornerback at the line of scrimmage and all but wrestling him to the ground when the Giants tried, unsuccessfully, to play the kind of physical man-to-man coverage—what a defensive coordinator would call press coverage—that had worked so well for the Packers in the early stages of the game. This replay provided a little football seminar sandwiched between two plays. The viewer had already seen the *what*—a touchdown catch—but this replay revealed the hidden why.

While today's task is picking apart the A-Team's last pre–Super Bowl performance, Kempner is not above taking a step back to look at the big picture. "I think we had a really good broadcast. The crew was equal to the elements and the great game we had," he says. "We didn't leave anything out there." On one level, he's right. But he's also suppressing the truth just a little; he knows it, and he knows that I know it. The game may have been a Mona Lisa, but a Mona Lisa with one giant zit in the middle of her forehead.

Because then comes the penalty. The Packers are moving into Giants territory, and New York appears to have come up with a key third-down stop on the periphery of field goal range. Long after the whistle is blown, Sam Madison of the Giants is called for an unsportsmanlike-conduct penalty, which gives Green Bay an automatic first down.

"This is as important as any penalty in the game," Buck tells the viewers.

And Artie Kempner and Richie Zyontz don't have a replay.

This is the result of a convergence of factors. The offensive player—utility running back Vernand Morency—didn't merit isolation coverage. The contretemps between Morency and Madison happened well away from the ball. And it happened well after the play had been blown dead. There are twelve cameras, as well as the coach's quality-control cam, and not a single one of them got a replay of what Aikman and Buck saw from the booth. While they have video of Madison pleading his case to the official, none of the replays show what he did to earn that unsports-manlike-conduct penalty.

The high camera that might have caught the penalty zoomed in on Favre instead of staying with a wider shot of the play. It's a blown coverage, to be sure, but under most circumstances it's a venial sin, not a mortal one, the sort of minor mental error that every football player suffers a couple of times a game.

Kempner rewinds and plays it again, almost hoping against hope that the phantom replay will magically appear. "I don't know that anyone else would have had it," he says, shaking his head.

Still, it's a nightmare scenario. It was a game-changing play—a third-down stop on the outskirts of field goal position that turned into a drive-extending first down. It would take on even greater importance as the Packers capitalized on the opportunity and scored a touchdown. This one stupid penalty easily could have determined who went to the Super Bowl.

"Richie is dying with this," says Kempner. "We did a great game and we blew one replay and that's all anyone's talking about."

Still, Kempner knows that it could have been worse. The fact that the game went into overtime and the Giants ultimately prevailed took some of the emphasis off the penalty. How else could it have been worse? It could have happened in the Super Bowl.

20

THE GAME

Seven Days

It's raining in Phoenix. As Super Bowl week officially begins, on the Sunday before the game, the heavens have opened up in a way that seems to happen only in the desert. The parking lot at my hotel was underwater from curb to curb and my rental car balked at the abrupt change in humidity, the little Subaru grunting and coughing before it finally started.

It doesn't rain often in Phoenix—the locals tell me that the last real precipitation came in December during the NFL meetings, which was, coincidentally, my last visit. The historical trends, of course, point toward desert sunshine. For the full month of January, the average rainfall in Phoenix is a scant 0.6 inches. However, over the last twenty-four hours, the rainfall in parts of this drought-stricken city has reached an ark-worthy 1.42 inches.

Although it's still a week away, everything somehow comes back to the Big Game. Would this be a continuation of a trend toward less-than-super weather for the Super Bowl? After all, it was rainy and cold all week in Jacksonville, it snowed on Super Bowl Eve in Detroit, and last year in Miami it was the first foul-weather Super Bowl ever. Even in the darkest cloud, there could be a silver lining. In my hotel lobby, a Giants fan asked me beseechingly if the rain might help his team. I reminded him gently that there's a retractable roof on the University of Phoenix Stadium.

As I looked at the puddle, I was reminded of how a friend who lives in town explained Phoenix's growing pains to me.

"When Phoenix really started to grow, twenty, thirty years ago, they hired some city planners and they said, 'This city is going to really get big. So now's the time to build some infrastructure—roads, schools, mass transit.' The city looked into it, and they realized that all of this was going to cost money. A lot of money," he said. "So they figured that if they just kept things more or less the way they were, people would stay away and that would solve all the problems."

It's the "if we don't build it, they won't come" theory of urban planning. It didn't quite work. And I'm reminded of the long-term cost of short-term thinking all week as I watch sewers struggling against the deluge, search in vain for places to park, and hear a reporter gnash his teeth as he recounts the saga of a media bus that missed a press conference because it got stuck in a rather routine rush-hour traffic jam.

Rain or shine, this is the city we have chosen.

Call it Anklegate. That's why media from all around the nation gathered in the pouring rain in a giant tent pitched next to the Patriots' hotel. They're waiting for the team to arrive, poised to learn not what the star quarterback would say but how gingerly he'd walk to the podium. The week before Super Bowl week consists of the usual patter—the Patriots' pursuit of perfection, the Giants' hope for a huge upset, and a bit about New England's Spygate videotaping scandal—plus one very juicy nugget.

On Monday, Patriots quarterback Tom Brady was caught on tape by a crew of video paparazzi. He was in New York City outside the apartment of his girlfriend, supermodel Gisele Bundchen, wearing a walking cast on his right foot. If this hadn't been the Super Bowl—just the AFC Championship Game—or if Brady had been dating an equally stunning but less famous young lady, the biggest football news leading up to any Super Bowl in recent memory likely would have remained a secret.

The smoking-gun footage was shot not by ESPN or a local sports television crew but by a cameraman from TMZ, the celebrity gossip outlet. A look at the footage reveals that this crew was focused first and foremost on Gisele. "Were you there with him at the game?" they asked with mock politesse. "Are you excited that he's going to the Super Bowl?"

Like a true veteran, without so much as a word or a glance, the supermodel hustled from the black SUV across the street and up the steps of her Greenwich Village brownstone. The only reaction was a growl from the tiny dog she was carrying in her bag. Almost as an afterthought, the crew turned their cameras on Brady, who was limping noticeably as he crossed the street carrying a small flower arrangement, letting two walking-around guys handle the luggage. "How you doing, Tom? Congratulations on going to the Super Bowl, buddy," they harassed. "Tom, anything at all? You're going to the Super Bowl. Not even a smile, bro?" The line of thinking was obvious. If he wouldn't talk, perhaps they could get Brady annoyed enough to take a multimillion-dollar swing at the guy with the mic. The fact that no one asked a single question about his gimpy foot revealed that this crew had much more experience in trailing Britney Spears than Peyton Manning.

This wasn't the first go-round between Tom, Gisele, and the paparazzi. A little more than a year earlier, a TMZ still photographer had snagged a shot of the newly minted couple approaching her Manhattan apartment. When they spotted the photographer, they pulled their jackets over their heads in perfect unison. Later that year, TMZ scored yet another Brady-related scoop when the QB was spotted wearing a Yankees cap.

Anklegate makes one thing perfectly clear: The Super Bowl is first and foremost an entertainment story, and never so much as when the star quarterback is dating the star of the Victoria's Secret catalog.

Why is the straight sports media playing catch-up on this huge story? They understand Brady's unquestionable importance to his team. He has started 126 consecutive games, a streak that dates to the beginning of the Patriots' Super Bowl run, and there isn't a more valuable—and irreplaceable—player in all of professional sports. And if Brady really is hurt, the Patriots clearly don't have much in the way of options. The team's two backup quarterbacks, Matt Cassell and Matt Gutierrez, have thrown a grand total of forty career passes between them.

Blame it on Bill Belichick. The New England head coach runs the tightest ship in the NFL. Unlike many other NFL coaches, he doesn't allow his assistant coaches to talk to the media at all. And while the collective bargaining agreement prevents him from muzzling his players in the same way, he does continually remind them that loose lips do indeed sink ships. (Even Brady himself acknowledged this: "I just try not to say too much to get my coach mad at me.")

Many of the sportswriters who have converged on Phoenix are convinced Brady's walking cast is a misdirection play aimed not at the Giants but at the media. On one level, the theory makes perfect sense. Letting the media speculate about Brady's foot is like throwing a rawhide bone to your dog while you're grilling rib eyes. If the reporters are busy covering Anklegate, that means they're not piling on with more "perfect season" stories—and "perfect season" pressure. If they're covering Anklegate, they're not dredging up Spygate stories from early in the season, wondering if a figurative asterisk should be attached to the Patriots' 18–0 mark.

Even the Giants add to the doubt factor. "I don't buy it," says Michael Strahan, a defensive lineman who will have the responsibility of harassing Brady on Sunday. "If he was really that injured, he'd probably be getting treatment up in Boston, even if he said, 'I can wrap ice on it at my girlfriend's apartment.'"

And there's certainly precedent. Just look at the Patriots' injury report for any game over the last four seasons. Right at the top, quarterback Tom Brady is listed as "probable: right shoulder." But every week he played, completely unhampered by his sore arm. (Only once during this streak did the line differ: On December 15, 2005, he was listed as "questionable: shoulder/shin," although he played.)

This escapade started when the NFL fined the Patriots for leaving an injured player off its weekly injury report. Miffed, Belichick added Brady to the list the very next week, and the fact that he continues to do so every week four years later is a testament to his elephantine memory. Tellingly, in a postgame press conference after the Patriots beat the Chargers in the AFC Championship Game, the assembled sportswriters don't even bother to ask Belichick about Brady's health, so the Patriots coach doesn't even have to fib about his quarterback's condition.

And of course, this being turn-of-the-millennium America, this charade is spun into a marketing opportunity. Brady is a paid endorser for a topical pain reliever called Myo-Med, and a November 2007 press release cites Brady's chronic shoulder injuries.

"I use Myo-Med two or three times a day to keep my shoulder and other joints and muscles mobile and pain free," the release quotes Brady, in his very best spokesperson pitch. "The toxin-free formula is great for athletes that need frequent application. It wouldn't help my overall game to destroy my digestive track [sic] with too many anti-inflammatory drugs like ibuprofen just to get rid of pain in my shoulder. My success depends on overall performance. I also like that Myo-Med doesn't leave me smelling like a tube of menthol." It's well known, of course, that supermodels despise the smell of menthol.

With the rain, the Patriots are late arriving at their hotel, and in the press tent, the natives are getting restless. With the two-hour time difference, deadlines are looming for journalists in Boston and New York, and editors are clamoring for Anklegate updates. There is no food, and the rain pounding relentlessly on the roof of the tent provides a flashback to the camping trip from hell. Camera crews cluster around the podium where Brady is likely to speak, those in the front guarding their spaces jealously, while those in the back are perched on stepstools in hopes of a bird's-eye view of the proceedings.

I head across to the hotel lobby in search of real people.

"No, I'm not Tom Brady," says Bridget Bennett as she turns around wearing a jersey bearing the quarterback's number.

"But she's hobbling too," quips her husband, Phil. They've come from Santa Teresa, New Mexico, for this. Bridget is sporting Pats colors and limping more than a bit after recent knee surgery.

The lobby, where the Bennetts and a handful of other fans have congregated, hoping for even a quick glimpse of their heroes, provides a welcome respite from the cynicism of the pressroom. Bridget Bennett is fortysomething with strawberry-blond hair, and she is wearing the kind of inviting smile that the Irish national tourist office ought to build an ad campaign around. She beams, happy just to peer out the window and watch the same drizzle that is drenching Brady, Belichick, and Tedy Bruschi.

"This is better than Disney," she laughs, stealing another glance out the window just in case a Patriot has appeared.

She is happy to tell her story, which may not be quite Ellis Island but still explains a lot about why the Super Bowl has become so special.

"I came here eighteen years ago on Super Bowl Sunday," she says proudly. She didn't understand the intricacies of American football at first, but the passion it inspired needed no translation. "I watched him almost cry," she said, recalling those Sundays when the Patriots—and her husband—would suffer a particularly tough loss. And at that point, in the days before the team's renaissance, there was plenty to cry about in Patriots Nation.

Then, when Bennett spent an entire winter on bed rest during her pregnancy, it all started making sense. Through that whole winter, she watched game tapes and highlight shows, devoured books, newspapers, and magazines. When the Patriots obliged with their first Super Bowl win, a fan was born.

But even now that she understands the intricacies of the safety blitz, the simple love of her team is what draws her to the game. "Isn't it good to have something to be passionate about?" she asks rhetorically, finding common ground with fans of other teams jealous of New England's success. "I've never been told 'I hate you' with such dancing eyes."

In the sodden tent, Belichick makes his entrance, long past fashionably late. He's the Vince Lombardi of the digital age, as well prepared, as cordial, and as forthcoming as a White House press secretary.

"How's Tom's foot?" comes the question from the front row.

"You'll have to ask him."

Then came the real moment of truth. Entering the press tent through a side door, Brady looks like a spread for a men's fashion magazine. He is wearing a dark three-piece suit, a white shirt with no tie, and a fashionable thirty-six-hour growth of stubble. No crutches. No cane. No walking cast. In fact, he's wearing a pair of cowboy boots. Even with his alternative entrance strategy, stage left, he is still surrounded by a gaggle of camera crews. Brady could easily trip over a cameraman, a boom mic operator, or a cable, and in a split second the coverage itself could become the news.

Brady walks to the podium without a limp. As he stands throughout the twenty-minute-long press conference, he seems to be favoring his uninjured *left* foot. Maybe it's the Myo-Med.

The first question, and really the only one: "How's the ankle, Tom?"

"What did the coach say?" Brady replies.

There are plenty of rules in the press box. The most obvious things that govern the conduct of the media are printed on the back of every credential: restrictions against live unauthorized broadcasting and prohibitions on asking players for autographs. But there are other unwritten rules that are just as rigidly enforced. No cheering in the press box. No shorts. No jeans. No T-shirts. No sneakers. It's a way to lend gravitas to a profession that involves whiling away hours watching games and talking sports. The sportswriter's uniform of Dockers and Rockports and box-plaid button-down shirts is an attempt to be taken seriously.

But Media Day at the Super Bowl, held at the University of Phoenix Stadium on Tuesday of Super Bowl week, is like a cross between Boxing Day and Mardi Gras, the one day of the sports year that all these strictures go out the window and anything truly goes. It's just another indication of the way that the Super Bowl has become more than a football game.

It's a giant attention grab, the one day in the world of sports journalism when the interviewer can trump the interviewee. Media outlets are ostensibly there to cover what the players say. But for those interested in talking about pass coverage and run blocking, there is access to the players at the team hotels. Media Day is most aptly named. It's the day when the media turns out en masse to cover the media.

With all this background noise, it takes an awful lot to get attention. Last year, for example, a Miami-based reporter set up a table with a game of Rock 'Em Sock 'Em Robots. It seemed like a pretty good schtick. It's got an old-school kitsch factor, and the game is quick, visual, and easy enough to explain to players raised on PlayStation. And can anyone really resist the tagline "Hey, you knocked my block off"? Unfortunately, while the reporter snagged a few rookies and benchwarmers, for most of the day the blocks remained unknocked.

This year, outlets seem to have refined their pitch, taking a cue from the world of advertising. Madison Avenue knows that there are three things that are all but irresistible: pretty girls, little kids, and cute puppies—and two of the three are very much in evidence on Media Day.

The biggest story is also the most obvious one. Ines Gómez Mont of TV Azteca, dressed up in a short white wedding dress complete with a veil, muscles her way through the crowd toward Tom Brady's podium.

"The woman in the wedding dress," says Brady.

"I'm in love with you," says Gómez.

"Are you really?"

"Will you marry me, please?"

"I've never had a proposal," says the man who is perhaps America's most eligible bachelor, lying through his teeth. "What's your name?"

"Ines."

"That's a beautiful name."

"I'm the real Miss Brady."

"I've got a few Miss Bradys in my life."

"Can I be one of them?"

"I'm a one-woman man. But you're a beautiful woman, and anyone who would have the opportunity to marry you would be a lucky man."

When the Giants have their turn to meet the press, Gómez poses the same question to Eli Manning.

"Manning, Manning, I love you. Will you marry me?"

Judging from his reaction, this may well be Manning's first proposal. He just shakes his head in embarrassment, looking for a way to hide under the podium. Gómez tosses him a "Marry Me Manning" T-shirt, and he obliges by holding it up to the camera shyly.

It's a classic example of making the most of your assets. Gómez isn't model-pretty and her English isn't especially good. But what her move lacks in refinement, it more than makes up for in sheer chutzpah. It also says something about the two quarterbacks. As a sixth-round draft pick who came from the bench to win a Super Bowl, Brady's been Teflon-coated his whole career. Manning, on the other hand, has been Mr. Velcro. Throughout his whole career he's been stuck with unfavorable comparisons, first to his brother Peyton and then to quarterbacks like Ben Roethlisberger and Philip Rivers, who were drafted after him but enjoyed more early success. No wonder he's a little gun-shy.

Other outlets resort to pure sex appeal. Televisa enlists Marisol González, a former Miss Mexico, to don short shorts and long boots, and get a cadre of Patriot benchwarmers to show her their victory dance. Not to be outdone, ESPN920, a Las Vegas radio station, has Veronica Grabowski, Miss Nevada, do a video blog while wearing her contest sash lest anyone think she's just another pretty face. She admits that her maiden foray into Super Bowl journalism hasn't been quite what she expected.

"I did about thirty interviews," she reports. Interviews in which she was the subject, she adds a little sheepishly. How many pictures has she posed for? "I lost count," she says, as yet another journalist hovers, hoping for a snapshot.

When it isn't the beauty queens, it's the kids. Brock Domann, the nine-year-old son of sports agent Craig Domann, reporting for *Scholastic News*, asks Eli Manning, "When you and Peyton used to play football, who would be the quarterback since you guys are both quarterbacks?" asks Domann. Eli says Peyton made him play center, because he was older. The boy barks right back, explaining that when he and his older brother play, *he* takes the snaps.

Even the legitimate journalists see how well this strategy works and try to get the pint-sized pundits to ask their questions. Ten-year-old Jason Krause of Chicago works his way through the crowd surrounding Tom Coughlin and asks a question that an ESPN producer whispered in his ear.

"Coach!" he yells. "I hear you've been a lot nicer this year."

"Who put you up to that question?" Coughlin wonders.

"Well, you've certainly been much nicer than Belichick," says Krause.

Earlier he asked another Giant, "Do you have a girlfriend?" and followed up with "Do you want one?"

Which is not to say that anything goes. A bunch of Patriots are sitting in the stands taking it all in, and a reporter from a Boston paper comes over. "So who's hotter? Gisele or Jessica Simpson?"

On the surface, it seems clever: the Battle of the Quarterback Girl-friends. Except that the Patriots players are too well trained, realizing instinctively that there's no diplomatic answer to that question.

"No comment."

And since he has nothing but a notebook, there isn't even a way for the reporter to edit the footage into a funny little montage of party-line answers. He has nothing. Zilch. Zippo.

"C'mon, guys, gimme something."

In the world of the Patriots, even on Super Bowl Media Day, if you say the wrong thing you can end up in Belichick's doghouse. "You try to avoid being the guy who gets the 'This isn't what we're looking for' speech. And it happens weekly," veteran Larry Izzo explains. "Sometimes it's just, 'Shut the fuck up.'"

While the Super Bowl seems to most outsiders to run like a well-oiled machine, that's not always the case backstage. History—which includes legends like the halftime show staging that wouldn't fit through a stadium door—has taught the NFL to expect the unexpected.

NFL vice president of media relations Brian McCarthy tells a story that typifies the logistical nightmare that is the Super Bowl. On Wednesday, the NFL is holding a press conference to unveil a new Tiffany-designed trophy to go to the MVP of the Pro Bowl. The shiny new hardware arrives in a timely manner safely ensconced in a Brinks security case. Only one problem—the keys to the case are locked inside.

A panicked call to a locksmith ensues, but McCarthy realizes that the assembled media, and the players, including Ben Roethlisberger, Matt Hasselbeck, and Larry Fitzgerald, won't wait, so he plans to start the press conference without the hardware.

"I'm talking about the award and the new trophy," says McCarthy. "And as I say that, I look to my left and there's my guy with the trophy. It looked as if we planned it."

Murphy's Law is hard at work at the stadium as well. With a warm-weather Super Bowl site, Frank Supovitz, the NFL's Super Bowl czar had expected cooperation from Mother Nature. But this week in Phoenix it's not just chilly but downright cold, getting down into the thirties overnight. And that adds a whole layer of complications. The plan was to put the movable field outside after Media Day and let the fresh sod, which was grown in Alabama and laid just for the game, soak up the desert sun, then move it inside for the game starting on Friday. No such luck.

The unseasonable temperatures call for a change in plans. The very real fear of a turf-killing frost make it necessary to bring the field in at night and roll it back out during the day.

"It's like tucking it into bed," Supovitz explains.

But since it takes ninety minutes to move the field in or out, and virtually all the work in the building has to stop while the field is being moved, this adds another three hours to every workday all over the site.

Think of it as Revenge of the Nerds. Veteran sports journalists grumble all week about Media Day and the stupid questions and blatant self-promotion from entertainment reporters, who can't tell the players without a scorecard. And yet this exchange was overheard between two veteran reporters as Tom Petty and the Heartbreakers were about to enter for their Thursday afternoon halftime-show press conference.

"Who's Tom Petty? I don't know any of his songs."

"Did you see *The Silence of the Lambs*? The fat girl was singing 'American Girl' in the car."

When the press conference starts in earnest, it gets worse. One reporter asks Petty, who has made it a point to reject all commercial requests for his music, "What's the goofiest request you've ever turned down?" and then with a straight face asks Petty to give a shout-out to 103.7 the Mountain in Seattle.

"I don't know, they're all pretty goofy," says Petty, more confused than annoyed. "I don't know how to answer that. But I will shout out."

Even moderator Brian McCarthy of the NFL can't let the exchange pass without comment. "We have a *real* question on the other side of the room."

You have to pay close attention to label use," says Chris Brown, an architect with DLP Group, as he aligns a can of generic cream of mushroom with the red portion carefully hidden. Think that stacking cans is the province of Apu at the Quickie Mart? Meet Canstruction.

Outside the Sears at the Chandler Fashion Center mall on the other side of Phoenix, well away from the Super Bowl hoopla, a team of architects and volunteers got up at the crack of dawn to build a replica of University of Phoenix Stadium completely out of stacked canned goods, flanked by tin can replicas of the team's helmets.

While the Canstructors actively solicited food donations from the general public, most of the 10,000 or so cans in use were donated by Safeway. After the game, the unopened canned goods will be donated to St. Mary's Food Bank Alliance.

The soup du jour on the stadium build is cream of mushroom, positioned so that a tan soup bowl on the label was visible. "This was the closest we could get to silver," laments Brown. The irony, of course, is that stripped of their labels, these cans mimic the color of the stadium almost perfectly, but then they couldn't be distributed and eaten afterward. The top, covered with the naked lids from chunk light tuna, provided a hint of what might have been.

The other big issue in Canstruction is structural integrity. The build team works from detailed blueprints, with each three-can-deep row carefully placed on Masonite templates. The Phoenix Canstruction team learned about the gravity factor the hard way—in an earlier build, a prototype of the Seattle Space Needle project collapsed overnight, setting off the alarms in the firm's offices.

"What if we don't go by the plans?" asks Kristin Stewart, a Scottsdale stay-at-home mom and novice Canstructor looking to celebrate Super Bowl week in her own way.

"It's going to fall apart," warns Brown.

You're not allowed on the carpet without your booties," chides Bari Henderson. When she notices her double entendre, she lets out a little giggle in spite of herself.

It's Wednesday afternoon at Wild Horse Pass, and the site of the Playboy Party is abuzz with activity. A pert brunette with a clipboard and a walkie-talkie, Henderson is an event manager from Relevent, the party-planning company, but on this operation, she's functioning more like a construction foreman or even a field sergeant. And foremen don't giggle.

Right now, her biggest enemy is dirt. And in that capacity, she barks a warning at anyone who so much as *thinks* about tracking dirt on the newly laid black carpeting, handing out the kind of surgical booties that would feel right at home in the middle of an operating theater.

The worst seems to be over, but Henderson's not about to declare victory just yet.

When a dozen tractor-trailers arrived in Arizona from New York and LA packed to the gills with gear yesterday, they were met with a surprise. That torrential rainstorm that soaked greater Phoenix over the weekend left the concrete floor of the giant tented structure plastered with a thick layer of mud.

"It looked like someone steamrolled a chocolate cake onto the floor," she explains.

So before any serious unloading could be done, this mess had to be cleaned up. The first attack at the crud removal was accomplished with a pair of Zamboni-like floor cleaners that ran laps of the giant building for the better part of nine hours. That was followed by mops and brooms, and by this morning the hard concrete floor was clean enough to eat off. But the unpaved parking lot is still a minefield of stray mud puddles threatening to bring dirty red clay onto the virgin carpet.

"We're very clean here," says Henderson, by way of explanation.

A set of large speakers are blasting music, an eclectic mix of Latin dance tunes, hip-hop, and classic rock. And in a way, the schizophrenic nature of the mix tape reflects the kind of day it is here, with each of several different crews still working single-mindedly in pursuit of its own agenda, not in direct conflict, but not exactly in complete harmony either. It's as if the framers and the finish carpenters were both on a house site at the same time.

Occupying the center of the cavernous room is a heavy-lifting operation: the sound and lighting truss. Constructing and hanging the massive truss, which holds lights and speakers well above the party floor, is the biggest task of the party prep. The truss is made up of aluminum sections, each about ten feet long. Each section is about twelve inches tall and eighteen inches wide, with diagonal and horizontal braces TIG-welded like a mountain bike frame. Imagine making a box kite out of aluminum extension ladders and you'll get the idea.

The sections, some straight and some curved, are held together with serious nuts and bolts, each roughly as big as my finger.

"It's like a giant Erector Set," Henderson explains.

The floor cleaning put the truss construction just a little behind schedule, but things are moving along efficiently. Right now the truss hovers about three feet off the floor, dangling from chains that are attached to the steel skeleton of the building. This is called "floating" the truss. At this stage, the lighting cans and the speakers are mounted according to an intricate lighting plan. They're wired and then tested to make sure they're working flawlessly.

The next step is "flying" the truss—hoisting it up to the rafters. Once it's flown, the truss should stay airborne until the party's over.

On another end of the truss, a guy with a little beard wearing a punk rock T-shirt is lashing the cables onto the truss with electrical tape. "We're trying to keep it clean so that you don't see the cable mess," says

James Fee. "We want them to go 'Wow' and focus on the design." It's all about keeping everything neat and in its place, especially since its place will soon be fifty feet in the air.

"I love the smell of carpet glue," says Fee. "It's almost like clothes coming out of the dryer." To me it's more like the fragrance of birthday candles that have been allowed to burn just a little too long, but whatever the analogy, the scent is enticing.

On the other side of the room, the carpet guys are transforming the concrete floors. It's a straightforward process—unroll the carpet, butt it up tight against the row that's already down, and then run a seamer that fuses the plastic backing of the carpeting together, hence that waxy aroma. It's a quick process, in contrast to the painstaking detail work being done on the still-hovering truss. However, the weather is playing havoc with this as well. The forty-degree swings in temperature between day and night are causing the carpet to expand and contract, which causes wrinkles and even a few failed seams. The solution is to trot out the emergency space heaters that Tony Berger had ordered as a party-night backup.

Over in the corner, the true nature of the party is beginning to reveal itself. A seven-foot-tall martini glass has just been unpacked and is sitting upside down, stem in the air, waiting to be assembled. The walls of the glass are more than an inch thick, reaching that critical point where tapping doesn't reveal any clues as to what it's made of. Plexiglas? Tempered glass? Some space-age composite that's a peace dividend of the Cold War? I tap again, but the glass still ain't talkin'.

What did they say about it?" asks Peter Eisenman, expectantly.

The grad student in the sweatshirt had just raised the issue of the local response from players and fans to the University of Phoenix stadium and the architect has risen to the bait.

"They said, 'It looks like the world's largest toaster,'" says the student, getting a laugh. "They liked it."

"Maybe they like toast," Eisenman quips right back.

Eisenman is on stage before an auditorium full of architecture students on the campus of Arizona State on the Thursday night before the Super Bowl. The architect never seems so alive as when he's in front of an audience, and this one is perfectly suited to the occasion, feisty and deferential at the same time. While the interplay becomes heated at times, they're never fighting, just sparring.

When the laughter settles, Eisenman gets serious for a moment. "A critic at the *New York Times* wrote that maybe Peter's too much of a football fan to build a great stadium. You know, I've always been criticized that I don't look after clients enough. I guess the *New York Times* doesn't think that football fans are clients. I've really been interested as a fan, to build a place that's exciting to watch a football game. And it is," he says. "I guess the *New York Times* isn't much into football. Thank God for toasters."

Eisenman has a sentimental attachment to his brainchild and is quick to leap to its defense. When they played the BCS championship game at the stadium, he arrived four hours early and watched the building fill up one fan at a time. Eisenman is in town this weekend because IBM asked him to give a Super Bowl morning talk to a select group of their biggest clients, a room representing billions of dollars worth of business.

When the lecture is over, the conversation, as it always does with Eisenman, circles back to football and his beloved Giants. "I'm just not sure New England has it in them to go 19–0. And they haven't covered the spread the last five games. My biggest worry? This is a fast track, the fastest field the Giants have played on, and Randy Moss is faster than Corey Webster."

When pushed for a prediction, he pauses for a moment and says. "Giants 28–24. My Giants could play a perfect game and lose," he continues. "And I don't know if they have another perfect game in them." I tell him that the only other people I encountered all week predicting an outright Giants win were the waitresses at a local Hooters.

He smiles and shrugs. Underdogs or not, his team is still in the Super Bowl in a stadium he built. "I think it'll be a good game."

So where can I get a parking pass?" I ask the guy in the red jacket, who bears more than a slight resemblance to Don Knotts. He squints hard, shifts a little from foot to foot, and then looks at me as though I'm speaking a foreign language.

In the office on the second floor of the building in the center of Westgate, across from Margaritaville just outside of University of Phoenix Stadium, they do one thing and one thing only: issue credentials. Like the rest of the world, the Super Bowl runs on credentials. In the real world it's about where you went to school and who you've worked with. In Phoenix this week, it's all about what you're wearing. Around your neck, that is.

A week-of-game Super Bowl credential is a plastic laminated card that measures about five by seven inches. It includes the bearer's name and affiliation as well as a photo. My picture is several years old and shows me wearing an old pair of glasses, but on balance, it's more flattering than the photo on my driver's license. It dangles from a lanyard that clips on two holes on either side, and it is the ultimate currency during the week before the game.

To get the credential, I had to fill out a form, complete with a request for the kind of personal information that used to be the province of mortgage applications. But in the post-9/11 world, this kind of background check has become just standard operating procedure for events of this magnitude.

My credential has gotten me most of the places I need this week, from the Media Center to Media Day at the stadium. But my week-of-game credential lacks one thing specifically: the letter S, as in *stadium*. So here I am, in what could pass for an outpost of the DMV, waiting for the appropriate piece of plastic that will allow me access to the stadium on the Friday before the game. The good news is that I am the only guest invited to Artie Kempner's Super Bowl pregame rehearsal in the FOX truck. But before I can get into the stadium, now well into its pregame security lockdown, I absolutely, positively need that particular piece of plastic. No exceptions. No excuses.

My quest is not going well. It is now 12:24. I need to get a day credential with stadium access, figure out where to park my car, and get over to the FOX Broadcast compound by 1:00 P.M. I explain the urgency of my mission.

"Wait in line, sir," says Don Knotts unsympathetically.

I creep to the front of the line. The good news? I'm on the credential list. The bad news? They still need to actually *find* my credential. I ask about a parking pass. From the look I get, I could just as well be asking for a soldering iron or a copy of the Magna Carta.

"This is the credential office. We don't know anything about parking," says Don Knotts' partner in bureaucracy, slowly, enunciating every syllable very carefully, as if talking to a particularly thick eight-year-old.

"Um, I can't imagine that all of these people *walked* here," I implore. "Where did *they* park?"

"I don't know, sir. Please take a number and wait in line."

So like a guy at the deli looking to buy a pound and a half of Boar's Head smoked turkey, I stand in the waiting-for-my-actual-credential line, clutching my little paper ticket with the number 2347 as though it were a lottery winner.

At 12:42 I finally get my actual credential. No parking pass. At 12:43 I make the executive decision to abandon my Subaru rental car outside the office and start hoofing it over toward the stadium. As I walk around the concrete barrier and find a gap in the chain-link fence, I hear "Next gate, sir." And then "Next gate, sir." Followed by "Next gate, sir," with a quarter mile between each gate. And finally I find a helpful volunteer willing to examine my credential, check it for the appropriate S, search my backpack, walk me through the metal detector, and afford me entrance into the University of Phoenix Stadium.

It's 1:03 and I'm in.

As I walk toward the south end zone—the business end of the stadium, where the field rolls in and out—where the FOX compound is situated, I run into the Greenway Demons high school football team lined up near the corridor that leads from the visiting locker room.

They've got that work-in-progress look that's typical of high school football players. They're trying to act casual but not succeeding, looking around a little too intensely, laughing a bit too hard at each other's jokes. It's not without good reason. It's fifteen minutes before their fifteen minutes of fame. In fifty-one hours, the New England Patriots will trot down this same corridor, waiting to be introduced.

And now these teens are the stand-ins, the body doubles for Tom Brady and Randy Moss, for Eli Manning and Michael Strahan. Their job this day is simple enough. They'll run through plays while the FOX broadcast team checks to make sure all the cameras are working and the camera operators know their assignments. Or more accurately, the teens will walk slowly through the plays so as not to bruise the delicate turf so close to game time.

"Hey, Ryan Seacrest," shouts middle linebacker Brenin Brooks. Seacrest, the host of *American Idol* as well as FOX's pregame red carpet show, is walking briskly toward the field and is almost out of range by the time Brooks bellows. Still, the teen claims credit for a full-fledged brush with greatness.

"Hey, I talked to Ryan Seacrest," he says as he does a little mock stage dive into a clutch of his teammates. It turns out that for Brooks, who will mimic Patriots veteran Junior Seau, this was only the beginning of his brush with greatness. Two minutes later Seacrest returns and stops to exchange high fives and pose for a few pictures. He makes a point to schmooze with his most vocal fan.

"Wassup, man?" says the *American Idol* host as he shakes Brooks' hand. And when he's done, he sidles up to Brooks' teammates. "Now you get to haze him," he says conspiratorially before he walks on.

As I make my way into the familiar confines of the FOX truck, I realize it's nothing so much as a sensory-deprivation unit that isolates the crew from the distractions of the outside world. For FOX's A-Team, once the door closes, this could be week one in Dallas or a playoff game in frigid Green Bay. Still, for all the layers of insulation—literal and figurative—it soon becomes apparent that this is not just another week for the FOX A-Team.

For example, this very operation—a dress rehearsal—is unique. As a rule, television crews don't rehearse. During a typical week, Zyontz holds a production meeting, usually on Saturday, to go over the big-picture issues of the telecast. On Sunday morning, Kempner holds a camera meeting to go over the specifics of what to expect from each team and how that relates to each camera operator's assignment. And that's it.

Take a step back and you can see how remarkable this is. From the beginning of training camp, each NFL team goes through thousands of "reps," running through each play a minimum of several dozen times at varying levels of game simulation—from walk-throughs to intersquad scrimmages to full-blown preseason games—before a play is ever trotted out in a game that counts.

As for the other elements of the Super Bowl pageantry, there is planning aplenty in evidence. Tom Petty and the Heartbreakers practiced their twelve minutes of music for at least twelve hours, while the technical aspects of the program—from the logistics of rolling the stage on and off the field to the roles of the hundreds of extras to the placement of the pyrotechnics—were practiced even more without the band on hand.

Even Jordin Sparks' rendition of the National Anthem—two minutes and nine seconds long—was practiced again and again. Her game-day protestations that she had hardly rehearsed reminded me of a kid who tells her friends that she hasn't studied at all for the big exam, just in case she comes back with a B+ instead of her accustomed A.

The FOX broadcast team? They have a single hour, give or take, to prepare for three and a half hours of live coverage that will be seen by more than a hundred million people around the globe. No pressure, though.

And yet this rehearsal is an afterthought on so many levels. In Jacksonville, Kempner scrambled to find a French junior team to stand in for the Eagles and the Patriots. This time, it's Greenway High.

One of the most pressing issues is running through the player introductions. It was one of FOX's biggest problems in their last Super Bowl. In Jacksonville, the crew was ready, only to find that the Eagles weren't, and there was a very long thirty seconds of vamping until the NFC champions appeared. Given his natural tendency to blame himself, Zyontz assumed that, despite plenty of preparation, he had somehow mistimed the introductions. And it wasn't until this very day, three years later, that he learned the truth. The Eagles, it turned out, were delayed by a water main leak somewhere in the bowels of Alltel Stadium en route to the field.

"I'll be ready to go in about two minutes," says Kempner to the rest of the FOX crew, savoring the fact that for once he, not the NFL, gets to decide when something starts.

"On Sunday it's a game. Until then it's a *megillah*," says Zyontz, breaking into Yiddish to explain a week full of waiting. When I look over quizzically, he explains. "There are a lot of people walking around without much to do."

And then they launch into the Super Bowl, minus the urgency, and for that matter minus the game.

"One. Two. Three. Four," intones Joe Buck, doing what is likely the 3,714th mic check of his relatively young broadcasting career. "Six. Seven. Eight comes after seven. Then ten."

Buck goes into Mr. Announcer Man mode and starts reading the player introduction script. There's a montage highlighting each team's season up on the video board. One of the points in the Patriots' piece is Spygate.

Richie Zyontz looks at this quizzically. "It's a part of the season," he reasons. "But then again, so was Eli getting booed and Coughlin almost getting fired." The Super Bowl is a time for celebration, not inquisition. The Spygate segment will be gone by game time.

The Greenway High kids walk out onto the field, moving slowly through a couple of plays.

"The players seem sluggish. Must be Super Bowl nerves," says one of the wags in the back of the truck. They are running through a handful of Giants plays in the Patriots' red zone when FOX president Ed Goren walks in.

"We have a failure to communicate," he announces. The NFL was never particularly happy about the idea of the FOX dress rehearsal, and when the kids started trodding across the delicate logos on the already stressed turf on the playing field, the problem came to a head and Frank Supovitz pulled the plug. Typical of Super Bowl week, this tiny tempest has reached the highest levels, with Supovitz taking it up with FOX chairman David Hill. Ten minutes, a half dozen plays, rehearsal's over. On to the game.

After the rehearsal, one of the assistants comes over to Kempner and asks, "Do you want to know the Las Vegas line on the number of times Archie Manning will appear on TV?"

"No, I don't," says Kempner emphatically. He is, of course, the guy who will determine how many times Eli Manning's father will appear on the FOX broadcast.

This unusual betting line is called a proposition bet, "prop" for short. These are offbeat, easy-to-understand wagers designed to entice the casual better who's intimidated by point spreads and over-under lines.

The prop bet began with the simplest prop of all—who'll win the coin toss. The prop really became a mainstay of the Super Bowl betting world in 1985, when behemoth lineman William "Refrigerator" Perry scored a touchdown for the Chicago Bears, against long odds.

Now Las Vegas sports books offer literally hundreds of props, ranging from how long it will take Jordin Sparks to sing the National Anthem to the color of the liquid that the winning head coach will be doused with. There's even a 2,500-to-1 shot that Tom Petty would smoke a joint during the halftime show.

Because of the long odds—and the fact that many of these props can be influenced or researched—casinos typically limit the size of the bets to $500 or less. Still, prop bets make up about half of the nearly $100 million wagered at legal Las Vegas sports books on the Super Bowl.

Gimme a Diet Coke," says the middle-aged guy at the bar, wearing jeans and a shirt buttoned but untucked. The bartender, a pretty brunette, looks up from mixing a Flirtini and some other concoction involving grapefruit juice and top-shelf vodka.

"I don't need a glass. Just gimme a can."

The exchange, midway through Friday night's Maxim party, is certainly simple enough, and unremarkable but for one thing: The guy ordering the soft drink is Tom Arnold. And in some way, this is what Super Bowl week is all about. It's the random chance of rubbing elbows with a midlevel celebrity. An hour ago, I was at the ESPN party, and the evening's first brush with near-greatness involved Jared, from Subway. The Biggest Loser is standing in a clutch of friends and admirers, looking around to see if anyone is recognizing him. When he catches me looking, he grins knowingly, as if to say, *Wassup, homes?*

On the way into the Maxim bash, Kevin Dillon pressed his way through the crowd with that wide-eyed, slightly self-conscious physicality that made his character Johnny "Drama" Chase so appealing on *Entourage*. The true A-listers want to be left alone, or at least they really believe they do. But further down on the totem pole, there's a more delicate dance between the perils and perks of fame. To borrow from Oscar Wilde, the only thing worse than being recognized is *not* being recognized.

Tom Arnold is standing two feet away from me, and I could wrap my arm around his shoulder and make some crack about his ex-wife singing the National Anthem, or tell him how wrong he was about TO on *The Best Damm Sports Show Period* and how much I loved him in that movie with, you know, the other guy and the hot chick that I caught on HBO last week. But that's not the Super Bowl way. I turn for a quick glance as he disappears into the crowd, Diet Coke in hand, and turn my attention to procuring a drink of my own, with alcohol, in a glass.

As I walked into the Maxim party at the Fairmont Princess in Scottsdale, I was seduced by the smell. Not expensive cologne, spilled drinks, or even a critical mass of pheromones from eligible bachelors and bachelorettes. No, what wafted through the air was sweet and savory wood smoke that smelled like the semifinals of a world championship barbecue cookoff. Brisket? Pork shoulder? Short ribs? I couldn't pin it down, but whatever it was it made me very hungry. And as I wandered around the party, I realized that subconsciously, I was on the prowl, hunting for whatever it was that smelled so good. I never found it. I will learn later that it wasn't food at all but the firewood—a special brand of juniper that the resort uses in its fireplaces and fire pits.

And my Tom Arnold encounter notwithstanding, the whole Maxim party is a bit like this, an exercise in expectations never quite fulfilled.

The Fairmont Princess is a spectacular property, as they say in the event business. And I'm sure that it looked remarkable to party planners who scoped it out, as well as to any civilians who might have been in on the decision. But on party day, filled with more than a thousand revelers, it's not without its problems.

The first issue is the weather. It's not a disaster. A disaster would have been the rainstorm that soaked greater Phoenix a week ago. Still, it's beyond chilly, verging on downright cold, forty-five degrees, maybe forty. Like most of the parties in Phoenix this week, the exclusive Maxim bash is almost entirely outdoors, and the tall radiant kerosene heaters that have been ubiquitous at every event this week can only do so much to fend off the elements.

The unseasonable weather leaves the female partygoers—which, after all, are the most volatile element in any party equation—faced with the coat conundrum. It's hard to party while wearing a coat. It's hard to party while holding a coat. Which means surrendering your outerwear to the coat check. Dropping a coat off isn't the problem. Picking it back up, *that's* the issue. It'll take time, which prevents a smooth and speedy escape. And of course, most single female partygoers hope that the evening's escape might come in the company of an eligible guest of the opposite sex, ideally a wide receiver with a guaranteed contract. So when it's time to go, there's a very real quandary: the coat or the wideout? Not an easy decision.

The bigger issue speaks to my wood-smoke-inspired wanderings. The Fairmont Princess is a sprawling property, and the pink stucco buildings with their Spanish tile roofs are built tight to the ground, never more than a couple of stories high, connected by short stairways, low balconies, and open hallways. There are perches aplenty from which you can see the pool or the fragrance garden, the bar or the dance floor. Revelers sway perilously close to the edge of the pool, over which Kanye West has set up a stage.

Still, it seems like the real party is happening somewhere else. No matter how good it is where you are—no matter how close your proximity to Tom Arnold—you're always faced with the nagging sense that you're missing something even better over there. From a hundred yards away, the girls seem hotter, the music seems better, the bar lines seem shorter, and every distant clutch of partygoers contains a limitless list of A-list celebrities.

This is the hottest party on the planet on Super Bowl Friday, and if you don't work it to its full potential—and the news crews and bloggers will be only too happy to tell you what and whom you missed—you'll truly hate yourself in the morning. It's an intensified version of the vague anxiety that plagues every Super Bowl–goer all week: *What am I missing?*

I came all the way from LA," says the balding guy, while the moderately attractive blonde standing by his side wonders just how much juice he's really got. "I'm a friend of Brett Ratner's."

A pause.

"The director."

You half expect him to whip out his BlackBerry and surf to Ratner's page on IMDb. "Look—*Rush Hour 3, Rush Hour 2, Red Dragon* . . ."

Tony Berger is moving a couple of the barricades, making last-minute adjustments to Lauren Malone's press area in the entrance to the Playboy party at Wild Horse Pass. And while it wasn't planned this way, it seems appropriate that Berger is on the inside of the barrier and Mr. LA Story is very much on the outside looking in.

It's three o'clock in the afternoon, six hours before the party, and Brett Ratner's friend has the honor of being the first to attempt to slither into the party. But he certainly won't be the last.

"Well, we set the guest list really far in advance," says Berger sympathetically, with a sly wink to Lauren. Mr. LA Story is pleading his case, such as it is, to the freelance party planner, not the Playboy executive who actually controls the guest list. "Months, really."

"But Brett said it'd be okay. He knows Hugh," Mr. LA continues.

"Maybe you should just have Brett make a call, then," says Berger diplomatically. "We can't really make changes to the guest list at this point."

Slowly but surely, Mr. LA is getting the hint. Berger has called his bluff. But his big mistake was when he tried to drop the name of the *Playboy* founder. To those outside the inner circle, he is Mr. Hefner. To his friends, he is Hef. Hugh? That's what his mother called him. And so Mr. LA and his date smile and turn away, perhaps pondering the likelihood of sneaking into a less-exclusive party.

On the very first page of *The Great Gatsby*, a novel largely about great parties, narrator Nick Carraway muses that "reserving judgment is a matter of infinite hope." True enough. But it also made him "the victim of not a few veteran bores and privy to the secret griefs of wild, unknown men." And so it was at the door of the Playboy party.

Like Carraway, the Playboy gatekeepers subject themselves to more than a few veteran bores. And the secret griefs of wild, unknown men? That they've got. Of course, with few exceptions, it's difficult to immediately and accurately parse the worthy from the unworthy, the real friend of Brett Ratner's from the guy whose brother-in-law installed a big-screen TV in the basement of the director's beach house. And of course, the downside to insulting an actual friend of a friend is huge, while the cost of treating even the most obvious scammers with a certain level of dignity is simply disaster insurance. And, perhaps, a tiny slice of infinite hope.

I walk into the giant tent, and I am so truly shocked by what I see that I double-check the time on my Omega Speedmaster. It's 2:47 P.M. on Super Bowl Eve, less than seven hours before the doors open. I recall last year's near-chaos at a similar hour, where the party could be charitably called a work in progress and less charitably a disaster in the making. Not so this year. The crew isn't installing the chrome lamps, they're polishing them. The bars are not being constructed, they're being stocked with 840 bottles of Cuervo tequila. The 80,000 feet of black drapes have been hung. The 33 cooks are putting the finishing touches on 8,000 appetizers—ranging from honey walnut tacos to miniature Beef Wellingtons—on 600 sheet pans. The heaviest piece of equipment in use seems to be a vacuum cleaner. Hef's private bathroom has been set up ("PRIVATE: Mr. Hefner, Holly, Bridget, Kendra, and Playboy Playmates ONLY" reads the sign). The giant martini glass sits high above the bar, not so much a prop as a declaration of victory. Sure, there are things to be done, but there seems to be nothing more than residual doubt that they'll get done in time. The vibe is one of anticipation, not panic.

And the Playboy Party Team? There they are—Lisa, Donna, Lauren, and Dana. They're sitting on a couch, huddling up on some last-minute guest-list issues, but they're also coordinating hairstylist appointments. They've come a long way from Miami. Chalk it up as a triumph for The List.

As the driver rolls up to Rawhide unfashionably early, I don't recognize the place. The strange venue at the kind of place you go to when you can't afford Disney World has been miraculously transformed. Playboy's Desert Oasis? This place shimmers in the distance like a mirage. The giant tent glows, lighted from within by colored floodlights, overlaid with a retro-cool sixties pattern. Last year, the American Airlines Arena was commandeered for an evening. This place seems to have been built from the ground up.

As I push my way through the thick crowd at the door—is Mr. LA Story still attempting to schmooze his way in?—I almost wish I had a fullback to block for me. And it's déjà vu all over again. As they're finding my name on the guest list, I peek over to my left toward an attractive young woman. I smile, but she pretends not to notice. It's Alyssa Milano. Without a word, she turns away and heads down the red carpet as I again trail behind. We'll always have Miami.

The red carpet is buzzing. Kevin Connolly of *Entourage* is trying to answer a question from an *EW* crew without seeming too jaded when his co-star Kevin Dillon grabs him and starts punching him playfully in the head. Regaining his equilibrium, literally and figuratively, Connolly smiles and tells the camera crew, "I'm thirty-four years old and he puts me in a headlock and gives me a noogie like I'm twelve." Boys will be boys.

The star of the red carpet, of course, is Peter Pan incarnate, the ageless Hugh Hefner. Tonight, he's got the Girls Next Door in tow. Holly Madison, Bridget Marquardt, and Kendra Wilkinson starred in an E! reality series about life at the Mansion, with special guests ranging from Howard Stern to Prince Albert of Monaco. The question isn't whether Hef is the hippest octogenarian on the planet. It's whether he has any competition at all.

Sure, he answers questions politely from the camera crews, but quite frankly, he doesn't need to say much. He just needs to be. It's easy to forget what a revolutionary figure Hef was, partially because the world has caught up with him so completely. But it wasn't that way in the 1950s when he launched the magazine and, really, a way of life. At a time when America was gray suits and white shirts and skinny ties and dinner on the table at five, Hef was all about silk pajamas, smoking jackets, and parties that went on all night. America was just beginning to begin to understand its place as a world power, and Hef made a powerful case for what to do with its newfound wealth and leisure time. Hefner's vision of gender politics may have been flawed, but there is no doubt that his worldview was, and is, hugely influential.

Once you make the U-turn at the end of the red carpet and take a quick right, you end up facing The Wall. With its narrow tan brick, it exudes the vibe of California construction from the days when muscle cars ruled the earth. The sign—PLAYBOY DESERT OASIS—in a suitably retro font continues the theme. A couple of dramatically placed floodlights emphasize its rough-hewn texture and all but invite every party guest to touch it. And touch they did.

There is a constant stream of partygoers stopping at The Wall to take a picture. Some are couples; some are guys who've borrowed an accommodating Playmate or two for a quick pose.

As simple as it is, The Wall has become the party's touchstone. These are "wish you were here" shots that announce to anyone and everyone that you've made it past the gatekeepers into one of the world's most exclusive parties.

And of course, like so much of Super Bowl week, it's all an illusion. The Wall is a partition constructed hastily from two-by-fours and sheets of plywood. On top of the plywood is a layer of passable fake brick. And none of this was here even two days ago. The Playboy bunny smiling for the picture with the guy in the dark suit? She's not his date, but a trained professional who smiles fetchingly, looks astonishing in a swimsuit, and flirts within very well-defined boundaries. At this moment, none of it matters. It may be an illusion, but it's a shared illusion, and that's what really counts tonight.

As I step inside to the party proper, it all begins to make sense. Even as it came together during construction this week, this giant tent always seemed like a curious place to have a party, empty and oddly proportioned, plopped down in the middle of nowhere. But as the room fills, my questions are answered. It's indoors, so it's neither too warm nor too cold, and the coat factor is a nonissue. The high ceilings and the canvas sides to the building keep the noise down to a murmur.

Yet another low-tech special effect, the giant martini glass, now has a Femlin perched in it, literally and figuratively above it all. The centerpieces of the party are all human in scale. Off to the corner is a retro-style photo booth, perfect for canoodling. In another is a faux fireplace with a couple of couches. And near a bar is a space-age television that looks like it came from George Jetson's living room. In this giant room, there's never a sense that someone else is having more fun than you are. It's democracy with a DJ.

As DJ Reach spins tunes, the place pulses. Literally. I place my hand on a table and it vibrates with the beat. The risers, they throb too. In front of the DJ booth is a simple riser about thirty feet long and three feet high with a railing, and a posse of attractive girls in short skirts seem to have staked it out as their own, oblivious to the gravity-defying Playmates holding court in the corners of the room. Later on, the New England Patriots cheerleaders will take their turn up on the platform.

"Y'all gonna make me lose my mind," blasts the DMX song.

But DJ Reach transforms it into an almost gospel-style call-and-response.

"Up in here! Up in here!" reply the faithful congregation.

And then as the clock takes the evening's big tick, the party takes on a new level of gravitas.

"It's Super Bowl Sunday, y'all!" says Reach, and the place erupts.

Of course, this level of revelry is possible because the details are sweated. At twelve-thirty I see Donna Tavoso looking disapprovingly at a bar line that's getting long and moving slowly, manned by pleasant but frazzled bartenders who have never seen a crowd quite this big. Presto—

relief is on the way. Not ten minutes later, a platoon of waitresses appears holding trays of martinis.

Even after the clock strikes one, the party continues to rev up like a flywheel, slowly gathering momentum. And then comes the one problem that no amount of planning could overcome. "Five minutes," mouths one of the security guys to the dark-haired bartender as she mixes yet another in an endless stream of vodka-and-tonics. The Arizona Alcohol Control Board has the final say, and at 2:00 A.M. precisely the Playboy Super Bowl party reaches its witching hour.

On the way out, near The Wall, I see Lisa Natale and Donna Tavoso.

"Good party," I say.

They each smile an I'm-going-to-Disney-World smile.

"Yeah, it was."

21
THE GAME

Game Day

It's 7:57 A.M., and like many Americans, I don't need an alarm clock to wake up on Super Bowl Sunday. My circadian rhythms are more than enough to counteract the fact that I had rolled in at around a quarter to three from the Playboy party. Shower, shave, and flip on *SportsCenter*, not necessarily in that order, all with a sense of urgency that belies the fact that the game was still more than six hours away. But I'm not alone—it's Super Bowl morning in America. From the quarterbacks to the scalpers, from the Madison Avenue ad guy to the delivery driver at the local pizza parlor, from the NFL's Super Bowl czar to the guy who bet ten dollars on the coin toss, the faithful are popping out of bed powered by sheer anticipation.

I think about the space that the Playboy team created last night, and about the space that Peter Eisenman has created for the game this afternoon. And then it hits me. The Super Bowl isn't so much a *thing*. It's a vessel. For all its sleek skin, Peter Eisenman's stadium is really just a $450 million receptacle. The Playboy party, a year in the planning? At its most basic level, it's simply an excuse to get people to the same place at the same time, and what happens after that is up for grabs.

It's the same with the game. Over the past four years, the NFL sweated a million details. FOX is ready to broadcast to 100 million people all over America. Still, this Super Bowl is a question mark, a story whose ending remains unwritten, a mystery without any clues. And that, perhaps, is the reason why this game continues to grow at a time when the rest of the world is fragmenting. It's a rare chance to see something unfold, moment by moment, something that's more real than any reality show. Super Bowl Sunday provides breaking news with only one guarantee: Someone's going to win.

Let the Billion Dollar Game begin.

Almost twenty years later, Paul Costello is still hearing about his first trip to the Super Bowl. He's just sitting down to the buffet breakfast in the pale, pastel dining room at the Doubletree near the Phoenix airport, proudly wearing his Justin Tuck jersey. His two sons—Evan, fourteen, wearing a Plaxico Burress jersey, and James, seventeen, sporting an Ahmad Bradshaw jersey—are already chowing down on the pancakes, scrambled eggs, and link sausages.

They came all the way from Sparta, New Jersey, to watch their Giants. This is Costello's third Super Bowl. His first trip to the Super Bowl was less than a scrapbook experience. He traveled to Tampa with a buddy to see the Giants take on the Bills. "We were young and we didn't have much money." He smiles and shrugs a little. "So we watched the game in the bar."

His wife still ribs him about that, eighteen years down the road. I sense not a tinge of regret. Somehow sharing a zip code with his heroes, as Scott Norwood missed his decisive field goal, seemed to be enough.

The relationship between a real fan and a team is just that. Good times and bad. Elation, frustration, and everything in between. "I remember rooting for them when they were terrible," he recalls. "Joe Pisarcik. I was at that game when he fumbled." He's referring to the most infamous moment in Giants history. Pisarcik, the quarterback, could have simply taken a knee and run out the clock. Instead he decided to make the handoff to fullback Larry Czonka. But he fumbled the snap, and Herman Edwards picked up the ball and scored one of the most improbable touchdowns in football history. For football fans, a moment like this was a reminder of the preposterous things that can happen when human beings get together and play for the right to possess an air-filled oblong object. For the Giants' faithful, that play, in which defeat was snatched from the jaws of victory, remains the ultimate embarrassment. Living through moments like these made the trips to the Super Bowl that much sweeter.

The Costellos are serious Giants fans and they wear it proudly on their back. They don't do face paint. They roll it old-school. No Manning or Strahan jerseys or, God forbid, Jeremy Shockey. Tuck is the unsung member of the defense. Back in the day, the elder Costello probably wore a Carl Banks jersey. Or maybe Harry Carson.

How did they get Super Bowl tickets? How does anyone get Super Bowl tickets? "We had a friend who had a friend," he explains. "It just all came together."

The Costellos are a part of Giants Nation, but this week they are also citizens of Football Nation. They flew out of Philadelphia and were traveling with a bunch of Patriots fans. By the third hour of the long transcontinental flight, made longer by the headwinds, all pretenses were down. They were talking trash about Brady's ankle and Spygate and Michael Strahan's inability to stay retired. "On Sunday, every football fan is like a part of your family," he says. "On Tuesday, those same guys won't look at you on the train."

And in the airport, Eagles fans came up to them. Now, normally Giants fans and Eagles fans are like the Shiites and the Sunnis. But division pride, conference pride, and the fact that the Patriots beat the Eagles in Philadelphia's last trip to the Super Bowl trumped their intramural differences, at least for this week. "Kick their ass," said the Philadelphia fans conspiratorially. My enemy's enemy is my friend, indeed.

This trip was a MasterCard commercial come to life. Tickets: $6,000. Airfare and hotel: $4,000. Going to the Super Bowl with your two sons: *priceless.* And they were hardly alone in this. More than 125,000 visitors converged on greater Phoenix during Super Bowl week, more than half of them without a ticket to the game or the prospect of getting one.

Costello was more than willing to pony up for the ultimate cool-dad moment. Thanks to Dad's juice and a few thousand dollars out of the savings account, the family's annual Super Bowl party had somehow morphed into a guys' trip to the game. Paul texted the boys a teaser at school. "Even though they're not supposed to have their phones on, they texted me right back," he laughs. James got right to the point: *Spill your guts, old man.*

Football is one of the things that a dad and two teenage boys can do together without crossing any of the boundaries that teenagers erect. For three hours every Sunday, they can roll back the clock, set aside their differences, and cheer on Big Blue.

"If it was just me, I probably wouldn't have done it," Costello admits.

This is more than a football game. He could mark the passage of time by the Giants' appearances in the Super Bowl. That first time, he was young, a new father, and still transitioning to life as an adult. "You were just a baby," he said to James, now a solid six-footer. "And you were just a twinkle in your mom's eye," he says to Evan, who barely looks up from his breakfast plate.

"Everyone should get to at least one—" He pauses to correct himself. "At least *two* Super Bowls. I'm hoping that by the time the Giants are in the Super Bowl again they'll be old enough to buy their old man tickets."

And what of Mom? "She'll open a bottle of wine and watch the game with one of her friends." But she'll do so while wearing her Brandon Jacobs jersey. She supported the trip, especially since they would watch the game from the stadium rather than a Phoenix sports bar, but her tempered enthusiasm had nothing to do with the money and everything with that parental instinct to protect your kids from disappointment. She remembers what it was like in 2000 when Costello traveled to Tampa again and this time watched the game from *inside* the stadium, only to see the Giants get crushed by the Ravens.

"My wife keeps me grounded," he says. "It's an awfully long way to go to watch your team lose." His job today is similar: "I'm trying to help them manage their expectations," says Paul Costello. "It could be pretty depressing in about six hours."

Interstate 10 is moving quite nicely, with most of greater Phoenix evidently still padding around in slippers. As Rick Rosson, Peter Eisenman's partner, turns the little rental SUV onto Loop 101, in the distance looms what has been the center of the sporting world for the last week. And on Super Bowl Sunday, arguably you can reasonably eliminate the word *sporting* from that phrase.

Today, the University of Phoenix Stadium doesn't gleam in the desert sun. On one of Arizona's rare cloudy days, its shiny silver skin blends with the slate-gray sky. If a stadium is a vessel, this one has remained, well, empty. Rosson was there a year and a half ago when the stadium opened with some pomp and circumstance. But the Cardinals have never played a really meaningful game here. There have been a couple

239

of nice wins, like the one against Pittsburgh earlier in the year, but the truth is that the team is struggling toward respectability and not much more. And while there was a BCS Championship game played here at the beginning of 2007, this is not primarily a college football venue.

No, today is the coming-out party for the University of Phoenix Stadium. The first Super Bowl. And if things go well, not the last.

But Rosson, Peter Eisenman's longtime partner, isn't thinking about the big picture. He's just trying to find a way in. Just because you built the stadium doesn't mean that you can get into the parking lot. Peter, his girlfriend, Sandra Hemingway, and I watch the bumper of the car in front of us and make small talk.

"What'll you give me if I jump the fence?" I say as we sit motionless. It's still only around 11:00 A.M. Were it an hour later, I'm not sure I'd be exhibiting such restraint. Others, however, are not quite so patient. We watch four Patriots fans get out of their car, hop that very fence, cross a drainage canal, and then hop another fence. We expect to see them get pounced on by a SWAT team, on general principle. But strangely, nothing happens. They climb over a small concrete barrier and continue to make their way to the stadium as we sit in the car, slightly dumbfounded.

"I don't see any snipers on the roof," Peter says matter-of-factly.

I peer over and I don't see anything either. But perhaps that's the point.

At the request of Arizona governor Janet Napolitano, the Department of Homeland Security has designated the Super Bowl as a Level One security risk. This puts it in the same category as events like visits from foreign heads of state, the State of the Union address, and presidential inaugurations. This isn't a pro forma designation. Last year's Super Bowl received Level One status, but before that you had to go back to the 2002 game in New Orleans, just months after the September 11 attacks, for a Super Bowl that went fully federal in terms of security. At its most basic level, this Level One designation means that federal law enforcement gets involved, with the Secret Service overseeing and coordinating all security measures, bringing in resources from the FBI, the Bureau of Alcohol, Tobacco, and Firearms, the National Guard, and other organizations as needed. That's the official statement.

As for the nitty-gritty details, security at the Super Bowl is on a need-to-know basis. And the NFL has made it clear that the press doesn't need to know. On Monday of Super Bowl week, the NFL held a press conference with representatives of federal authorities as well as state and local police, to discuss security. Or not, as the case may be. The practical reason was to inform the general public about things like road closures as well as the security measures that would be in place at the game. There would be airport-like security—metal detectors, potential pat-down searches, and X-ray screening of small items like purses. Bigger bags and parcels would be strictly prohibited. Beyond that, the institutional thinking is "the less said the better." In Tampa in 2000, for example, it was revealed that local police used cutting-edge face-recognition software on their security cameras. This raised a small fuss and the agencies involved distanced themselves from the program.

As for the bigger-picture items, the panelists made a nonspecific mention about a no-fly zone around the stadium, and beyond that everyone was in loose-lips-sink-ships mode. However, security experts have speculated that the security measures enforcing the no-fly zone include F-18 fighter jets, Black Hawk helicopters, an AWACS airborne command center, and probably handheld Stinger antiaircraft missiles. Of course, these airborne defenses are largely hidden from view. In Detroit, where Ford Field lies in close proximity to the Detroit River, a heavily armed 225-foot Coast Guard cutter called the *Hollyhock* was a prominent reminder of the gravity of the situation.

The Super Bowl is perhaps the ultimate target-rich environment, with close to half the country already in front of their televisions. And it's been that even before terms like "target-rich" have become part of the lexicon. The novel *Black Sunday* by Thomas Harris, who would later crawl into our collective psyche as the creator of Hannibal Lecter, was inspired by the terrorist siege at the Munich Olympics. The plot of the book, which was later made into a movie by John Frankenheimer starring Bruce Dern and Roy Scheider, involved an attention-starved Vietnam vet turning an explosives-laden blimp into a weapon of mass destruction at a stadium with 80,000 people, including the president of the United States, in attendance. At the time, both the movie and the book were well received but mildly criticized for being totally implausible. In 2008, that is not the case.

Fortunately, real-world Super Bowl security breaches have been very minor. In 2004, a man dressed as an official got onto the field, took off his clothes, and streaked across the turf. This was the year of the Janet Jackson wardrobe malfunction, so this incident wasn't widely reported. Last year an Internet prankster claimed that he "hacked the Super Bowl" by distributing hundreds of light-up devices to fans just before the halftime show. While the elaborate prank was supposed to flash a secret message with the address of a Web site promoting his new book, it wasn't actually visible to anyone in the stadium or at home. And while his Web site does feature what appears to be documentary evidence of the prankster and his accomplices moving cartons of the devices in, even if it's legitimate, the security breach is far less serious than it seems. While the "Prince Party Team Fan Packs" were unauthorized, they weren't dangerous, and as such weren't the target of the security measures in place.

After the press conference, I sidle up to Milt Ahlerich, the NFL's director of security. Tall, bespectacled, and dapper in a dark suit, Ahlerich looks like everyone's grandpa, the kind of guy whom you could see entertaining kids with card tricks or losing on purpose at checkers. But Ahlerich lives in the land where most of us fear to tread.

"We look hard and we think about the worst-case scenario," he says.

"The ATF, the things they bring to sniff out bad devices. The protection from the air. I don't know that I'd want to come to the game if that wasn't in place. I really don't." he says. "We touched on it lightly. It's there. It's there. It makes me all warm and fuzzy to know that it's there." He smiles a worried smile.

"We have scrubbed this thing," says Ahlerich. He describes the previous weekend's "tabletop exercise" in which they played out a scenario where a suspicious "device" was discovered ten miles away. Having thought the unthinkable, they still didn't feel any need to change tactics at the last minute. "Should we do more sweeps of the stadium? No, we have confidence in the plan, that we're doing it right."

Ahlerich is smiling when he says all this, but I wonder if this keeps him up at night.

"Look at my hair," he says with a laugh, pointing to his snowy white regulation haircut. "They pay me to worry."

But the thing that really keeps Ahlerich up at night is the lone crazy. A massive conspiracy tends to leave footprints, often very large ones, which is why these threats are often disrupted in the planning stages. But one crazy guy? From John Wilkes Booth on down, a troubled individual with a weapon has proven capable of doing serious damage while remaining undetected until it was too late.

Around the time that Rick, Sandra, and I are sitting in traffic, about a quarter mile away in the Jobing.com Arena parking lot, a man named Kurt William Havelock is considering his future. Havelock is angry. He is a normal guy, or so the neighbors said. He lives in an apartment with two small kids, two large dogs, and his fiancée. Of course, there is the small matter of the white hearse he owns with the vanity license plate DRTNAP, but he has never been in trouble with the law. The month before, he had applied for a liquor license in his hometown of Tempe. Normally the city council rubber-stamps such applications before passing them on to the state liquor control board. But Havelock planned to open a Halloween-themed bar called the Haunted Castle, and neighborhood scuttlebutt suggested that it would be popularly known as Drunkenstein's, so local merchants put pressure on town officials and Havelock's application was denied. His dream was over before it began.

Havelock's next step was to buy an $899 AR-15 semiautomatic assault rifle from the Scottsdale Gun Club along with 250 rounds of .233 caliber ammunition. This is a serious weapon, essentially the civilian version of the M-16 automatic assault rifle that is the weapon of choice for the U.S. military. Even in civilian trim, it's deadly accurate, with a range of 600 meters, or almost a third of a mile.

Havelock has typed up copies of an eight-page manifesto and mailed them to various media outlets.

"I will test the theory that bullets speak louder than words. Perhaps the blood of the inculpable will cause a paradigm shift . . . someone has to start the revolution but no one wants to be first . . . I will slay your children. I will shed the blood of the innocent. No one destroys my dream. No one. I will not be bullied by the financial institutions and their puppet politicians . . . All this boils down to an econopolitical confrontation. I cannot outvote, outspend, outtax or outincarcerate my enemies . . . but for a brief moment, I can outgun them . . . The Patriots versus the Giants . . . do you see an ironic parallel? How many dollars will you lose? And all because you took my right to work, to own a business, from me . . . Perhaps [Web sites] will print up some cool T-shirts like 'I Survived Super Bowl XLII.'"

He headed to the gun club for target practice, but the facility was closed for a private event. He considered heading to the Desert Ridge Marketplace mall. Instead he drove to Glendale. He scribbled a quick-and-dirty living will, telling anyone who might read it that he didn't want to be resuscitated, and stuffed it in the glove compartment of his car.

Then he walks over to the Jobing.com Arena, which is outside the security perimeter of the game but very much a part of the pregame festivities. He surveys the scene, the fans of all ages, all easily within range. There is absolutely nothing to stop him. He watches for about a minute, pondering the attention he could get, the damage he could do, the innocent blood he could shed.

And then something happens inside Kurt William Havelock's head. The manifesto-writing madman is shouted down by the regular guy who had kids and dogs and who just wanted to open a bar. He never opens the bag with the gun, six 30-round magazines, and 20 loose rounds.

Instead, Havelock picks up his cell phone, calls his fiancée, sobbing, then meets his parents at his condominium, a forty-minute drive away. His father takes the gun and the ammunition, and Kurt William Havelock surrenders to Tempe police and is arrested and charged with mailing threatening communications. He is subjected to a psychiatric evaluation, which found "no mental defects."

Judge Edward V. Ross, who presides over a hearing in U.S. District Court, orders him held without bail, saying, "I haven't read more chilling words, and I've been doing this a long time."

Sometimes, even when you've got F-18s on alert and snipers on the roof, you need to catch a break.

So, Joey, what words of advice would you give to Britney Spears now?"

Joey Fatone, erstwhile member of 'N Sync, looks into the camera solemnly.

"Well, I would tell her to find a place where she's safe, and I'd tell her that there are a lot of people who love her."

What does this have to do with the Super Bowl? It used to be that celebrities just headed on into the game, hustling past fans, hiding under baseball caps. Not anymore. While the red carpet had been a staple of

Super Bowl parties for years, a red carpet for the game itself was un-charted territory until FOX chairman David Hill made it happen, fur-ther blurring the lines between sports and entertainment. That this is a red carpet that could have been taking place at the Emmys, the Gram-mys, or the Oscars was made very clear a few minutes later. Soon after Fatone slips inside, an older guy wearing a slightly rumpled suit walks down the runway unrecognized and unmolested. It is baseball commis-sioner Bud Selig, certainly one of the five most powerful men in sports.

The payoff for FOX? Carefully orchestrated cross-promotion. Hugh Laurie, the star of *House*, a FOX drama about a cantankerous, contrarian physician and the interns he bullies into solving medical mysteries, is patiently bantering with camera crew after camera crew. Laurie, who's English (although the character he plays is American), has never seen a football game. That only adds to the fun. "It's very different than rugby. It's an amazing spectacle," he tells *Entertainment Tonight*. "And I know there are people out there who would kill for my tickets."

In one way, he's one of the stars of the evening. This evening's very special episode of *House*, which airs immediately after the Super Bowl, gets the mother of all lead-ins. And while Laurie is probably a little fuzzy about what happens on third down, he understands the real and direct relationship between the quality of the game and the magnitude of his ratings tonight.

"Because *House* is on after the game, I'm hoping for a one-point game that goes down to the last thirty seconds," he says when asked for a prediction.

Next down the carpet is Jordin Sparks. Her story is almost too good to be true. She grew up in Glendale, just down the road from the sta-dium. Her father is Philippi Sparks, a former Giant. At the tender age of seventeen, she won *American Idol*, FOX's highest-rated show. And now she'll be singing the National Anthem at the Super Bowl. Who would dare script something like this?

Although she'll wear Armani for the anthem, now she's wearing a Giants jersey and bouncing off the walls with the energy that helped her win a battle that's part singing competition and part personality contest.

"Just trying to keep it real," she tells the first camera crew. "I didn't think it could be bigger than *American Idol*. *American Idol* is huge, but a billion people watch the Super Bowl. It's a step up."

What's it like performing in your hometown, Jordin?

"I have so much support in Glendale. They're like 'Congratulations, don't forget the words.'"

Forget the words?

"I know the song, but I don't practice it too much. I overanalyze it. I think when I go out there I'll be okay. There's more pressure than usual."

Philippi, what advice would you give your daughter?

"Breathe."

"It's getting more and more real," Jordin tells the next camera crew.

"It's the biggest moment of her life," Philippi intones.

"No pressure, Dad."

"You are a ball full of energy," comments an anchor from a local station.

"It's one of the perks of being eighteen," says Jordin Sparks, beaming.

Open or closed. That's the question that Frank Supovitz, the NFL's Super Bowl czar, is wrestling with. It's only a few hours before game time, and he's got to make a final decision about whether or not to open the retractable roof of the stadium. About a week out from the game, Supovitz got the word that it might rain on Super Bowl Sunday. And having seen firsthand the Sunday before just what a Phoenix downpour looks like, he is taking the threat seriously.

So he watches the weather report and ponders.

To open or not to open, that is the question.

Pro: There can be a lot more pyrotechnics during the pregame and halftime shows. The sound in the building is better with the roof open. And fans would be able to see—or at least hear—the flyover of the fighter jets.

Con: It could rain.

The teams, of course, want an answer as soon as possible. The production crews, on the other hand, want to wait as long as possible, hoping for a definitive break in the weather. And then there are practical considerations. During Super Bowl XXXVIII at Houston's Reliant Stadium, the roof got stuck halfway open.

If this were a league championship game rather than the Super Bowl, this would be primarily a football decision, with a handful of people consulted. How many weighed in on this?

"Dozens," says Supovitz, shrugging while he smiles.

The other factor is that this is an irrevocable decision. If Supovitz decides to open the roof and a downpour starts, the NFL would be committed to keeping it open for the duration of the game to keep the conditions the same for both teams. On the other hand, if they close the roof and the pyrotechnics from the pregame and halftime shows were to fill the building with smoke, they would have to deal with that. Unlike a fully enclosed stadium, the University of Phoenix Stadium doesn't have a smoke-removal system to pull air out of the building. The building's elegant solution to that problem—open the roof—won't work on Super Bowl Sunday except in a true emergency.

So literally minutes before the doors are to open, the production crews are doing pyro tests, just to see how much they can use without overwhelming the room.

Supovitz checks and ponders and waits and weighs input from all sides. And then he makes the only rational decision: Close it. "When you're dealing with the league's biggest game, you have to err on the side of being conservative," he reasons. If the halftime show has to suffer a bit in the service of the game, so be it.

For the most part, the rain will stay away. There will be some wind and a bit of drizzle, but nothing more. Supovitz will be second-guessed by some for keeping the roof closed. But, of course, he won't get any credit for the superbly played game, the spectacular catches that might not have been made if the ball and the turf were a little wet. It comes with the territory.

It's a corridor, not a tunnel, that leads onto the field at the University of Phoenix Stadium. On one side is a concrete wall; on the other are the supports for the portable stands. This is the business end of the stadium, where the field rolls in and out. And it's one place in which the vomitoria that Peter Eisenman detests might have come in handy. Instead, the walls make this passage feel like a slot canyon, or maybe one of those narrow streets in lower Manhattan where you can see only a sliver of the sky.

Still, the reveal is spectacular. My gaze soars to the almost translucent roof and the light and airy trusses that support it 300 feet above. The close-cropped turf is solid but just a little spongy. The PA announcements are echoing off the walls just a bit. It's more than an hour before game time, but the stands are nearly filled.

Is there anyplace better than the sidelines of the Super Bowl before kickoff? My purple nylon Reebok vest is tacky, but it's my ticket to a place few ever get to see.

The NFL has made one subtle but important change to the game-day schedule. The pregame show, starring Alicia Keys, will come before, rather than after, the warm-ups. It allows the players to move straight from the warm-ups to the game. It allows fans to actually see the warm-ups.

It also sends a message about 2008's prevailing back-to-basics trend—*it's the game, stupid.*

The kickers are the first to arrive. They both start at the Patriots' end zone, and New England's Stephen Gostkowski, who has been money on short field goals, starts deep. New York's Lawrence Tynes, who has a strong leg but has been erratic on shorter attempts, starts with a couple of chip shots.

Kickers are a strange breed, always a little apart from the rest of the team. They rarely tackle or get tackled, but their job is crucial. Each of the Patriots' three Super Bowl wins were by a single field goal, and the Giants won a Super Bowl on a last-second miss by Buffalo's Scott Norwood. If football is a team game, for better or for worse the kicker stands alone.

Eli Manning stands in the middle of the field. Without the ball, he shuffles languidly, with the awkward gait of a teenager who's grown a little too fast and still isn't quite comfortable with his body. It's this body language that has frustrated Giants fans, who contrast it with the gunslinger swagger of a quarterback like Ben Roethlisberger or even Manning's big brother, Peyton. But when Eli Manning gets a football in his hand today, he is transformed. His movements turn deliberate as he takes two steps up in the pocket and throws, finding Plaxico Burress in midstride. Four other Giants are loitering in the Patriots' end zone, a place they hope to visit early and often once the game starts. Brandon Jacobs tosses a ball back using an awkward, sidearm motion and almost hits Ahmad Bradshaw in the helmet.

At the other end of the field, Tom Brady whips one over to Randy Moss. The ball has plenty of zip on it—Brady's arm is deceptively strong—but it's not crisp. It wobbles a little in flight, and it's a little low and a little behind the world-class wideout. Could his ankle really be hurting? Coach Bill Belichick watches his QB with concern, picks up a stray ball with annoyance, and chucks it over to the sidelines.

On the Patriots' sideline, there's an odd mix of NFL personnel and A-list celebrities. Kurt Russell and Kate Hudson are there, making small talk to Patriots owner Bob Kraft. "I've always been a Patriots fan," Russell says. "But this is my first Super Bowl."

Hudson beams and says it's a Christmas present. "I always wanted to take my dad to the Super Bowl."

Bob Kraft comes over to his tween-age grandson, who's wearing an old-school Boston Patriots T-shirt, gives him a hug, and kisses him gently on the top of his mop of hair. The various factions of the Kraft family assemble for a family photo, waiting to get everyone together like the wedding scene from *The Godfather*. Maybe the very rich aren't different after all.

My magic purple vest allows me back onto the field for halftime as well, and in addition to seeing Tom Petty, I get to watch the last few plays of the first half and the first few of the second from field level. This is a perspective that every fan should experience when the game looks just a little bit too easy on television. From the high camera angles that Kempner and company afford the viewer, the field looks like a chessboard, and a slant pattern to the wide receiver seems like it should be as simple to pull off as rook to queen's bishop 2. But even the shortest glimpse of a football game at field level will set you straight on that one.

Watching Tom Brady drop back to pass with his back to his own end zone, one thing becomes painfully obvious: The main component of the quarterback's job is belief. Brady's not throwing to a receiver. He's throwing to a spot on the football field in the hope that Wes Welker, who is now four yards past the line of scrimmage and just making his first move on the defender, will shake the coverage and arrive at those particular coordinates at the precise moment that the ball does. He is very much living in the present—the defensive ends, outside linebackers, and blitzing safeties see to that—but his success or failure depends on a sequence of events that's very much a work in progress when he releases the football.

Up close, the game is remarkably fast. When Eli Manning calls a play-action fake, he fakes more than the defender. I'm watching Ahmad Bradshaw pile into the line while Manning is standing in the pocket checking off one receiver and then another before making his throw. I've been faked, too.

Standing at field level, it's also remarkable that either team ever gets a play off. Even under normal circumstances, it is all but impossible to hear the signals that the quarterback shouts. In this way, the Super Bowl represents something close to a best-case scenario. The capacity crowd may be modestly excited, but most of them are relatively nonpartisan, or at least aren't displaying their rooting interests by shouting so loudly that they drown out the opposing quarterback's snap count.

And Eli Manning is sacked." Five words that Joe Buck will forever be grateful that he did not utter. It's third and five with 1:15 left on the game clock, and a play that may go down as the greatest moment in Super Bowl history is developing. As he drops back to pass, Eli Manning finds himself about to be sacked by a fierce New England pass rush.

"Pressure from [Adalius] Thomas on the edge," says Buck. "And Eli Manning . . ."

This is the pause to end all pauses, the moment when Buck is about to blurt out something that could haunt him for his whole career, the play-by-play man's equivalent of "Dewey Beats Truman." But the same internal editor that keeps Buck from dropping F-bombs on the air today keeps him from jumping the call. A split second later, Manning somehow squirts out of the pile of blue shirts like a grape seed.

". . . stays on his feet," Buck continues. "Airs it out down the field. It is *caught* by Tyree."

"We didn't have Tyree on the catch." That's what Richie Zyontz is saying in the FOX truck, living his greatest nightmare for about four seconds.

"Yeah, we have Tyree, I guarantee it," replies Artie Kempner calmly.

The isolation replay of this landmark play is on a different tape machine than it would have been during a regular-season game, so it took Zyontz a split second to locate it.

And when it's cued up, the replay proves as poetic as the play itself.

From field level, the camera shows just how close Manning came to getting sacked as Jarvis Green grabs his jersey and Richard Seymour looks ready to wrap him up. It pans left as Manning scrambles, and widens out just a little as he prepares to throw. The ball stays perfectly framed throughout its improbable flight and the shot ends with a perfect silhouette of David Tyree jumping for the ball with Rodney Harrison all over his back like a suit off the sale rack. It's the sort of complex shot a Hollywood director would have spent three days planning, but today it's the result of a skilled cameraman following Kempner's A-Team game plan to a tee in real time.

The extra-slow-motion isolation replay that follows illustrates even more graphically just how improbable Tyree's catch was, and in the booth Troy Aikman picks up on the visual cue. "Rodney Harrison was in position behind Tyree. And when the ball came out it looked like it was going to be overthrown and Rodney Harrison was going to have an easy interception."

Zyontz adds a couple of quick cutaways—Tyree's jubilation, Manning's relief, and Harrison's disbelief—but this sequence is all about The Catch. And the producer just lets it breathe.

The game-winning score a moment later is memorable for what Buck and Aikman *don't* say. When Plaxico Burress catches what would prove to be the championship-winning touchdown, Buck says simply, "Burress alone. Touchdown New York."

And then for a full 46 seconds an announcing team at the very top of its game says absolutely nothing, letting Artie Kempner's montage of great pictures tell this improbable tale.

We had to reload the cannon." That's what Frank Supovitz calls it. The cannon was the Super Bowl postgame festivities that began with a second still on the clock.

The monitor in the stadium's mission control reads one second to play, but then Supovitz looks out the window and sees there are players and media streaming onto the field.

He turns to Mike Pereira, vice president of officiating. Is it really over?

No.

With that, the question turns to reversing the scenario. Supovitz turns to Milt Ahlerich, head of security, to help get the field cleared. And almost as quickly as it boiled over into chaos, order is restored. It's still a monumental task to herd these interlopers, but the NFL has one big advantage.

"These weren't crazed fans. These were members of the media and other people with legitimate reasons to be there. When they realized they were on the field before the game was over, they were embarrassed. It wasn't hard to convince them to leave."

Just how do they produce those Super Bowl championship caps mere minutes after the game is over? Through the magic of heat pressing.

Sharp-eyed consumers will note that the design of the official Rebook Super Bowl champion cap itself is deceptively modular and the team logo on the upper-left-hand corner is the only team-specific element. So when the Giants pulled off Sunday's upset, a miniature hat factory set up in a conference room of a Phoenix hotel springs into action.

"It's a high-tech version of an iron-on patch," explains Ben Erps, president of All Pro Championships, a Louisville, Kentucky, sports merchandising firm. Embroidering a whole hat can take a half hour, but these patches can be affixed in only thirty seconds. Batches of freshly minted Giants World Championship hats are on their way to fourteen area hotels within the hour.

"Pardon the expression, but we wanted to strike while the iron was hot," says Erps. Jubilant Giants fans will buy up all 2,000 hats within minutes of their arrival.

During the week, the generic Super Bowl XLII merchandise formed the basis of another cottage industry. Instead of packing the merchandise up every evening and setting it out fresh in the morning, the All Pro reps simply covered it with a sheet and turned the stand over to college students who were moonlighting as night watchmen of sorts. They'd do some homework, watch a movie on a laptop, and keep an eye on the apparel. "They'd just babysit the merchandise," says Erps.

With the New York Giants having just pulled off what might be the greatest upset in Super Bowl history, you might think that their locker room would be celebration central, but that isn't the case after Sunday night's improbable win. While a World Series locker room is an orgy of champagne showers and attaboys, the Giants' post-championship locker room is surprisingly businesslike, with only a few bits of stray confetti on the carpet signifying that this is more than just a mere mid-October road game.

"My fucking shoulder hurts," announces Plaxico Burress to no one in particular as he limps from the shower to his locker buck naked, his "Everything Happens for a Reason" tattoo spanning both preposterously muscled shoulder blades. As he towels off methodically, a small cadre of reporters stand by his locker strangely silent. When another journalist invades the scrum and breaks the silence with a question, Burress ignores it and simply slips on a pair of black briefs with his back to the assembled scribes. "He's not going to do an interview until he's dressed," explains a Giants beat regular to the interloper.

"Thanks, Plax," says a female reporter from NESN, a Boston cable outlet, with thinly veiled sarcasm.

On the other side of the room, Michael Strahan chides a Japanese camera crew. "I don't like people taking my picture when I'm not fully dressed," he says as he knots the black and red silk tie that matches his dark gray pin-striped three-piece suit.

Wide receiver Steve Smith is facing the sort of crisis that besets NFL rookies. Freshly showered, he arrives at his locker, puts on his suit, and then discovers he has lost his diamond earrings. He picks up towels, flips over bags, and drops more than a few F-bombs. No luck. The rookie heads toward the bus, his shirt untucked, his eyes still scanning the floor.

Tank Daniels is dealing with his own set of issues. "I've got fifty-three text messages," he says, looking at his cell phone in disbelief. "I can't return all of these."

"My battery would die if I had that many messages," agrees Antonio Pierce.

Daniels is in full multitasking mode. He is in charge of his four-and-a-half-year-old son, Jackson, who is wearing a Super Bowl jersey with "Daddy" on the back. It is well past his bedtime, but playing with his father's tangle of credentials keeps a meltdown at bay, at least for the moment.

Domenik Hixon, for his part, is encountering swag issues. His commemorative Super Bowl bathrobe won't fit in his bag, so he has to sling it under one arm, still wrapped in plastic. Earlier, without thinking, he had opened his silver New York Giants Super Bowl Championship commemorative Gatorade bottle. "I was thirsty," he says. Now the special-teams specialist went from cooler to cooler in search of an unopened one. "I'm not going to crack this one," he says.

While pundits will bluster about the Giants roller coaster season, it's truly been that and more for Hixon. The backup wide receiver started the season playing for the Denver Broncos. While returning a kickoff in his first NFL game, he was hit by Buffalo's Kevin Everett. It was a clean tackle and a routine play. Except that Everett didn't get up. He lay motionless on the turf for 15 minutes, paralyzed, and doctors feared for his life. Quick action from medical personnel on the scene, administering chilled saline to lower Everett's body temperature probably prevented permanent paralysis. His recovery, like the Giants victory, has been called a miracle.

For his part, Hixon began having nightmares—in which it is he, not Everett—lying motionless on the field. In another line of work, he might have been given counseling. But this is the NFL, and he was cut by the Broncos. "It was a long day and a half," says Hixon. But it was a phone call from the New York Giants that led him to this confetti-littered locker room and a storybook ending to an all-too-real football season.

"Buses leave in three minutes," bellows a Giants representative about ten minutes after a previous five-minute warning.

"You won't leave *me*," announces a now fully dressed Burress as he bounds across the room.

Although the buses are ready to leave, Shaun O'Hara is not. While most of his teammates are ready to pull out, the veteran center makes his way back to the field at the University of Phoenix Stadium, his championship hat looking surprisingly appropriate with his dark suit. He scans the scene with his camcorder, executing a slow panorama of the now-empty stands. "This is the stadium," he says softly to his camcorder. "That's a nice shot. The trophy up there on the scoreboard." He takes one more long look, before switching his camcorder off. "Now, it's time to party."

Super Bowl XLII is now over.

What is the final tab on Super Bowl XLII? The NFL doesn't calculate a grand total for its signature game and no independent entities have attempted to fully quantify the excess of America's Biggest Day. But here's a quick-and-dirty accounting of the big game.

According to a study done by the W.P. Carey School of Business at Arizona State University, the economic impact of Super Bowl XLII, which includes bevy of local parties, the Playboy Party among them, totaled a record $500.6 million. The University of Phoenix Stadium, which wouldn't have been built without the promise of a Super Bowl, was completed at a cost of $422 million.

The street value of a stadium full of Super Bowl tickets is $511 million.

FOX paid the NFL an estimated $712.5 million for the broadcast rights for the 2007–2008 season, including the rights to Super Bowl XLII. The value of the commercials on the FOX broadcast was approximately $162 million.

Bridgestone's sponsorship of Tom Petty's halftime show cost more than $12 million. Tom Petty's *Greatest Hits* reached number one on Billboard's album charts the week after the Super Bowl, while his *Anthology* collection ranked sixth, with both records selling a combined 40,000 copies. Tickets for Petty's thirty-six-stop national arena tour went on sale the Monday after the Super Bowl and sold briskly.

NFL Licensing sold $140 million worth of Super Bowl–related clothing and branded merchandise.

The legal betting handle for Super Bowl XLII in Las Vegas was $92.1 million. With the large point spread coupled with the Giants upset, bookmakers actually lost $2.6 million, the first time since the San Francisco 49ers blowout win over the San Diego Chargers in 1995 that the bookmakers lost money. Some have estimated that illegal betting on the game may approach $1 billion.

Add all that together and the bottom line for the Super Bowl is approximately $2.5 billion. If the Super Bowl were a nation, it would have a Gross Domestic Product about the size of North Korea, and its economy would be larger than that of forty-nine other nations.

But as mind-boggling as these numbers are, the Super Bowl is not about the money, or not *only* about the money. From the days when the cavemen would gather around the fire after the day's hunt, societies have always needed a time and a place to come together. And Super Bowl Sunday is ours, a time when, for a few short hours, America simply stops.

It's sixty minutes of professional football, played on the first Sunday in February. It's also a time for hopes and dreams. A time when we gather together to scream at our flat-screen televisions, not quite believing that Eli Manning eluded the rush and David Tyree held on to the ball.

Sure, this billion dollar game harbors the crass and the commercial. But for a few short hours at least, the truly base and the evil must wait outside the door because we're watching the game. The Super Bowl is possibility, it is opportunity, it is hope, it is dreams. And what can be more American than that?

EPILOGUE

The morning after the Playboy Super Bowl Party, Darren Rovell of CNBC, who is the Mr. Blackwell of Super Bowl week, wrote, "In the ultimate battle of men's magazine Super Bowl parties, *Playboy* beat out *Maxim* by perhaps the widest margin since the two began competing in 2001."

Super Bowl XLII was the highest-rated sporting event of all time, with 97.5 million viewers. Only the *M*A*S*H* series finale, with 106 million viewers in 1983, drew a larger audience. More Americans watched the game than voted in the 2004 presidential election.

The Budweiser commercial "Clydesdale Team" won the *USA Today* Ad Meter poll, the company's tenth consecutive victory. The spot continued to air later in the year during the Summer Olympics.

The 2012 Super Bowl was awarded not to the Arizona Cardinals but to the Indianapolis Colts, who will move into a new domed stadium before the game.

Despite the Giants' Super Bowl win, the Dow Jones Industrial Average fell from 12,800 on January 4, 2008 to 9,323 on November 4, seemingly well on its way to defying the Super Bowl Indicator.

The NFL raised the face value of some Super Bowl tickets to $1,000. The prices of 1,000 other tickets were dropped from $700 to $500, the first time the league has cut prices of Super Bowl tickets.

Bruce Springsteen has agreed to be the halftime performer for Super Bowl XLIII.

ACKNOWLEDGMENTS

Trying to get a grasp on an enterprise as large and complex as the Super Bowl, I sometimes felt a little like the blind man trying to describe an elephant. That said, it helps to have someone to help direct you toward the trunk. I was lucky enough to have a group of pros who did just that. Lauren Melone of Playboy, Brian McCarthy of the NFL, and Lou D'Ermilio and Tim Buckman of FOX Sports invited me behind the scenes, found me the right people to talk to, and answered my stupid questions with patience and expertise. Malcolm Gladwell would call them "connectors" which means "people with a special gift for putting the world together." I just call them lifesavers.

Thanks to everyone at the NFL, especially Frank Supovitz, Charles Coplin, Joan Ryan-Canu, Jack Groh, Milt Ahlerlich, Shandon Melvin, and Greg Aiello. Thanks also to Steve Sabol of NFL Films, Jim Steeg of the San Diego Chargers, as well as the late Don Weiss, whose memoir, *The Making of a Super Bowl*, provided valuable insight into the early days of the game.

Peter Eisenman and Rick Rosson would have made great sports talk hosts if they weren't such great architects. A giant thank you to Bob Lachky of Anheuser-Busch, who took time out from the craziest weeks of his busy schedule to explain it all to me. I'm hugely grateful to everyone at FOX Sports, especially David Hill, Ed Goren, Joe Buck, Troy Aikman, Richie Zyontz, Colby Bourgeois, Fred Aldous and the rest of the A-Team.

Acknowledgments

Special thanks goes to my tour guide Artie Kempner, and his wife Marcy, and his sons Matt, Ethan, and Jack. Early on, Richie Zyontz told me "Artie's all access" and, as usual, he was right.

In Phoenix, Mike Kennedy, Bob Sullivan, Christina Estes, and Julie Frisoni were among those who provided ample insight and abundant hospitality. And a huge thank you to the Playboy Party Team—Lisa Natale, Donna Tavoso, and Dana Rosenthal, as well as Tony Berger and everyone at Relevent—I'll never think about a party the same way again.

I can't say enough about my editor Jason Kaufman who came up with the idea for this book, and then let me write it my way. Every writer should be lucky enough to have an editor as supportive as Jason, but I know he's one of a kind. His assistant the ever-capable Rob Bloom, has big shoes to fill, and occupies them admirably. Chris Fortunato and Tina Henderson transformed my manuscript into a book with staggering speed and silky smoothness while copyeditor Sue Warga doggedly stripped the inaccurate and the inelegant from every page.

Let me thank my own crew, including the ever-reliable Sam Kissinger, who worked like a young pro from beginning to end, while research guru Matt Shepatin and intern Tommy Crawford made some key contributions. My great friends, Jerry Beilinson and Al Mercuro read this manuscript as it was taking shape and made valuable suggestions, while my favorite editor, my wife Sally, found the key to Chapter 3. The indomitable Emily Sklar transcribed dozens of hours of interviews, keeping carpal tunnel syndrome—and insanity—at bay. What can I say about my agent, Mark Reiter? He's a wartime consigliere. And thanks to Lee Garfinkel for a crucial connection and my buddy Wayne Henderson who let me sleep in his spare room during a crucial crunch week, and often shamed me into working when I just didn't feel like it. A shout out to my Super Bowl running buddies including Adam Thompson, Russell Adams, Hannah Karp, Aaron Kuriloff and also to Sam Waker and Jill

Kirschenbaum who edited the wsj.com blog that helped to inform my reporting on Super Bowl XLII.

Now the hard part. How do you thank the people who give you a reason to get up in the morning? My amazing wife Sally, and my remarkably talented kids Ethan and Emma inspired every single word in *The Billion Dollar Game*. Gracias, Danke, Merci, Arigato, and just plain thanks.

Finally, to Clover, our spunky pet chicken, who lived a full and happy life while this book was being written, rest in peace.